FOREIGN ENTERPRISE IN NIGERIA

Laws and Policies

The American Society of International Law

STUDIES IN FOREIGN INVESTMENT

AND

ECONOMIC DEVELOPMENT

Previously published

Foreign Enterprise in India: Laws and Policies by Matthew J. Kust
Foreign Enterprise in Colombia: Laws and Policies by Seymour W. Wurfel

FOREIGN ENTERPRISE
IN NIGERIA

Laws and Policies

By PAUL O. PROEHL

THE UNIVERSITY OF NORTH CAROLINA PRESS · CHAPEL HILL

Copyright © *1965 by*
THE UNIVERSITY OF NORTH CAROLINA PRESS

Library of Congress Catalog Card Number 65-19387

Foreword

Professor Proehl's study of *Foreign Enterprise in Nigeria: Laws and Policies* is one of several studies of the legal environment for foreign investment in selected countries, in the context of the political, economic, and social development in each country. The studies are being carried out under research fellowships granted by the American Society of International Law in its research program on foreign investment and economic development. Studies on India and Colombia have already been published. Others in the series will cover Japan and Mexico.

The aims of the society's program are to describe and analyze the legal institutions in selected countries that affect the participation of foreign capital and technology in their economic development and to clarify the factors that impede or facilitate foreign participation. It is a further aim to give the political, economic, and social background necessary to an understanding of why and how national laws and policies have developed as they have.

It is recognized that the factors affecting private investment decisions are not primarily "legal" ones. Nevertheless, important policies usually find expression in legal form, and the adequacy or inadequacy of the legal framework for investment may influence the decisions of investors seeking opportunities in other countries that, for their part, need foreign capital and technology. Moreover, the actual practice of various governments in dealing with foreign investment can throw light on the norms of international behavior that concern the international lawyer.

John R. Stevenson, in practice in New York City, was chairman of the society's committee that developed plans for the series of studies. Mr. Stevenson, Covey T. Oliver (then Professor of Law at the University of Pennsylvania, now United States Ambassador to Colombia), Myres S. McDougal (Professor of Law, Yale University), Lester Nurick (Assistant General Counsel, The International Bank for Reconstruction and Development), and Walter Sterling Surrey, in practice in Washington, D.C., assisted by the staff of the society, drew up the "Guidelines" that served as a general guide to the scope and contents of each book.

In the series of country studies each research fellow has been assisted by an advisory group including economists and political scientists as well as lawyers at the bar, in business, in government, and in universities, who have special competence on the country under study. The following have participated in the advisory group for the Nigeria project: John S. Bainbridge, Assistant Dean, Columbia University Law School; Karol N. Gess and James N. Hyde, both in practice in New York City; William A. W. Krebs and Richard T. Murphy, Jr., Arthur B. Little Co.; Lawrence C. McQuade, formerly in practice in New York City; Soia Mentschikoff, Professor of Law, University of Chicago; J. D. Nyhart, School of Industrial Management, Massachusetts Institute of Technology; Arnold Rivkin, International Bank for Reconstruction and Development; Charles Runyon, Assistant Legal Adviser for African Affairs, Department of State; and A. Arthur Schiller, Professor of Law, Columbia University.

Neither the society nor the advisory group, of course, is responsible for the statements and views expressed, which are solely the responsibility of the author. Indeed, as one would hope and expect, comments and suggestions from the advisory group reflected a diversity of views on legal, political, and economic questions.

I would like to thank, on behalf of the society, the members of the advisory group for the time and attention they gave to Professor Proehl's valuable study. A grant from the Ford Foundation to the society has made possible the series of country studies; we are grateful for their interest and support.

H. C. L. Merillat
Executive Director
American Society of International Law

Washington, D.C.
January, 1965

Preface

To describe any dynamic institution in print that does not appear almost immediately is a precarious undertaking. Language is swiftly overtaken by events, and the author experiences the hapless predicament of the dismounted rider who sees his horse galloping off into the distance.

When the institution under study is the conglomeration of forces and factors that constitute a new and developing nation, the task is even more hazardous. Ideologies shift; constitutions are altered; governments change; volumes of new legislation are passed; ministers and ministries are reshuffled; a sudden downdraft in the production or in the world market price of a critical export commodity, or in external reserves, may require the realignment of the entire economy; political parties wax and wane; sectional, racial, or linguistic differences erupt and divide the people along new lines.

Even where the internal political and economic elements remain relatively constant, the reliability factor in the delineation of the law and policy of a new nation toward foreign investment is doubtful for other reasons. Pertinent documents are hard to come by; responsible officials lack information that falls within the ambit of their authority; laws as amended exist only in hand-made annotations in the possession of a few conscientious bureaucrats; contradictions are found between the written and the spoken word; statistics are scarce and of doubtful accuracy. The mass of factual material that one is able to uncover, verify, and relate rests on shifting sands: laws, regulations, policies, and practices have not become sufficiently institutionalized to give assurance of continuity or consistency of application. Overlying the mass and obscuring its outlines is an administrative gloss derived from the conviction that the problems of nation-building and the stimulation of economic growth against heavy odds permit, or even dictate, wide latitude in the exercise of executive discretion.

Other vices follow when time and temperament have not permitted more than a casual approximation of a government of law rather than of men, when personalities and power dominate the experimental and formative period, which is so often also a period of permissive reaction against the constraints identified, most often erroneously, with the politics of colonialism. What national leaders identify as essential flexibility and selectivity, in determining means and goals within severe limitations of human and material resources, provide an easy avenue to corruption. Lacking experience, adequate criteria and controls, and, above all, a national consciousness, it is easy for the government official to favor his region, his tribe, his friends, and, finally, himself.

No nation, developing or established, is entirely free of such faults, and, among the new and developing, there are wide differences of susceptibility. Nigeria is, happily, among those few of the new nations that, while prone to all of the symptoms mentioned above, suffers least from what the outsider views, not as flexibility and selectivity, but as the tendency toward arbitrary and partisan action that puts the foreigner at a serious disadvantage and robs the future of any predictability as to the safety of alien-owned property against non-market risks. Nigeria, also, has a relatively efficient government apparatus, both at the national and regional level; its officials are generally knowledgeable; laws and regulations are rather readily obtainable; and, perhaps most important for the foreign investor, most government ministries—and particularly the Ministry of Finance, whose role is critical—have developed fairly consistent approaches to the reception and treatment of foreign investment. Cabinet shifts have been rare.

Essentially, Nigeria enjoys a rule of law based on a constitution respected by its leaders and enforced by its courts. Some of it is façade, to be sure, especially in the authoritarian north, but there is solid reality as well. It may, perhaps, be said that the question for Nigeria is not whether the federal constitution, with its safeguards for individual rights and its controls over executive action, can contain the ambitions and preconceptions of its politicians, but whether it—and the Federation of Nigeria with it—can survive the recurrent tensions of regional suspicions, jealousies, and antagonisms. Is a federation viable in which the possession of power and the possession of human and material resources are divided, where deep antipathies resting on cultural and ethnic differences exist?

At the close of 1964, the hardiest optimist could hardly have been expected to answer that question affirmatively with respect to Nigeria. The first national elections since independence were held on December 30, 1964, and the result was just short of disaster. Because of alleged pre-election irregularities in the Northern Region, aimed at capturing the north's 167 seats and, thus, the national Parliament itself for the Northern coalition, the election was widely boycotted by the coalition of Southern parties. The Eastern Region, using its newly found oil riches as a powerful lever, threatened to secede. President Azikiwe, who comes from the east, considered ignoring the election results and forming a "provisional" government. The latter would have been as fatal as secession because the north would not have recognized such a government and properly so, because the president has no power under the constitution to form a provisional government. It was just that argument, pressed by Nigeria's leading jurists—including the federal chief justice and the chief justice of Eastern Nigeria—that saved the day. Despite the fact that it apparently meant continued Northern domination for five more years, the president bowed to the language of the constitution. The Northern power base is, perhaps, of questionable legitimacy, but the remedy lies not in boycotts and unconstitutional action but in the appointment of a commission of inquiry into the alleged irregularities in the north. The people of Nigeria, it would seem, are as entitled to this as much as they were to the Coker Commission of Inquiry that investigated the misgovernment of the Action Group in the west in 1962-63.

This is the third serious crisis that Nigeria has experienced since 1960. The first, the Western Region Crisis of 1962-63, which is described in Chapter X, pitted the ruling coalition of Northerners and Easterners against the Action Group of the west and culminated in the imprisonment of the leaders of the Action Group upon their conviction for felonious treason. The second crisis came in the form of labor unrest generated by rising living costs in the face of wage-levels that had remained static for five years. Government held firm at first but finally capitulated in the face of a general strike. The settlement will require that funds earmarked for economic development be used to meet higher recurring costs.

But Nigeria has met and mastered each of these crises. There has been some violence, and there has been lawlessness in both high places and low, but a fundamental adherence to orderly processes has never been abandoned by the responsible federal officials. It has asserted itself strongly even in the midst of crisis, in the face of outrage and despair. Some partisans view this as weakness, and some critics say that what passes for orderly processes are, indeed, the trappings of legitimacy in which the exercise of power is cloaked. The only true measure of how much substance rests beneath the form is to observe closely the courts and judges of Nigeria. (The Nigerian press is free but partisan, sensationalist, and poorly informed.) Their burden is heavy, as the Sardauna of Sokoto himself has suggested in the headnote to Chapter I. It is not only the burden of convincing foreigners that their capital is safe in Nigeria but also that of holding faith for all Nigerians in an ideal amply set forth in the Nigerian Constitution although, as yet, it is an ideal only imperfectly realized.

Some readers may find some of my comments too frank. My purpose was not to write to please anyone but to make an honest appraisal of things as I found them. My Nigerian friends know that I am animated by the warmest feelings for Nigeria and its people, and I would ask the reader to keep this in mind if he finds that in his opinion I have overstated the case.

The obligations incurred en route to this final act of writing a preface are too many to enumerate. I should like, however, to express my thanks to the American Society of International Law, sponsor of the project, and to its executive vice president, H. C. L. Merillat, for his assistance and patience. I am also grateful to the many government officials, lawyers, bankers, and businessmen—Nigerian, American, and British—who provided information and assisted me in my endeavors, and to the many individuals who read parts of the manuscript and offered their criticisms and suggestions. Lastly, I should like to express appreciation to James H. Giffen, who put the footnotes in order, and to my wife, who excused my prolonged absences in Nigeria and aided me in preparing the manuscript.

The opinions expressed are my own and should not be attributed to any other individual or be taken to express any national bias. The inevitable errors and shortcomings are likewise mine.

Paul O. Proehl

Bordeaux, France
February 10, 1965

Contents

Foreword vii

Preface ix

I. THE SETTING 3

II. ECONOMIC DEVELOPMENT IN NIGERIA 13

III. NIGERIAN LAW: SOURCES AND PROSPECTS 37

IV. ENTREPRENEURSHIP, FORMS OF ESTABLISHMENT, AND PROTECTION OF INTANGIBLE PROPERTY 71

V. LABOR 89

VI. TAXATION, INCENTIVES, AND HANDICAPS 117

VII. LAND TENURE 137

VIII. CREDIT TRANSACTIONS 145

IX. NATIONALIZATION, SOCIALISM, AND NIGERIANIZATION 159

X. THE WESTERN REGION CRISIS OF 1962-1963 175

Abbreviations 195

Notes 197

Index 239

FOREIGN ENTERPRISE IN NIGERIA

Laws and Policies

I

The Setting

States, like individuals who observe their engagements, are respected and trusted; while the reverse is the fate of those who pursue an opposite conduct.
Alexander Hamilton

Honourable Members will appreciate that our future prosperity as a Region will depend largely upon the confidence which the world at large places in the probity of our institutions and especially the courts and the system of law which they administer. If there is any lack of confidence the result will inevitably be that we shall fail to obtain the foreign capital and investment which we need in order to expand our economy and develop our social services.
Alhaji Sir Ahmadu Bello
in My Life, *1963.*

BACKGROUND

On October 1, 1960, Nigeria emerged from the status of protectorate to that of independent nationhood under the personal sovereignty of Queen Elizabeth II. On the third anniversary of that date, October 1, 1963, this tie between the queen and Nigeria was severed, and Nigeria became a republic within the Commonwealth. Dr. Nnamdi Azikiwe, a leader in the peaceful struggle for independence and governor general since 1960, assumed the office of president.

The change-over had symbolic and emotional meaning rather than profound political significance. Nigeria was already exercising all of the political prerogatives of sovereignty; in 1963 it assumed sovereignty in name as well as in fact. The most important immediate legal consequence was the abolition of the appeal from the Nigerian Supreme Court to the Judicial Committee of the Privy Council, and this connection might have survived had the Nigerians chosen to preserve it. But it, too, was an incident of subordination—and a more real one than the role of the queen—that clouded the image of independence.

The record of British dominion over this heterogeneous land of some 50 million persons—one-fifth of the population of Africa—is impressive and, on the whole, bright. It is generally a record of dedicated, enlightened, and frequently imaginative colonial governors and civil servants who, over many decades of tutelage, put as much, or more, into Nigeria as British commercial interests took out: modern government, the whole range of administrative and legal institutions and apparatus above the tribal level, the basis for a modern economy, the educational system, and a good part of Nigeria's modern, urban culture. These contributions were what made it possible for Nigeria, immediately upon her accession to independence, to step forward and claim her place as a respected member of the family of nations and a power to be reckoned with. There has never been any question of Nigeria's right or ability to thus assert herself, and Nigeria's representatives have done so with vigor in international councils.

Few of the new nations that have emerged in the postwar era, and certainly none in sub-Saharan Africa, have so clearly made their mark for stability and sophistication as has Nigeria. Indeed, nations both old and new might well stand in wonder of the achievements of Nigeria. While Nigeria represents "Africa's ethnic and cultural heterogeneity in its richest and most diversified form,"[1] it is slowly but surely creating a national consciousness. Regional, tribal, linguistic, religious, and cultural differences remain strong, to be sure. These have twice already threatened Nigerian unity and may do so again, but it is believed that Nigeria will survive. The disparate tensions that these internal differences create from time to time tend to strengthen and preserve (aided by the federal system of government) the spirit of tolerance and mutuality that would not obtain if power could be exercised without regard for such differences and their almost continuous interplay.

Nigeria's program of economic development demonstrates a sensible appreciation of necessary priorities as well as of the limitations under which Nigeria, with relatively scarce material resources, seeks to raise its standard of living, which is now based on a per capita income of $84.00. The discovery of oil in large quantities has greatly enlarged the possibilities of sustaining economic development over a long period.

Nor have the Nigerians turned inward in contemplation of their domestic problems. The leaders and representatives of Nigeria have participated widely and meaningfully in United Nations, African, and other international affairs. Their participation has rarely been marked by the flamboyance and extremism so often displayed by the representatives of the new nations, and their counsel has generally been one of moderation.

The concrete achievements of Nigeria in these three areas—domestic politics, economic development, and international relations—are numerous. The central administration and the federal parliament have operated smoothly, efficiently, and effectively. A strong civil service of Nigerians has been built on the foundations laid by the colonial civil service. The top posts are now all held by Nigerians, although expatriates continue in technical positions, such as in audits and accounts, until Nigerians are trained to take over.

Nigeria is placing great emphasis upon education as the essential requirement for sustained growth and ultimate self-reliance. A careful, far-reaching survey and recommendations made in 1960 by a committee of experts[2] serve as a master plan for a program to which a large share of development funds is being devoted. Four universities have been established since independence, three in the provinces and one in the national capital, in addition to the excellent University of Ibadan, founded by the British as a college of the University of London in 1948. American teachers and administrators serve on the staffs of all five institutions, and a number of American universities are helping in the development of Nigerian universities and secondary schools under U.S. AID contracts. It is hoped that, by 1968, the five Nigerian universities will have ten thousand full-time students enrolled, 75 per cent of them taking pure and applied science courses. By 1975, Nigeria expects to produce four hundred doctors per year; there is now only one doctor for every thirty-five thousand Nigerians.

A heritage of the British colonial era, which Nigerians have treasured and perpetuated, is the highly developed legal system based on English statutes, common law, equity, and, at local levels, on customary law. The superior courts are administered by a corps of well-trained, experienced, and able judges. Several have attained international prominence: the Federal Chief Justice, Sir Adetokunbo Ademola, for his role in helping sponsor and formulate the "Law of Lagos," a statement of basic law made under the auspices of the International Commission of Jurists, and his participation in the World Rule of Law Movement; and Sir Louis Mbanefo, Chief Justice of Eastern Nigeria, who has served on the International Court of Justice as an *ad hoc* judge in the *South West Africa* cases.

English statutes, as originally enacted or as modified for Nigerian purposes, continue in force, although since independence only the Nigerian legislatures may legislate for Nigeria. There has been no indiscriminate rush to "remake" the laws of the country or tendency to engage in what has aptly been described as "legislative incontinence." The new laws enacted by the Nigerian Parliament, as well as by the regional legislatures, generally reflect care and caution in the legislative process, as well as a high order of legal draftsmanship, a skill not often found in new nations. Modern British statutes continue to serve as models.

On the economic front, Nigeria is showing consistent annual increases in gross national product. It hopes to reach an annual growth rate of 4.5 per cent in 1966. A six-year economic development plan was put into effect in 1962. This calls for total new investment in productive assets and facilities of £1.1 billion. Of this, £549 million is to come from domestic savings, both public and private—the difference between national income and consumption. It is hoped that £327 million will be provided by foreign governments and international agencies in loans and grants. The United States has already pledged £80 million, and the commitments of other nations and international agencies, principally the World Bank, left a gap (after allowing for underspending) of £105 million by mid-1964. Finally, private investors are expected to bring £200 million into Nigeria as capital, to match the £200 million (included in the above £549 domestic-savings figure) of Nigerian capital to be invested in the private sector.

Private capital investment since independence has not yet achieved the high mark of 1960; while domestic private investment has been sustained, foreign private investment has not lived up to expectations. The lag in foreign investment since independence is attributable to a number of factors: a "wait-and-see" attitude on the part of foreign investors after Nigeria struck off on its own; lack of knowledge and interest on the part of American investors; the world-wide economic slowdown of 1962; and the political crisis in Western Nigeria, which began in May, 1962, and darkened the future of Nigeria for well over a year.

The crisis came at a critical time, just as foreign interest and confidence in Nigeria were gaining hold. An intraparty struggle for control of the ruling political party in the west, which was also the opposition party at the federal level, erupted in a riot in the regional legislature. The federal government, acting under emergency legislation authorized by the Nigerian Constitution, suspended the regional government and appointed a federal administrator for the region. Subsequently, a commission of inquiry uncovered widespread mismanagement of Western Nigerian funds. Evidence was also produced that Action Group leaders had planned to take power by force in September, 1962, and the trials and sentencing of the accused on charges of felonious treason continued through 1963. To many observers, and particularly to those who were considering investment in Nigeria, these events augured a period of unrest in which economic activity would stagnate or, worse, a time in which Nigeria might go the way of the Congo. Nigeria, many thought, was no different; it, too, was heir to the radical disease of the emerging nation—instability.

The firm steps taken by the Nigerian government to meet the challenge of the Action Group effectively put down any threat that existed. Foreign investors appear to have been reassured of the government's ability to preserve law and order, and significant new investments appeared on the horizon by the end of 1963, including an American automobile assembly plant still under discussion at the end of 1964. British interests are expanding their commitments in Nigeria, and Dutch, German, and Italian investors are among those most vigorously seeking new opportunities.[3]

These new investors have been persuaded that their property is safe in Nigeria and that they will be able to get their profits, and eventually their capital, back to their homelands. The chapters that follow are intended to help the American investor make that judgment for himself. It is still too early to judge the effect on foreign investment of the election crisis of December, 1964, and January, 1965; but it does appear, in the spring of 1965, that the opinion prevails that Nigeria has the strength and resilience to withstand recurring crises.

For the prospective investor who reaches an affirmative judgment (and it is believed he can reasonably do so), Nigeria offers substantial inducements. Qualification of his project as a "pioneer industry" entitles the foreign entrepreneur to a tax holiday, favorable write-offs of capital equipment, and tariff protection, if he needs it, to ward off competition from imports while his business is in the "infant industry" stage. Capital may be forthcoming from the newly established Nigerian Industrial Development Bank. Government will assist in securing land for factories; industrial estates, planned areas that are close to shipping facilities and markets and have roads and utilities already in place, have been developed near several cities.

Of course, there are handicaps to overcome. Non-political factors mentioned most frequently by foreign businessmen as hampering foreign investment in Nigeria are the bureaucratic obstacles encountered. Visas are mysteriously hard to come by, even by representatives of established, reputable firms; personnel issuing visas are not helpful; when a visa is finally granted, it is often restricted to too short a stay to permit the businessman to make an adequate survey. Approval of "pioneer industry" status drags on interminably; files are lost or misplaced; responsibility is often shrugged off or, as frequently, asserted vis-à-vis another government department or agency. As late as 1964, there was still no centralized authority for inviting, receiving, and helping a prospective foreign investor; and often the complaint has been that Nigerian officials appear to be in the role of dispensing favors, while the foreign investor's view is that Nigeria must aggressively seek the investor.

For the American investor, Africa, including Nigeria, is still at the bottom of any list of potential sites for investment abroad, except for investment in the exploration for, and the production of, oil. American capital and entrepreneurship that has transnational or overseas aspirations turns first to Canada and western Europe, then to Japan, and then to the developing countries with which the United States has traditional ties: the Philippines and Latin America. Africa tags along at the end because, until recently, Americans knew little of Africa and were discouraged from entering what were then French and British colonies. Today we know much more of Africa but not enough of the individual nations that comprise it, and we tend to generalize from the examples of those that have demonstrated that the foreign investor enters at his own risk. Finally, from a business point of view, most African nations do not provide the mass market to which American businessmen are accustomed and which they prefer. The American investor, therefore, believes that he is the one to be persuaded to bring his capital and his know-how into Nigeria.

Few Nigerians appreciate how vital foreign capital and know-how —particularly the latter—are to Nigeria's economic growth. Proud of their independence, convinced of their bright future, and inexperienced in the stringent and inexorable demands of the modern economy they desire, Nigerians view the foreign investor's role in Nigeria as a privileged, rather than an essential, one. When Nigeria reaches the "take-off" stage, some decades hence, they may indeed be right. Nigeria does provide the largest mass market in Africa, where limited-scale mass production can be economically initiated now and can be escalated as the wants and needs of 45 to 50 million persons rise. One example may suffice: in a Hausa village in Northern Nigeria, comprising perhaps five hundred persons, entirely agricultural in its economy, and where no English is spoken, the chief informed the writer that, in 1960, there were three transistor radios in the village. In 1962, there were thirty. Also, over the next decade or two, as Africa moves to create a common market, or at least as a division of labor among the West African nations evolves, Nigeria may serve as the natural industrial center from which goods will flow throughout West Africa and perhaps, indeed, throughout sub-Saharan Africa.

Given the stability that Nigeria seems to promise, the future appears to be hopeful. With a few exceptions, there is a need for almost every kind of manufacturing plant. Already several large textile mills (one American-owned) are in production. Trucks are being assembled. Flour is produced by an American-owned mill.

Tires, plywood, plastics, soap, margarine, beer, cigarettes, soft drinks, clothing, furniture, paints, cement, and drugs are manufactured in modern plants. Oil is being extracted from what may prove to be one of the world's great pools, and an oil refinery ultimately capable of supplying all of Nigeria's needs is to come into operation in 1965. The great Niger Dam project, the first stage of which is to be completed by the end of the decade, will produce vast quantities of electricity, supplying industry with cheap power and intensifying the demand for electrical goods and appliances in remote but densely populated areas.

Despite the lack of a central Nigerian facility, the businessman who visits Nigeria can find assistance and advice in the Ministry of Commerce and Industry and, in particular, from the representatives of the A. D. Little Company attached to the ministry under a U.S. AID contract. This team has made a survey to determine immediate investment opportunities, and the list comprises a hundred items that possibly can be profitably manufactured in Nigeria. The list includes a wide variety of goods: peanut butter, shoes, clothing, paper, fertilizer, petrochemicals, pharmaceuticals, nails, screws, stoves, and storage batteries.

The need for marshaling limited resources and the desire to raise living standards quickly often appear to make attractive measures of expediency or totalitarian methods of economic development, attractive, for they avoid the difficulties and delays inherent in a democratic society where a consensus is required and where the people retain a wide freedom of choice and action. Unlike some of the other new nations of Africa, Nigeria has resisted the temptation to fight the war of economic development by shifting to a highly centralized form of government in which the regions are reduced to mere administrative components of the government at Lagos or in which the role of the legislature is subordinated to the will of the executive and the rights of individuals are submerged in a vast campaign that gives absolute priority to the attainment of national objectives. While the federal government is supreme, Nigeria was created as, and remains, a federation: the regions have substantial powers and areas of responsibility; parliament functions as a vigorous and creative organ; the press criticizes freely; and the Nigerian citizen enjoys the full range of civil rights guaranteed by his constitution.[4]

The numbers of able persons which a new nation is able to project onto the international scene and how they conduct their business there are always worthy of note. They demonstrate the intellectual level and the vitality of the nation's leadership, and they indicate whether power and prestige are widely shared or whether they are the prerogative of a small group or, perhaps, of one man. Nigeria and Nigerians have performed well in this respect. Chief Justice Ademola and Sir Louis Mbanefo have already been mentioned. Others who have distinguished both Nigeria and themselves include Godfrey K. Amachree, former solicitor general and now undersecretary of the United Nations; United Nations Ambassador S. O. Adebo; Dr. T. O. Elias, Attorney General and Minister of Justice, author of numerous books on law, and member of the International Law Commission; Chief Joseph M. Johnson, Minister of Labor, who was elected president in 1963 of the General Conference of the International Labor Organization, although he shortly resigned in protest against the presence of South African representatives; and Dr. Moses Majekodunmi, Minister of Health and the second African to be elected to the presidency of the World Health Organization.

In international affairs, Nigeria's position is usually a moderate one. One rarely finds Nigerian leadership in accord with the extreme positions advocated by other African leaders, and for this reason, Nigeria has not yet assumed the role of leadership in Pan-African affairs which, by virtue of its size, its resources, and the abilities of its leaders, is certainly destined to be hers, once bravado, demagoguery, and imprudent experimentation have run their course elsewhere on the continent. While Nigeria is building and husbanding its strength, there is no compromise on essentials; its positions against racism in South Africa and the remnants of colonialism in the African area are clear. And while Nigeria generally acts with great caution in foreign affairs, when its leaders believe occasion warrants, they act with boldness and, if necessary, alone. This was demonstrated by Nigeria's break in diplomatic relations with France (not yet repaired in 1965) when France conducted its first atomic test explosion in the Sahara. The principle at stake—keeping Africa clear of any type of nuclear explosive device—was one not as profoundly appreciated elsewhere.

In sum, any assessment of Nigeria's record of accomplishment in the brief years since independence cannot but impress one, both in relative and absolute terms. To be sure, there are entries on both sides of the ledger. The Nigerians themselves would be the first to admit it; but they would insist, and they would be right to do so, that the credit entries greatly exceed the debit items.

II

Economic Development in Nigeria

Genuinely bootstrap development is possible, as the history of Japan showed. The development of Japan came almost wholly from internal reorganization and by the acquisition of knowledge rather than capital from abroad. For this recipe to be successful, however, a fairly authoritarian social structure seems to be necessary. Whether this is feudal as in the case of Japan, or Communist as in the case of China, bootstrap development means holding down consumption, holding down real wages, and squeezing the farmer as hard as he can be squeezed in order to extract every last ounce of subsistence for capital accumulation. In looser and more democratic societies this is hard to achieve. It is hard to resist the clamor of the people for a present share of future benefits. Under these circumstances it is hard to keep real wages from rising, which means it is hard to keep consumption from rising, which means it is hard to keep production ahead of consumption, which means it is hard to accumulate. Under these circumstances a careful use of foreign investment seems almost necessary. If the investor can be rewarded with friendly attitudes and with long-term security, the recipient society will not have to pay so much hard cash. With an unfriendly and querulous attitude ... foreign investment can only be attracted at a high price. The ability to make good bargains with foreign investors is a very important element in ... success. ...

                K. E. Boulding in The U.S. and Revolution, *1961.*

PLANNING SINCE 1945

Long-term economic planning began in Nigeria in 1945, with a ten-year development plan laid out by the British colonial administration under the United Kingdom Colonial Development and Welfare Act, 1945.[1] It was only partially successful as comprehensive economic planning was still a very new art. The 1945 plan was not an integrated program that marshaled the needs of the nation and its economy as a whole and then assigned necessary priorities. Rather, the plan was an aggregation of projects put forward by various administrative departments of the colonial government without regard for the needs and capabilities of each sector of economic activity. Ten years also proved to be too long a planning period; methods and goals blueprinted in 1945 were no longer relevant after a few years of swift movement and transformation. There proved also to have been too much spending on non-productive social welfare projects whose desirability could not be argued but which did not produce income. Instead, the improved educational, medical, and health services that resulted made recurrent and constantly higher demands on annual budgets.[2]

New impetus was given to economic planning in Nigeria in 1955, with the establishment of the National Economic Council, a cabinet-level[3] consultative body that was "to give maximum encouragement to the development of national economic policy and to close co-operation towards that end among the four governments of the Federation."[4] The Joint Planning Committee, established in 1959, became the "working arm" of the council, chaired by the economic adviser to the federal government and staffed by senior Nigerian officials. The committee "has the specific functions of preparing statements of fundamental objectives for guidance of the planning authorities of the four governments in the formulation of their development plans, and of examining the plans of the governments and making recommendations ... in light of the agreed fundamental objective ... [and] bringing the plans together within the national development framework."[5] Regional ministries of economic planning were set up after the council came into being, but not in the north until October, 1961.

New five-year plans were initiated in 1955 by the federal government and by the regions established under the 1954 Constitution. These were formulated against the background of the lessons learned in the previous decade. In 1960, when independence was about to be granted, the goals had not yet been met, except perhaps in the Western Region, which, in 1960, embarked on a second five-year plan. Meanwhile, the other 1955-60 plans were extended to 1962.

Whether these earlier plans were entirely adequate or not, the decade of 1950 to 1960 was one of considerable growth. It demonstrated what the Nigerian economy was truly capable of and furnished a base for greater achievements. Production in Nigeria grew at the annual rate of approximately 4 per cent in the decade while population only increased by between 2 to 2.5 per cent per year.[6] Agricultural production rose by 30 per cent, and the value of merchandise exports was almost doubled. Five times as many manufacturing establishments existed in 1960 as existed in 1950; construction activity had increased by 200 per cent; and electricity and water supplies were quadrupled. While aggregate consumption remained almost constant at 92 per cent of gross domestic product (GDP), private consumption was reduced from 87 per cent of GDP in 1955 to 84 per cent in 1959. The absolute increases, however, in consumption were about 42 per cent over the decade. The move toward a greater degree of self-government and the costs of social welfare schemes made a corresponding rise in government expenditure inevitable, from 3.5 per cent of GDP in 1950 to 7.5 per cent in 1960. Savings throughout the decade thus ran at about 8 per cent of income. Investment during that time, nevertheless, averaged 11.3 per cent of GDP. This was made possible principally by augmenting domestic product with external resources: the influx of foreign capital and the drawing down of Nigerian-owned sterling reserves.

Nigerian sterling reserves stood at a high of £263.1 million in 1955, but by 1960 these had declined to £171.35 million. The amount of foreign capital invested in Nigeria in the six-year period between 1954 and 1960 amounted to £118 million. Public borrowing had also brought in £11 million and donations, principally colonial development and welfare grants, totaled £25 million. Thus, in the seven-year period, of a total gross expenditure in fixed capital estimated to have been £763 million, 4.7 per cent came from foreign public sources, 15.5 per cent from foreign private sources, and 10.7 per cent from Nigerian exchange reserves. The balance, of course, came from personal savings (39.3 per cent), taxes, government surplus, and other forms of national saving (28.4 per cent).

The 1960 reserves of £171.35 million were quite adequate for the time being in terms of Nigeria's annual rate of imports,[7] but it was obvious that if the rate of drain continued, not only growth but economic stability would be threatened. Priorities had to be assigned which would have the effect of conserving existing foreign exchange reserves and insuring investment in capital assets capable of creating wealth more rapidly.[8]

THE 1962-68 PLAN

The result was the determination to launch a new development program in 1962, one which marshaled all of the resources of an independent Nigeria for the realization of a comprehensive plan that frankly depended in large measure on securing vast sums of external financing and was dedicated to increasing output. The plan originally was to run for five years, but it has been extended to six, to accommodate the goals rather than cut them back or attempt to achieve them in the shorter and, as it appeared, inadequate time. The plan was devised in the Economic Planning Unit of the Federal Ministry of Economic Development with the help of experts supplied by the World Bank and the Ford Foundation.[9] It established the general objectives of development, over-all quantified economic targets, priorities, and strategy.[10]

The National Development Plan, 1962-68, is described thus:

The basic objective of planning in Nigeria is not merely to accelerate the rate of economic growth and the rate at which the level of living of the population can be raised; it is also to give her an increasing measure of control over her own destiny. The present First National Plan is therefore seen as the first in a series which will bring Nigeria to the "take-off" stage. This means that within a reasonable period of time Nigeria should be in a position to generate from a diversified economy, sufficient income and savings of its own to finance a steady rate of growth with no more dependence on external sources for capital or manpower than is usual to obtain through the natural incentives of international commerce. This means also that it will by then be possible to have established at optimum efficiency the institutions, procedures, basic facilities and essential industries which will make such growth possible. This does not, however, mean that Nigeria forgets for a moment that she is a member of the family of nations—indeed the growth of the Nigerian economy is an essential complement to the growth of the expanding world economy and world trade—but it does mean that increasingly she intends to develop her economy so as to be less and less dependent upon such external factors of development as foreign financial and technical assistance, the behaviour of foreign private investment, and sudden changes in the prices of her primary export products.

Until that stage is reached, however, Nigeria will continue to need and indeed welcome foreign capital and skills.[11]

Specifically, the objectives of development have been stated to be:[12] (1) a maximum increase in the standard of living; (2) rapid development of trained manpower; (3) achievement of an equitable distribution of income, both geographically and socially; (4) achievement of a self-sustaining economy; (5) achievement of a more productive and diversified economy to minimize excessive dependence on any single physical or economic factor; (6) achievement of a modernized economy consistent with the democratic political and social conditions of the Nigerian people.

The "quantified economic targets"[13] are: (1) to increase the annual economic growth rate to 4.5 per cent by 1966 (GDP grew at the rate of 2 per cent in 1961-62 and at the rate of 3 per cent in 1963-64); (2) to hold the increase in per capita private consumption to 3.5 per cent per year; (3) to create 500,000 new non-agricultural jobs; (4) to raise the relatively lower standard of living in rural and depressed areas; (4) to maintain the investment rate at least at 15 per cent of domestic product;[14] (5) to achieve, over the six-year period, a total gross fixed investment of £1183.3 million (excluding defense expenditures), 67 per cent of which is to be within the public sector and 33 per cent in the private sector; (6) to reduce the large proportion of gross fixed investment taken up by construction works (60 per cent in 1960); (7) to shift investment into higher "pay-off" areas; and (8) to prevent price increases in consumer goods from rising more than 1 per cent per annum.

THE PUBLIC SECTOR

Of the public expenditures under the plan, both federal and regional, which are to amount to £676.8 million, 71.4 per cent is to be devoted to the sectors that will contribute directly to economic growth: primary production, trade, industry, electricity, transport, communications, irrigation, and industrial water supplies. Of these, primary production, trade, and industry have the highest priority; 27 per cent of the total public investment will go into these areas of activity, almost equally divided. Of the remainder, 10 per cent, or £68 million, will be spent on the huge Niger Dam project. Social overhead (education, health, town and country planning, social welfare, and information) will claim 20.8 per cent of the public investment, of which one-half (10.3 per cent) will go to education; 7.8 per cent will be required for administration.[15]

On "non-economic expenditures," one Nigerian commentator stated that "... there is still scope for further reductions in this sphere. While some, ... such as those on defense and internal security, are, in the nature of things, unavoidable, there are others—such as those on town and country planning, middle-class housing estates, impressive office buildings, over-lavish embassies, etc.—which can be further curtailed or even suspended without much harm to the great majority of the Nigerian population and without much damage to Nigerian prestige abroad."[16] Actually, none of these items except town and country planning appears as such in the plan; to the extent, however, that they appear in annual budgets they obviously affect the availability of resources for realization of the plan. Austerity in the plan can be set at naught by extravagance elsewhere. The 20.8 per cent to be devoted to social overhead is probably minimal in the face of rising popular demand for greater welfare benefits, which for many Nigerians is the tangible evidence of growth and, indeed, nationhood. In large measure, it is insurance for popular support and political stability.

THE PRIVATE SECTOR

Under the plan, the approximate ratio between government investment and private sector investment of 2 to 1 is not expected to shift radically. Private sources, it is hoped, will supply about £400 million in new investment to complement the public resources to be devoted to the plan. Half of the £400 milion is to come from indigenous sources and half from foreign private investors. On the whole, it is believed that the projected rate of private investment is not excessive, but the present imbalance between the indigenous and foreign capital components is a matter of some concern, since the future of Nigeria's foreign-exchange position rests on the planned inflow of private foreign capital. In both 1962 and 1963, private investment is estimated to have been £70 million per year, against a planned annual rate of £65 million, of which foreign capital was only £10 million to £15 million. Undoubtedly, the low rate may be ascribed to remittances made by trading firms to short-term creditors overseas and the substitution of Nigerian credit sources, particularly for financing exports in line with government policy to "Nigerianize" the credit base. The inflow of private capital into the manufacturing and processing industries, it should be noted, increased between 1961 and 1962, from £5 million to £12 million. The outflow has been mainly in the trading and services sector. Nevertheless, the private investment figure of £70 million per year is to be contrasted with the high level achieved in 1960 of £90 million to £95 million—9 per cent of GDP, of which foreign capital was £20 million to £25 million.

FOREIGN PUBLIC CAPITAL

The capital component that Nigeria hopes to raise abroad from public sources (international agencies and foreign nations), in both loans[17] and grants, amounts to £327 million, the contemplated deficit in foreign exchange without further drain on existing reserves and without any deduction for underspending. Less than half that amount was in sight at the end of the plan's first year, but by mid-1964 the gap had been reduced to £105 million, according to the Minister of Finance, who was probably taking underspending into account. The United States alone has committed itself to provide £80 million, exclusive of surplus food shipments under Public Law 480 and of loans extended before the plan. United Kingdom loans, grants, and commitments stood at £17 million in 1964, and principal aid commitments from other nations were as follows: Italy, £9 million; the Federal Republic of Germany, £8.5 million; Israel, £3 million (of which £1.16 was drawn prior to April 1, 1962); and the Netherlands, £2 million.[18] By late 1964 the World Bank (IBRD) had committed itself to loans totaling £44.82 beyond the £10 million committed before April 1, 1962. Thus the IBRD had already exceeded the expectations of £40 million which the planners hoped for from this source over the entire 1962-68 period. Nigeria has also received approximately £12.5 million from the International Development Association, £0.5 million from the International Finance Corporation, and £4.3 million from the United Nations Special Fund, of which £2.7 million is estimated to contribute to capital expenditures under the plan.

To encourage and co-ordinate foreign loans and grants to Nigeria, an IBRD Consultative Group was established in 1962, consisting of Belgium, Canada, the Federal Republic of Germany, Italy, Japan, the United Kingdom, the United States, and Switzerland. The group has met several times to exchange information on the programs of donor nations and of the IBRD.

The contemplated foreign-exchange deficit assumes, of course, that Nigeria will be able to sustain the currently high earnings of its seven principal export crops[19] and sales of crude oil. Oil may, indeed, prove to be the salvation of the plan if, as it now appears, Nigeria possesses one of the world's great oil pools. But the economy remains principally agricultural, and Nigeria's fortunes are closely tied to the movements of world commodity markets. However, Nigeria enjoys a considerable margin of safety in that it exports as many crops as it does, rather than only two or three, for price fluctuations are more likely to average out or at least ameliorate sharp and wide changes in national income. Public demand for imported consumer goods until 1962 was running constantly higher and was causing a heavy drain on foreign exchange; annual tariff increases since 1962 have cut back consumer imports somewhat but have increased revenues even more.[20]

Imports during 1963 totaled £207.5 million, a slight increase over 1962, reflecting purchases of machinery and equipment. Tariff increases and rising Nigerian production brought about a decline in imports of cement and consumer goods. The value of exports during 1963 was also slightly higher, amounting to £189.5 million. As a result, the over-all trade deficit in 1963 was only £18 million, exactly half of what it had been in 1962. However, payment for services and other transactions in "invisibles" took £12 million. On December 31, 1963, foreign-exchange reserves, therefore, stood at £94 million, down £30 million from 1962—the heaviest loss to date. By the end of March, 1964, reserves had dropped further to £87 million, sufficient for five months of imports at current prices.[21]

External-resource requirements will be further reduced to the extent that the £327 million of foreign exchange is realized through grants rather than loans, for the projected need is based on its entire fulfillment through loans and, therefore, includes a debt service cost of £52 million.[22]

FINANCING INTERNAL COSTS

How is Nigeria planning to pay for the internal costs of the six-year plan? All internal resources devoted to the plan must be generated as savings—that is, the difference between income and consumption, whether the expenditure is made in the governmental or the private sector. The major financing of the government's portion of the plan will be achieved by taking in approximately £1.2 billion in revenues and income, spending only £954 million on "running the household" and putting the balance into the plan. A portion of annual government budgets is always devoted to non-consumption items, such as buildings, which are capital investments rather than items of recurrent expenditure.[23] These are not necessarily related to the six-year plan; to the extent that they are, they serve the plan. However, they are not included in the specific public sector investment objective of £676 million.

Similarly, the plan will benefit from economies affected in non-capital government expenditures—what government "consumes" by way of civil service salaries, rentals paid, and other recurrent administrative expenses. Such savings generate a surplus on recurrent account if taxes and revenues remain constant or rise, for example, while spending on annual government costs declines. The difference may then be diverted to the development plan, and the plan envisages £27 million coming from this source over the six-year period. Despite the fact that government expenditures in 1962 increased by £20 million over 1961 and were estimated to increase by another £10 million during 1963, the Minister of Finance in April, 1963, predicted budget surpluses for the two years amounting to £17 million. In fact, a budget surplus of almost half that amount, £8.45 million, was achieved in the first year, but this fell to £3.13 million in the second year. Nevertheless, the sum of £11.5 million represents 40 per cent of the plan's capital funds expected to come from that source over the six-year period. Since government costs increased, the surplus obviously came from increased revenues, mainly the higher duties on imported goods imposed in 1962. Rivkin had in 1961 proposed an increased revenue on luxuries as capable of bringing in some £10 million to £15 million annually.[24]

Economies in government operation in a new and expanding society are unlikely (although underspending typically occurs in the public capital investment sector), but it may be possible to shift some of the heavy educational expenses now borne by the federal and regional governments to local authorities and to students. Even here, there is not likely to be any net gain. Additionally, it is believed that there is need in Nigeria, principally as the result of the Western Region crisis of 1962,[25] for the expansion of police and military forces, for naval units, and for an air force befitting Nigeria's status as an African power. An armaments factory has also been built. As apparently must happen to all nations, "defense" now looms as the most expensive item in the Nigerian budget; £12 million was budgeted for 1964-65. None of these factors, needless to say, is conducive to budget surpluses in the future, and while sizable surpluses were achieved in the first two years of the plan, they are not likely to recur in the same magnitude, if at all, especially in view of the 1964 wage increases. The government's ability to fulfill its contribution to the plan out of budget surpluses will now depend on finding additional revenue by way of direct taxes or excise duties.[26]

Developmental institutions have functioned at the regional level for several years, channeling funds obtained primarily from regional marketing-board surpluses into regional agricultural and industrial development. No comparable development corporation existed at the federal level, although the Ministry of Economic Development fulfilled for the federal government many of the functions performed for the regions by their development corporations. The federal government also channeled federal funds as equity investment into specific projects. But it lacked an "entrepreneurial, capital-mobilizing" institution. Thus, the creation in January, 1964, of the Nigerian Industrial Development Bank (NIDB)[27] became "another milestone in the economic march of Nigeria," as the Minister of Finance put it. NIDB is the successor of the wholly privately owned Investment Company of Nigeria (ICON), founded in 1959 with a capital of £1 million subscribed by Nigerian, British, Canadian, American, Swiss, French, and Dutch individuals, banks, insurance companies, and commercial engineering and manufacturing firms. ICON's purpose was to provide medium- and long-term loans and to purchase equity shares in Nigerian public and private companies. It also sought to stimulate the creation of technical and financial partnerships with Nigerian interests and played an important part in establishing the Lagos Stock Exchange; one of its announced goals was to "stimulate a share and security market." It also engaged in underwriting, encouraged foreign investors to come into Nigeria, and offered management and technical advice.

ICON might well have gone on its way as it was and very usefully. But as a "going concern" with a remarkable record of accomplishment, it attracted the attention of Nigerian authorities as a ready-made base for fulfilling the need for a national development bank. Thus ICON, after rather difficult negotiations, was reconstructed at the request of the Nigerian government, and NIDB, 51 per cent controlled by Nigerian interests, is the result.

Control is held by the Nigerian government (which has made an interest-free loan of £2 million), by the Central Bank, by the International Finance Corporation (which has undertaken to regard its shares as Nigerian), and by Nigerian shareholders whose total holdings at present amount to only £20,000. However, the portfolios of both the Central Bank and the International Finance Corporation will be opened to the Nigerian public. ICON shareholders have for the most part remained as part of the minority, while eight new banking and investment houses in the United States, Germany, Italy, Switzerland, and Japan have been brought in as shareholders.

NIDB will devote its funds and energies principally to investment in industry and in mining. Like its predecessor, NIDB will make or guarantee medium- and long-term loans, underwrite new issues of securities, invest its own funds, and provide technical and business management advice. The president of NIDB is Chief Ugochukwu, a self-made businessman who has been characterized as "a firmly free-enterprise man."

Beyond that secured from revenue sources, additional financing for the governmental share of the six-year program will have to be drawn from the private sector by loans made by institutions and individuals through the purchase of various types of government savings certificates.[28] This source depends on what private savers are able to accumulate after spending what they need for consumption, less what portion of such accumulations they choose to put into private sector investment. In a society with a low level of per capita income and increasing consumer demands, saving is a rare phenomenon. It is not merely a case of lack of thrift. It is simply that the necessities of life and rising levels of taste press against income. The lack of consumer credit facilities helps to create savings because individuals must save up for large purchases rather than buying on time. Although these are short-term funds, in the aggregate they constitute a relatively stable pool of savings that can be channeled by the institutions holding such funds in the form of postal savings, national savings certificates, or commercial savings accounts into government securities. This is true, of course, if such funds are put into savings institutions and are not buried or otherwise hidden, as is reputed to be widely the case in Africa, particularly among the poorly educated and rural population.

Results of efforts made, in 1963, to induce saving and to coax funds into savings channels and directly into the public sector through a nationwide campaign were disappointing. The volume of premium bonds and savings certificates stood at only £11,000 at the close of 1962 and had only risen to £59,000 by the end of November, 1963. Although the Minister of Finance said in his 1963 budget speech that he was "far from despondent" and expected to intensify the National Savings Campaign, there is real doubt whether voluntary small savings can contribute significantly to the plan. The campaign cannot induce saving where income does not permit. Savings facilities must not only be readily available but there must be knowledge of their use and confidence in their liquidity. The National Savings Campaign may thus be a useful educational program that will ultimately bear fruit, but not before some time has passed. Instilling the "idea" of saving, however, is, after all, itself a component of an economic growth program and essential to future development plans.

That other types of small savings are growing despite the obvious handicaps is reflected in rising commercial savings accounts. These increased from £21 million to £24.2 million during 1962 and increased again during 1963 to £28 million, probably reflecting principally traders and urban middle-class savers with higher-than-average incomes who were situated in communities having banks. Postal savings, on the other hand, whose facilities are available at every post office and by their nature attract low-income and rural savers, fell during 1962 and again during 1963.

Deposits in commercial banks rose from £87 million at the end of 1962 to £96 million at the end of 1963. However, loans and advances rose from £77 million to £89.5 million, so that credit was extended at a greater rate than savings were accumulated. The net result, of course, is that the plan derives no support from this sector at all; in fact, since only short-term funds are involved, the banks' credit policy is in aid of consumption rather than saving. Concern should also be expressed for the dangerous "overlending" that is taking place, from the viewpoint of sound banking practice.

Credit controls are, of course, available to the Minister of Finance, but they are politically awkward to institute and difficult to administer effectively. Minimum liquidity ratios squeeze the Nigerian bankers who have no overseas resources such as the expatriate bankers have. Selective instruments of control—such as informal requests of banks to restrict the financing of imports, a method currently employed—generally hurt the Nigerian trader first and foremost and do not seriously affect the established expatriate trading firm. The Central Bank rediscount rate has no appreciable influence on commercial lending because of the considerable gap that exists between the rediscount rate and the rates charged by banks for prime loans. It would seem that controls must eventually be used which more directly inhibit consumption, such as more restrictive import policies on consumer goods and restrictions on high-cost residential and office-building construction. The present policy of raising tariffs to discourage consumption of imports has two faults: it tends to be inflationary, and it tends to distinguish even more sharply the difference in the standards of living of expatriates and the Nigerian elite, on the one hand, and the Nigerian masses, on the other. There is no way to save except by not spending, and this requires an austerity that Nigerian officialdom has not yet been willing to impose upon itself.

The urban middle class is beginning to interest itself in life insurance, although the industry is in its infancy in Nigeria. But as actuarial studies demonstrate the insurability of larger numbers of Nigerians, this will become an important channel for savings and investment of funds in governmental and private-sector development. At present, at least, life insurance has become sufficiently important to require legislation passed in 1964[29] to the effect that all life insurance issued in Nigeria and covering Nigerians must be denominated in Nigerian currency and the whole of the premiums invested in Nigeria. Additionally, a powerful tax incentive exists to encourage the purchase of Nigerian policies and investment by foreign insurance companies in Nigeria of premiums paid by Nigerians in non-Nigerian currency, e.g., policies taken out by Nigerians while in the United Kingdom. The whole of such premiums are allowed to the insured (or the person paying the premium) as a deduction from taxable income; if the premiums are not invested in Nigeria, the maximum deduction is only one-third of the premium.[30]

A new outlet for private savings is the facility of the Lagos Stock Exchange, both with respect to the several successful new issues floated and the thirty-odd stocks now listed on the exchange. The exchange, which began operation on June 5, 1961, with four licensed brokers, supplements the cumbersome mode of transacting business in London by cable or letter, and provides a means of investing funds that for one reason or another must remain highly liquid. But even more important in the long run is the opportunity it provides to Nigerian savers to participate in risk-taking enterprise related to Nigerian economic development. At this point, only a small group of Nigerian individuals are active in this role: applications of Nigerian individuals to subscribe to the £2.1 million Nigerian Sugar Company issue of 1962 numbered 920, for a total of £125,780; in 1963, 495 Nigerians purchased £31,070 worth of the £50,000 ordinary stock issue of the *Daily Times* of Nigeria. Private financial institutions—insurance companies and pension and provident funds—have been the main support of new issues, and large blocks of stock continue to be placed in London.[31] Of the Nigerian sugar issue, £800,000 was subscribed by United Kingdom investors, £540,000 by the Nigerian government, and £760,000 by Nigerian private investors, both individuals and institutions. Nevertheless, the £760,000 represents the largest single accumulation of private capital resulting from a public offering.[32]

The issuance of securities is regulated by the Companies Act.[33] Prospectuses of shares offered by the Lagos Stock Exchange are in a sense "policed" by the Council of the Exchange and, for the present at least, by the English parent companies themselves or by the rigid requirements as to disclosure imposed by United Kingdom law firms, local law firms, and firms of chartered accountants that participate in the preparation of the issue. Of the companies that have thus far floated new issues through the exchange, only the Nigerian Sugar Company is not the subsidiary of a British firm. In that case, however, a Nigerian subsidiary of a British firm was appointed managing agent of Nigerian Sugar under a twelve-year contract, and the Nigerian subsidiary of another English firm agreed to "buy at Company's ruling selling price any part of the Company's sugar production in Nigeria which is not otherwise sold."[34]

The most usual form of issue is that of convertible debenture stock secured by a trust deed on the company's assets. However, Dunlop Nigerian Industries made an offering of ordinary stock in 1962, and the *Daily Times* issue was split between ordinary shares (£50,000) and 7 per cent first-mortgage convertible-debenture stock (£300,000).

Securities-trading in private issues at the exchange has roughly doubled in volume each year of operation, from a monthly average of £7,000 in 1961, to £12,000 in 1962, to £26,000 in 1963. While the total number of transactions in 1963 was only slightly higher than in 1962 (709 as against 695), the total value of all transactions more than doubled. Transactions in government stocks still dominate trading; in 1963 the 295 transactions in government securities represented a value of £4.9 million, and the 414 transactions in industrials had a value of only slightly more than £300,000.

Among institutional savers, the National Provident Fund (NPF), which was established in 1961[35] and began operations in April, 1962, promises eventually to channel considerable resources into investment but, for the time being, however, only into the public sector. This is a form of social security that covers retirement (at age fifty-five), survivorship, invalidity, and sickness. Like other systems, it is constantly adding to its reserves because it covers an ever-increasing work force that is compelled to contribute, as is the employer. In its first year, the fund took in £2 million. By the end of 1963, 390,646 workers with cumulative contributions of £4.5 million were in the scheme. Coverage is general for all wage earners, and exemptions are few. When extended to a new category of employees, participation becomes mandatory, and private plans, although they may continue in force, may not be offered in lieu thereof.

The Minister of Finance has decided that the income of the fund will be invested only in "securities enjoying trustee status and for the present this will be further limited to investment in Federal Government securities." An American observer, formerly associated with ICON, has described the Fund as a "quasi-taxation device" and suggests that "the Fund should be managed in the direct interests of its contributors, which would mean optimizing return on investment given certain restraints on risk, rather than in the sole interest of Government, which is to raise capital for public sector investment."[36] However, as the same observer points out, it is not clear that purchase by the fund of private securities would constitute any net gain for the private sector since "the Federal Government has supported the market by buying securities in its own name ... in effect transferring funds from NPF (and other sources) to Government and then putting them back into the private sector."[37]

Since benefits payable by the fund are set by statute and these will probably be determined by criteria other than available reserves, it is perhaps doubtful whether the contributors would be better served if the fund could purchase private "growth" securities. Caution and conservatism in administering this "public trust" are probably the considerations that dictated the minister's decision. It is important to note that, in regard to economic development, an employer-employee-financed social security program such as the fund creates savings whose demands as purchasing power are long postponed. It dampens consumption. Secondly, it relieves government of the expense of providing equivalent or similar benefits out of current revenues to pensioners whose claims will mature during the critical decades of development ahead. The existence of the fund also probably tends to diminish popular demand for more extensive government-supported welfare programs that might add to the burden of recurrent expenditure. Additionally, while the government has the use of these savings, they are held in trust and, in fact, remain private savings. The fund's proceeds, invested in government securities, come to the government as loans, not as revenues, and thus exert a conservative influence in the formation of development plans.

The fund does result in enforced savings, just as taxation does, but the effect is quite different. Although saving through the fund requires no individual initiative, the idea of individual participation is emphasized by the payroll deduction and by the individual's knowledge that he has a claim on the fund. This is preferable to meeting government's capital needs through general taxation and appropriation, where all initiative and ultimate control pass to government. There is, instead, under the fund, the meeting of an urgent social need through a desirable balance between private and public sectors.

The repatriation of capital, institutional savings, and to some extent the import of capital are reflected in the purchase of government development loan bonds and short-term treasury bills. Between 1959 and 1962, three development loans had raised £19 million. In early 1963, the Fourth Development Loan brought in £15 million,[38] and the Federal Republic of Nigeria First Development Loan in early 1964 raised £20 million. Treasury bills have been marketed since April, 1960 (on a weekly basis since January, 1963), and British commercial banks have been among purchasers of treasury bills; but loan bonds have not attracted foreign capital. The transfer of Nigerian-owned capital from abroad has been rather successfully encouraged and, on its return, has gone largely into loan bonds. In 1962, the Minister of Finance regarded the maximum long-term debt that could be sustained by the value of treasury bills permanently in issue at £10 million; in 1963, he raised this estimate by suggesting a range of £10 million to £15 million.[39]

The main subscribers are the Central Bank, the commercial banks, and the regional marketing boards. Individuals account for less than 0.5 per cent. Total internal borrowing by the federation, by April, 1963, including fixed long-term debt and treasury bills, amounted to £67 million, up from £14 million in 1959. The debt-to-income ratio then stood at less than 1 to 6, which is quite healthy.

FEDERAL PROJECTS AND ALLOCATIONS UNDER THE SIX-YEAR PLAN

The principal development project, which will require 10 per cent of the public expenditure contemplated under the plan, is the Niger River dam at Kainji in Northern Nigeria, which is to have an initial capacity of 280 megawatts, when completed in 1968, and an ultimate capacity of 880 megawatts. It is estimated to cost £72 million and will be financed out of the federal component of the plan.[40] Kainji is part of a long-term scheme for which a permanent statutory body has been set up, and it will eventually supply the greater part of Nigeria's electricity needs.[41] Two more dams are to be constructed as power needs increase.[42] The dam at Jebba, with a 500-megawatt capacity, is to be brought into use in 1982. The third, at Shiroro Gorge, will bring the total power output of the complex to 1,730 megawatts. Foreign financing committed directly to the Kainji Dam is: World Bank, £28 million; U.S., £5 million; U.K., £3 million; Italy, £9 million; Netherlands, £2 million (plus suppliers' credits amounting to £2 million). The dam system will also benefit agriculture through irrigation,[43] aid fisheries through the creation of lakes, establish flood control, and increase the navigational capacity of the Niger River.[44] It is contemplated that aluminum smelting will eventually be one of the major industrial uses of power.

The second major project to be financed at the federal level is a £30 million iron and steel complex to be located in Northern and Eastern Nigeria, using Nigerian iron ore, limestone, and power. Efforts are now being made to find a way to "coke" Nigerian coal, which is of a low grade. The mill is expected to go into production in 1966-67 and should reach its ultimate capacity of 250,000 tons in 1970-71. Initially, it will produce black and corrugated sheet steel, rods and bars, angles, channels, and other structural steel. It is contemplated that eventually the regional governments will join in financing the mill. A sum of £2 million was allocated for the oil refinery in the east, and its completion is planned for 1965. In addition, £5 million is to be used for direct investment in other types of industry, and £25 million has been designated for assistance to regional governments in expanding primary production.

Over-all, the federal government's "portion" of the £676.8 million plan is £412.5 million. This amount represents direct spending by the federal government (£238 million, or 58 per cent) and self-financing by statutory corporations, government-owned Nigerian National Lines, and government-owned Nigerian Airways. Within the federal sector, the following allocations have been made: transport (£104 million); trade and industry (£44 million); town and country planning (£23 million); and health (£10 million). The federal program breakdown has 72.3 per cent going into development, 16.5 per cent into social overhead, 10.7 per cent into administration, and 0.5 per cent to debt service.

Federal aid to higher education under the plan is to total £14 million and reflects the government's concern over Nigeria's pressing high-level manpower needs:[45] £5.5 million is for the University of Lagos, £4.5 million for the expansion of the University of Ibadan (which is also a federal institution), and £4 million for regional universities.[46] About one-half of the £10.3 million to be devoted to the federal government's health program will go to the expansion of the University of Ibadan Hospital and the newer University of Lagos Teaching Hospital. A target date of 1967-68 has been set, by which time the universities should have an enrollment of 10,000 full-time students, of which 7,580 are to be enrolled in pure and applied science courses.

REGIONAL PROJECTS AND ALLOCATIONS

In Western Nigeria the total 1962-68 government expenditure was projected at £240.1 million, of which capital expenditures are to equal £90.3. Hoped-for private-sector investment is £140 million. The objectives were stated to be increased productivity, modernization, diversification, increased employment (particularly to absorb the numbers of primary-school leavers), "to strengthen the development spirit of the community as a medium of fostering economic progress and to strengthen the private sector of the economy." In introducing its plan, the government of Western Nigeria also stated:

The approach of the 1962-68 Programme is fundamentally the same as that of the First Development Plan and of the 1960-65 Plan of which the present is a projection. The First Plan laid the foundations of a welfare society based on the true values of freedom and democracy and on respect for the individual; a social and economic order which tries to make equal opportunities available to all; an order in which there is a steady rise in income and standard of living—deriving from increased productive capacity, both agricultural and industrial—coupled with a very large measure of social justice.[47]

The proposed allocation of public capital investment was as follows: commerce and industry (£24.9 million); primary production (£18.4 million); public works, transport, and power (£17.7 million); social services (£21.8 million). Major categories of projects planned within that framework include: large-scale industry (£10 million); credit facilities, including contribution to the Western Region Development Bank (£6.8 million); urban water supplies (£6.25 million); roads and bridges (£6.25 million); farm settlements (£5.6 million); University of Ife (£5 million).

Eastern Nigeria proposes to spend a total of £108.9 million, of which £75.2 represents capital investment. A sum of £37 million is to go to agricultural and other primary production to diversify the region's economy and reduce the inordinate reliance on the production of palm oil, which until the discovery of oil in the east accounted for 90 per cent of the exports. Eastern Nigeria already has a good industrial base; during 1952-62, £65 million was invested there in industry, most of it by private foreign investors. Specific allocations under the plan are: education and technical training (£29.9 million); trade and industry (£13.5 million); transport and communications (£10.2 million); rural and urban water supplies (£6.2 million); town and country planning (£3.5 million); and health services (£3.2 million). Included is the Eastern Region's £2 million investment in the oil refinery.

Northern Nigeria plans to spend the largest amount during 1962-68, a total of £293.8 million.[48] It has the farthest to go, lagging considerably behind the southern regions in every phase of economic development except political stability and its commitment to private enterprise.[49] Capital expenditures are to total £98.8 million, of which £66.4 million is to be direct government expenditure and £32.4 million is to be channeled into development corporations from the Industrial Development Corporation. The latter is to operate "as a commercial company ... on a profit-making basis," engaging in projects either by itself or with a technical partner from the Agricultural Development Corporation or from the Housing

Corporation (successor to the former Native Authority Housing Corporation). These draw their financing from the Northern Nigerian Development Bank, which in turn is financed by the Marketing Board and by outside investment. A total of £17.7 million, it is hoped, will be made available to the bank over a six-year period, principally from marketing board surpluses.

The principal allocations in the north are: communications (£22.5 million); education (£18.9 million); rural and urban water supplies (£9.25 million); agriculture, fisheries, and animal resources (£8.8 million); and health services (£4.4 million).

THE FIRST TWO YEARS: 1962-64

The first survey of accomplishments under the 1962-68 Plan was released in March, 1964, covering only the federal portion of the plan[50] (regional reports were to be issued later in the year). "Shortfalls" and "imbalances" that appeared in the first two years were overshadowed by the 1963 census report, which, if accepted, would wipe out the predicate for Nigeria's growth; the plan assumed a population growth rate of 2 to 2.5 per cent, and the census revealed an annual population increase of 5.5 per cent. What deficiencies appeared in performance had to be viewed in the light of the initial difficulties in getting the plan moving evenly along all fronts and the slow generation of projects and expenditure of funds in the first years.

Nevertheless, in several important aspects, revisions and adjustments were suggested. First, costing of projects was apparently far too conservative; the federal government's share of financing the plan, £412 million, had risen by £70 million, or by about 16 per cent. The principal cost increases occurred in electricity, transport, and administration (including defense); additionally, the government decided to increase its direct investment in industry from £5 million to £8 million. Projects continued from the 1955-62 programs of development also cost more than anticipated.

Second, the report indicated an imbalance in spending between wealth-producing ("development sector") and social welfare ("social and administration sectors") schemes, in favor of the latter. A deficiency of 14 per cent in expenditures in the development sector was estimated and a corresponding "over-investment" in welfare, and the report asked that the pattern be "radically changed" if the objectives of the plan were not to be adversely affected.

Reasons for the imbalance were given as three: (1) delay in completing studies and designs for large-scale projects; (2) the rise in security and defense needs; and (3) the lag in agricultural development planning. For example, spending on research in the primary production sector, which includes agriculture, fell short of its goal by 4 per cent. The Food and Agriculture Organization mission surveying agriculture in Nigeria was slow in submitting its report, and the establishment of the National Agricultural Bank, for which £3 million was allocated, awaited the report. In trade and industry, investment was only half of what had been planned for the two years. The steel mill was "still at the preliminary stage," although £320,000 was spent on the project in 1963-64. Of the £5 million planned for direct investment, £2.2 million went into the Nigerian Sugar Company, Dunlop Rubber, Michelin Tyre, and the Nigerian Fermentation Company.

Excessive spending occurred in transportation, which accounted for 38.8 per cent (£15.9 million) of the money spent under the plan instead of the scheduled 25 per cent. This is within the "development sector," but the report admits that there has been "too much emphasis on the construction of roads and bridges."

The tendency to spend scarce resources on prestige items or what are considered incidents of nationhood were apparent in the following expenditures made in the first two years: broadcasting (and this is only the federal service) consumed 3.3 per cent (£1.4 million) of the 1962-64 capital expenditure total, six times the original amount planned (Nigeria has inaugurated External Service Broadcasts which may be heard twice daily in the United States); an ordnance factory, £811,000; military barracks at Enugu, £800,000; and warships, £470,000.

The third point made by the report was that financing of the plan was falling short of expectations as far as external capital input was concerned. Difficulties were also forecast in securing adequate local capital over the next few years. The report recommended "drastic measures ... to increase available resources." Whereas the plan envisaged that 50 per cent of expenditures over the 1962-68 period would be financed from foreign sources, in the first two years, only 14 per cent of the federal government's total capital expenditures came from abroad, and it is believed that the proportions with respect to regional plan expenditures were even lower. Of course, this low proportion in the first two years is governed by the nature of the projects undertaken. Over 33 per cent (£140 million) of the federal government's share of the plan[51] has been assured in terms of external resources, all of it tied to specific projects, some of which have not yet gotten underway.

On the domestic side, the largest share of plan expenditures came from drawing down Nigerian foreign reserves, to the extent of £10 million, twice what the draw-down was to be during this period under the plan.

During the plan's first year, borrowing from domestic sources provided £17 million, principally from the Fourth Development Loan. The First Republic of Nigeria Development Loan,[52] floated early in 1964, raised another £20 million. In both cases, as noted previously, the Central Bank was the chief subscriber. While total domestic borrowing is expected to obtain £63 million for the plan, the report suggests that £40 million is the limit of the Central Bank's contribution. To expect the bank to contribute more, the report says, would "impair monetary stability." Institutional investors are expected eventually to be the principal sources of the difference. Budget surpluses, as noted, may repeat the phenomenon of 1962-63, but it is hardly likely. Statutory corporations performed poorly in the first two years. They are expected to provide £89 million for their own development over the six-year period, but in the first year, only some £5.5 million of the £13.2 million they spent came from their own resources.

A concrete result of the survey of the first two years' performance was the decision, announced by President Azikiwe in his 1964 message to Parliament, to establish a Project Evaluation Unit and an Investment Unit, which are "to conduct feasibility studies and project evaluation on a nationwide scale to ensure that our industrialization programme is properly oriented to those industries which will ensure the maximum growth in our economy."[53] For the prospective foreign investor, the creation of the Investment Unit, long recommended to the Nigerian government by a number of experts and businessmen, was welcome news. This office was to serve both as an information center and liaison office for new investors and as a registry for industrial projects established in Nigeria. It was hoped that this facility would remedy the lack of "focus" that has prevailed in the Nigerian government's efforts to encourage new foreign investment, which has been evident in the dispersion of reliable information and authority. Unfortunately, by the end of 1964 the proposal had not yet been realized, and the only source of comprehensive information for the prospective investor continues to be members of the A. D. Little Company team, who are to be found in the offices of the U.S. AID mission or tucked away on the fifth floor of the Ministry of Commerce and Industry. The difference between wish and fact is sometimes appalling.

III

Nigerian Law: Sources and Prospects

In the majority of developing countries the adoption of a framework of law and regulations conducive to the full use by their citizens of productive resources that already exist would probably make a greater contribution toward their development than is now provided by all external assistance from both public and private sources.
     Emilio G. Collado in Foreign Affairs, *1963.*

THE RECEIVED LAW

As an offspring of the British colonial system, Nigeria fell heir to English law as British rule was extended, first to the Colony of Lagos, annexed to the British Empire in 1861, then to the Protectorate of Southern Nigeria (the former Oil Rivers Protectorate, established in 1885 and enlarged in 1893, when it became known as the Niger Coast Protectorate), and finally to the Protectorate of Northern Nigeria, which Britain took over from the Royal Niger Company on January 1, 1900.

Various ordinances and proclamations[1] gradually brought the judge-made common law and the doctrines of equity and English statutes of general application[2] to Lagos and the protectorates, so that, by 1906,[3] in theory and in law, at least, the three bodies of law applied throughout what was to become the Protectorate of Nigeria in 1914[4] and was ultimately to constitute the nation of Nigeria, except for the addition, in 1961, of the British Northern Cameroons.[5]

The result was to provide the colony and the protectorates—and after 1914, the Protectorate of Nigeria—with a ready-made body of legal doctrine, practice, precedents, and statutes. Furthermore, this was administered in Nigeria by English colonial civil servants, thus firmly implanting it, at least initially, in its "original purity." This received body of law was supplemented after 1900 by those "imperial statutes," passed by the British Parliament, that were of "general application"[6] and were made applicable to dependent territories by reference or by necessary implication, and by delegated legislation enacted by the Crown, under the authority of the Foreign Jurisdiction Act,[7] and promulgated by Orders in Council.[8] More frequently, as the years went by and the local legislative function was developed, the received law was augmented by English statutes that, as "model enactments," were adapted to Nigerian conditions and promulgated under the authority of the colonial administration by proclamation or by local legislation.

While the received body of unwritten common law and equity transplanted to Nigeria looms large in the statute books and practice of Nigerian courts even today, it was and is "residual law." While the lacunae that this received residual law filled were, indeed, very large, nevertheless, it did not supplant pre-existing native law that was not repugnant to "natural justice, equity, or good conscience."[9]

The high court laws of the federation and the regions direct in almost identical language that "The High Court shall observe and enforce the observance of every customary law which is applicable and is not repugnant to natural justice, equity, and good conscience, nor incompatible either directly or by implication with any written law for the time being in force, and nothing in this Law shall deprive any person of the benefit of any such customary law."[10]

Thus, where native law—or customary law, as it is now called—was well developed, as in the spheres of family relations, real property, succession, and inheritance, English common law or equity could only be a "law of last resort," at least where only Nigerians were involved. Both the received English common law and the pre-existing native law had to retreat in the face of British imperial statutes and local Nigerian legislation. Local legislation, in its turn, remained subordinate to applicable imperial statutes, orders, and regulations issued thereunder.[11] Additionally, the administration of this received law by colonial judges according to the criterion of general applicability also conditioned its acceptance. Thus, a statute or a principle of the common law might not be applied in Nigeria because examination revealed its source to be a peculiar local English condition (thus denying its generalness) or because of its unsuitability in the receiving country, by virtue of peculiar local conditions (thus denying its rational applicability).[12] In fact, Allott points out that not only the power to exclude but also the power to modify "objectionable rules of English law" was exercised by imaginative colonial judges.[13] Of course, colonial legislatures increasingly exercised the adaptive and creative functions, and English statutes were often considerably altered before their enactment as Nigerian law. Since this process of revision was one of up-dating law, as well as conforming it to local conditions, which were not always so highly peculiar, such legislative action often resulted in "bringing the colonial law closer to, instead of farther away from, the current law of England."[14] In other instances, because the application of the law would involve primarily Englishmen in Nigeria, or because no local criteria had been sufficiently developed, statutes were adopted without significant change, such as the English Companies Act of 1908.

Today, only Nigerians legislate for Nigeria.[15] Laws in existence in 1960 were continued in force by the Independence Constitution "as if they had been made in pursuance of this Order [in Council] . . . read and construed with such modifications, adaptations, qualifications, and exceptions as may be necessary to bring them into conformity with this Order." The Republican Constitution of 1963 has a similar provision: "§156.-(1) All existing law . . . shall, until that law is altered by an authority having power to do so, have effect with such modifications (whether by way of addition, alteration, or omission) as may be necessary to bring that law into conformity with this Constitution and the constitution of each Region."[16]

Since English decisions made before 1900 in the common law or equity, or with respect to statutes also applicable to Nigeria, were obviously part of the received English law, the problem regarding pre-1900 precedents binding on Nigerian courts was simply which English courts could render decisions binding the courts of Nigeria. Although that matter was never made crystal clear,[17] it has been generally assumed that the decisions of the English high court and courts superior to the high court were binding on colonial supreme courts.[18]

What of decisions made by high court judges in England after 1900 that expounded or modified equity and the common law as received in Nigeria in 1900? Is "the common law fixed and the judge's function . . . merely to find, reveal and apply the relevant rule"?[19] Or does the law stand as it did on the date of reception, because there does not, in fact, exist an "undiscovered" body of common law that was received *in toto*, whether or not enunciated on a cut-off date? Allott says that the first view is "untenable, although colonial courts appear constantly to treat such [post-1900] English decisions as binding on them."[20] Elias, on the other hand, says that post-1900 decisions "apply [and, presumably, he means "bind"] as long as they do not involve a change of any particular common-law doctrine or principle."[21] Thus, it would seem, a post-1900 decision of the English high court, applying an established common-law or equitable principle to a "new" post-1900 set of facts, would bind Nigerian courts if the same set of facts subsequently arose in Nigeria. While it may be argued that this circumstance—"old" principles applied to "new" facts—would itself be a "change" in the principle concerned, Dr. Elias' statement of the rule appears preferable. This also receives support from the recent analysis made by Park:

. . . Dr. Allott's arguments, upon close examination, do not hold good. And his position is not in accordance with the actual practice of the courts. For, notwithstanding the isolated *obiter dictum* of Petrides J. quoted above,[22] it is clear that they operate on the other interpretation. In deciding issues on points of common law and equity they base themselves on English cases without making any attempt to discriminate between those decided before and after 1900. Many examples could be given of cases in which only post-1900 English rulings have been used to establish the rule applied.[23]

However, where after 1900 an English court, whose decision in law or equity would otherwise be binding, has rendered a decision on a pre-1900 statute of general application or a post-1900 imperial statute applicable to Nigeria, the decision does not bind a Nigerian court. This follows because such decisions constitute neither common law nor doctrines of equity. And, as has been noted, where a principle of the common law or equity has been altered by Nigerian legislation, an English court's statement on the unaltered principle carries no weight in Nigeria.

It would seem logical to assume that, since Nigeria became a republic in 1963, only Nigerian judges can now create precedent binding on Nigerian courts, but this is not the case. The Republican Constitution in §155(3), by specific reference to the Interpretation Act,[24] retains "any right, privilege, obligation, or liability" saved by that statute's operation. Thus, if we accept the view of Elias and Park that post-1900 decisions of appropriate English courts are binding on Nigerian courts, since neither independence in 1960 nor the establishment of the republic in 1963 has interrupted the rule, it still obtains. The received law of England, which with respect to equity and common law does not remain static, thus continues to occupy a vital place in Nigeria. As Park says, "That, of course, does not prevent a body of Nigerian case law growing up around this received law. This has indeed occurred.... But it does prevent Nigerian common law and equity striking off on their own, and in places departing from the pattern of development in England."[25] What is to be awaited is revision of the various laws which strikes the words "of England" from the provision regarding the application of the common law in Nigeria; and development may not even await that technical change. As Park himself has said elsewhere: "The influx in a few years' time into the legal profession of lawyers well versed in the decisions of their own courts will without doubt substantially advance the replacement of English by Nigerian cases as the main source of authorities on the common law and the doctrines of equity."[26]

English precedent will then rank no higher than the decisions of other common-law countries, including other members of the Commonwealth and the United States, which in recent years have been increasingly cited by Nigerian courts. This has been especially true where the lineage of a particular body of law is traced to a nation other than England (*e.g.*, the Penal Code of Northern Nigeria, 1959, which came to the region from India through the Sudan) or where precise English precedent is lacking (*e.g.*, constitutional law developing under a written constitution, where reference is made to United States judgments or to those of Commonwealth countries).[27] For some years still, however, the substantive links with the past, reinforced by training, habit, and the limited reference books available, will probably result in more frequent citation of English cases as authority than of those of other common-law countries.

A NEW JURISPRUDENCE?

Perhaps, someday, demands will be heard in Nigeria for the development of a "mixed jurisprudence" rather than a "slavish" following of English-oriented law.[28] Certainly we can expect that nationalistic impulses will find expression in efforts to "Nigerianize" the law, i.e., to emphasize local origins and values.[29] Some voices to this effect have already been heard. Indeed, there is a renewed interest in and emphasis on customary law as an assertion of Nigerian identity; but the changes are likely to be more apparent than real, for the interests of Nigeria as an aspiring commercial and industrial nation coincide with the thrust of the body of transplanted English law. This needed body of modern law is nowhere to be found in existing indigenous norms that historically have been concerned largely with personal and family relationships, with land tenure, and with torts and contracts only on a relatively primitive level. There is no thought of undoing the changes made by the colonial administration in Nigerian customary law. After the enlightened postwar colonial rule of Nigeria and three years of independence under the Crown, very little of a fundamental nature remains to be undone in the way of imposed colonial legislation that was contrary to Nigerian values.

Efforts to introduce legal concepts and rules from non-common-law jurisdictions, on the other hand, may eventually pose a more serious threat to the "integrity" of the adopted legal system. This is not to suggest an eclecticism that would try to construct the ideal jurisprudence by combining the best of common-law and civil-law systems. But the felt needs of a developing nation for a jurisprudence incorporating a "statist" approach to development might seek legal norms in the systems of socialist or communist nations, which appear to be more compatible with its goals, particularly in areas where its interests and those of the former-colonial and other "capitalistic" powers are or appear to be in conflict.

Such a shift in legal values would proceed from a political decision of the greatest importance, assuming, of course, that it would be made within the constitutional framework. What may be said here is that the Nigerian judiciary and bar would, without doubt, resist any efforts to achieve a "mixed jurisprudence," whatever it might be. Most certainly, the initiative for such a change will not come from Nigerian lawyers. Beyond the positive factors of stability, certainty, and economy, which the judges and lawyers of Nigeria know inhere in retention of the present system, certain negative factors militate against experimentation of this kind. There is little knowledge among Nigerian judges and lawyers, all British trained, of non-common-law legal systems and principles. The difficulties posed by foreign languages and the non-availability of materials are further obstacles. Habit and inertia fortify these factors. The Nigerian public would have no interest in an effort to construct an "ideal" legal system that hinged on debating the comparative virtues of existing legal systems,[30] although an uninformed enthusiasm or, at least, support for an "African" or "Nigerian" system of law might be generated by political manipulation.

More likely is the further development of tendencies by intellectuals at the political level to look for guidance and sources in the legal systems of other young nations that, like Nigeria, were once colonies and have similar constitutional, political, and economic problems, and it is also likely that these intellectuals will promote such new norms. How Indian law has accommodated that country's program for economic development and its search for political stability is an attractive subject for the attention of Nigerians because an identity of interests exists here that the legal systems of white, developed nations do not provide, except through the "colonial tradition." An eclectic Western jurisprudence, where the choice between aspects of systems lies principally in sophisticated refinements of legal abstractions and procedure, is politically meaningless. But the affirmative rejection of accepted norms that are identified with the former colonial nations may have great political significance, particularly if a scapegoat must be produced. The relatively settled systems of Western jurisprudence are often criticized as not entirely responsive to the dynamics of the vast and profound social and economic change that India and Nigeria are undergoing. The law imposed by a colonial administration is somewhat suspect since its primary object is not viewed as being social justice. What begins as an "anti-colonial" attitude may by extension become anti-Western and anti-white; far oftener, it will be articulated as anti-capitalist. The appeal for a new legal approach may then be made in a more positive context. It may be proposed as "socialist," or, even more affirmatively, as "African socialist," or simply "African."

Nigeria, like all of Africa, is in search of itself. Although the preoccupations of newly-won independence distract the African nationalist from the larger scene, this identity will soon again be sought in the larger frameworks of regionalism; then of race or color; and, perhaps ultimately, in that seemingly logical but often wholly unnatural "unity" that geography may appear to provide, in this case, the continent of Africa. The negative forces of poverty, inexperience, and instability, which now and for some years will act centripetally on the divergent nations of Africa, will, as they are overcome (in individual nations), act as centrifugal forces. Nevertheless, the common effort to escape from what has brought these nations together may result in the development of "new" norms of constitutional and economic law, consciously or unconsciously borrowed from socialist legal systems but promulgated as African. Several channels exist for the indirect transmission of Marxist norms into an African *corpus juris* that would avoid the stigma of "foreign law" with which Africans already feel overburdened. They can come from Ghana, Guinea, or the new nations of North Africa or East Africa; or, indeed, they may gradually insinuate themselves as the necessary substance of what a good number of responsible Nigerians refer to rather loosely as "pragmatic socialism," "democratic socialism," or "African socialism,"[31] without explaining what is really meant.

In Nigeria, a number of forces work against any easy acceptance of legal norms developed or brought into Africa in this manner. First and most important is the position of leadership that Nigerians believe is theirs, by virtue of Nigeria's size, relative wealth in human and natural resources, and its moderately successful record for stability, democratic practice, and effective administration since independence. In large measure, this derives, it is submitted, from the successful manner in which Nigerians have assimilated the Western (or British) "heritage," compared with other African countries. This has led to a certain air of superiority among Nigerians vis-à-vis other African states, and much of it is justified. Nigeria will not assume a passive role in the development of new "African" norms and will be unreceptive to legal ideas having their genesis elsewhere on the African continent through a process in which Nigeria has not participated. The infusion of legal ideas into Nigeria is unlikely from certain West African nations toward which animus exists (such as Ghana),[32] from hinterland states that are frankly considered structurally and culturally inferior, or from North Africa, whose states are geographically, culturally, and racially remote from Nigeria.[33]

CUSTOMARY LAW AND COURTS

Customary law, it will be remembered, is the basic law of Nigeria—all other law is interstitial or superimposed. While the scope of customary law may be narrow, the vast bulk of litigation, which occurs at the customary court level, falls within its ambit.[34] The authority usually cited for the retention of customary law as law in English colonies is the statement of the Privy Council in *In re Southern Rhodesia*:[35]

Some tribes are so low in the scale of social organization that their usages and conceptions of rights and duties are not to be reconciled with the institutions or ideas of civilized society. . . . On the other hand, there are indigenous peoples whose legal conceptions, though differently developed, are hardly less precise than our own. When once they have been studied and understood they are no less enforceable than rights arising under English law.

In practice, it is pre-eminent, rather than co-equal with English common law and equity. As Allott points out,[36] it is doubtful whether the first portion of the quoted statement applies to any African legal system. "Among the Negroes of Africa," wrote one authority, "primitive jurisprudence attains its highest development. In precision and scope their code rivals that of the Ifugao,[37] but unlike the Ifugao, the Negroes have almost everywhere an orderly method of procedure before a constituted tribunal. They display a remarkable taste for juridical casuistry and a keen sense of forensic eloquence."[38]

However, as we have seen, customary law may be superseded by legislation, and the rule has always been that it may be applied only if it is not repugnant to natural justice, equity, and good conscience. These criteria are hardly as meaningful today as they once were. British colonial administration has long since eliminated the "barbarous" aspects of customary law that fell under the prohibition. Additionally, in practice, customary law is not necessarily applied if the case involves mixed elements of customary and received law;[39] if the parties have agreed that the transaction is to be governed by the received law; if the parties are not both Nigerians (although a non-Nigerian may agree to submit to customary law, and customary law may be applied without such consent if "it would be unjust to either party to apply English law");[40] or if the parties, though Nigerian, are subject to different norms of customary law pertaining to the case owing to differing tribal origins. Aside from its relation to real property,[41] customary law does not directly pertain to this study, except, perhaps, to the extent that it reveals the tendency to conservatism in retaining customary law or indicates a tendency to discard established norms and engage in legal experimentation, which is reflected in its abandonment or radical revision.

Now that Nigeria is independent, it may soon be incorrect to speak of a separate body of customary law, except to identify sources. There will be, more properly, a Nigerian "common law of mixed origins," free of new foreign influences except as imported formally by legislation and informally by judges in writing opinions.[42] The conscious political efforts to achieve internal unity in all areas of Nigerian life, both national and regional,[43] would appear to work against the further development of law restricted to particular tribal groups, as customary law is. The application of customary norms, as they now exist, will be hampered by the increasing mobility and urbanization of Nigerians. In Lagos, there are now no customary courts, although customary law may be applied in existing courts in appropriate circumstances and between appropriate parties.[44] Norms of more general applicability will be sought in legislation at the regional level, it can be predicted, and the body of distinct and viable customary law will recede as it is thus absorbed or displaced. For example, all customary law pertaining to crimes has been replaced throughout Nigeria by criminal codes, retaining in but a few instances only the most general of customary norms.[45]

In the north, the Islamic content of customary law is very large.[46] It is likely to remain so for some time, and customary law and the system of customary courts are likely to retain vitality there longer than in the south. The Northern Nigerian is conservative and traditionalist, and his reference to customary law is reinforced by his religion.

It is interesting to note that only in Northern Nigeria may a judge decide a case under "justice, equity, and good conscience"[47] when no rule of stated law, written or unwritten, appears applicable. As a result, analogous customary law may be applied, in the name of equity, in a case involving one or more non-Nigerians to whom customary law, as such, would not be properly applicable.[48] In effect, however, the result may be less objectionable than that following on application of the provision of the high-court laws of Lagos and the regions, under which customary law may be applied "also in causes and matters between Nigerians and non-Nigerians where it may appear to the court that substantial injustice would be done to either party by a strict adherence to any rules of law which would otherwise be applicable."[49]

While customary law may be applied in any Nigerian court, the customary courts, which apply both general law, as set forth in their constitutive legislation, and customary law (including Islamic law), have jurisdiction only over Nigerians in the Western Region.[50] In the Eastern Region, jurisdiction extends to "persons of African descent, provided that the mode of life of such persons is that of the general community,"[51] and to persons of non-African descent as directed by the governor in council to be so subject.[52] In the Northern Region, the native courts have jurisdiction over both permanent and temporary residents whose general mode of life is that of the general native community.[53] Non-Africans may, however, submit to the jurisdiction of these courts by consenting thereto, and they do so consent by instituting proceedings in customary courts. In all three regions, customary courts have both civil and criminal jurisdiction.[54] In the Eastern Region, for example, the civil jurisdiction of a district court (customary court) of grade A (the higher of two grades) is limited to claims not exceeding £50, while its criminal jurisdiction is confined to crimes punishable by not more than six months' imprisonment, twelve strokes of the cane (for juveniles), or a fine of not more than £50 or its equivalent under customary law.

In the Northern Region, there exist both Moslem and non-Moslem native courts,[55] the former applying Moslem law to Moslem parties in civil cases only; there is no distinction as to the criminal law applied by either type of court, since both are governed by the Northern Penal Code.[56] The Moslem courts are commonly known as Alkali courts, after the Moslem official who sits as president. Like the non-Moslem courts, they exist in five grades. Appeals in questions of Moslem law go from either the highest Alkali court or native courts to the Sharia Court of Appeal. The basic law applied there is that of the Maliki School,[57] but its frame of reference also includes "natural justice, equity and good conscience."[58] To resolve conflicts of jurisdiction between the Sharia Court of Appeal and the High Court of Justice of the Northern Region (the regional supreme court) a Court of Resolution was established in 1960.[59] The permanence of the law of Islam in the judicial system of the north is thus institutionally assured at all levels, in contrast to the south, where customary law may be hard-pressed to survive once it leaves the customary courts and enters the domain of lawyers and judges having little interest in perpetuating it.

The disinterest of lawyers in customary law derives not only from their lack of formal training in this branch of Nigerian jurisprudence but also from the more immediate fact that lawyers are excluded from representing clients in the customary courts except in the top grades, which the bulk of litigation does not reach.[60] As a result, there is neither the incentive to learn nor the opportunity to gain practical knowledge of customary law. Elias says that lawyers "tend to despise the, to them, non-technical rules of law and procedure followed in the Native Courts."[61] The English training of lawyers also "tends to breed in them a sneaking contempt for the indigenous laws [which for them have] neither the dignity of 'civilised' law nor the prestige of authority."[62] The establishment of Nigerian law schools may alter this in part by providing formal education in customary law,[63] but, at present, the subject can (and does) receive only cursory treatment in the curricula of law schools designed to train lawyers for practice—and the application of customary law does not, except by way of rare appeal,[64] involve the lawyer. The incentive is still lacking.

The gradual assimilation of customary law into bodies of regional statutes, as has already been accomplished by the criminal codes, where legislation is bound to replace large areas once occupied by tribal norms in order to facilitate economic development and credit expansion,[65] would appear to be the fate—and hope—of customary law in Nigeria. As long as lawyers' appearances before customary courts are limited, customary law remains unwritten, the judgments of such courts go unreported, and appeals are few, it is difficult to foresee the *evolution* of "general principles" (as distinguished from stating such principles as the result of unification and codification) of diverse systems of customary law into either a regional or national "common law."[66]

This is not to argue the indispensability of lawyers to the realization of justice in the customary courts but to assert their critical role in the process of creating and sustaining a viable system of general common law in a diverse society. Thus, if customary law is to be preserved, it would seem either that all the customary courts must be opened to lawyers or that it must be accomplished through unification and codification of customary law by the legislature, with the help of lawyers or legally-trained experts. The peculiarly local or tribal characteristics of law, in either case, will be lost and will be replaced by more generalized, external norms. This might precede and aid national or regional integration. Whether a legislature would dare to anticipate the processes of history and impose such general norms as a stimulus to national unity and to economic development is not free from doubt. The criminal codes do not furnish a ready precedent for the codification of the law of marriage, divorce, custody, and inheritance. The British impact on criminal norms, even at the customary level, was already considerable during the colonial period; the law of personal status and relations was generally left alone, except for certain flagrant "abuses."

It is difficult, in any event, to see how particular tribal norms can survive national and regional political and economic integration. Economic development requires the marshaling of human resources in cities and towns and in plantations and farm settlements. It means urbanization, mobility, and the disintegration of rural, tribe-centered life. New value groups, such as political parties and unions, will be substituted for the tribe. There will be a retreat from the loyalties to the extended family to a preoccupation for the needs and demands of the immediate family. All of these factors will foster the need for a general body of law governing personal status that is free of tribal idiosyncracies. This will be a process of decades, of course, perhaps of a century, but it seems reasonably certain that it will eventuate.

However, customary law has an important institutional prop. Chiefs and elders, who once had a larger role to play under the British system of indirect rule, must now cling to customary law as the mainstay of their declining power. Apart from conferred or inherited status, which is itself regulated by customary law (subject to regional legislation, of course), and the ceremony that attends the office, the holding of customary court is the sole demonstration of legitimate authority left to the chiefs and the major source of their claim to local pre-eminence. It is the one prerogative that chiefs may still consequentially exercise.

But chieftaincies and councils of elders cannot survive indefinitely as elite institutions. The "best man" principle in the selection of chiefs and customary-court magistrates in the Eastern Region (which never had traditional, inherited chieftaincies) is symptomatic of their decline. An increasingly educated, democratic-minded, and utilitarian society that is bent on modernization and the efficient use of scarce economic resources will hardly tolerate unearned status and privilege.

Even in the "feudal" north, where the emirs are firmly entrenched, a shift to an "efficient" oligarchy is taking place. In his autobiography,[67] the Sardauna of Sokoto, Premier of the Northern Region and the reputed power behind the Prime Minister of Nigeria, claims that

... the old Emirates were originally much more democratic than they were when the British left them, and ... we have been doing our best since then to put things back; to ensure that the Chiefs are surrounded by a wide body of suitable councillors, mostly chosen by election, whose advice they *must* take....

The immense prestige of their office is thus harnessed to the machine of modern progress.... To remove or endanger this prestige in *any way,* or even to remove any of their traditional trappings, would be to set the country back for years.... We must get away from the idea that they are effete, conservative, and diehard obstructionists: nothing could be farther from the truth....[68]

The institution of chiefs has been fortified by constitutional provisions that give chiefs legislative functions in the upper houses of both the federation and the regions. Under the federal constitution, two of the four senators representing the federal territory are the Oba of Lagos, who is an ex-officio member of the Senate, and "a chief selected in such a manner as may be prescribed by Parliament by the White-Cap Chiefs of Lagos and War Chiefs of Lagos from among their own number."[69] Each of the three regions selects twelve federal senators, nominated by the regional governor and elected by the regional legislature. Although senators representing the regions in the federal Parliament need not be chiefs, four chiefs now sit for Western Nigeria and five each sit for Eastern and Northern Nigeria. Each of the upper houses of the three regions is designated as "House of Chiefs," and only chiefs or traditional rulers may sit in these houses. In all four legislatures, the upper houses participate fully in the legislative process, except that in no case may the upper house originate "money" bills[70] nor defeat a "money" bill by a refusal to act on it, as long as the bill has been submitted to the upper house at least one month before the end of the session.[71]

Despite these extensive provisions, the place of chiefs in the government is generally regarded in the south of Nigeria as a transitional arrangement. However, this overlooks the difficulties that constitutional amendments in Nigeria would involve: altering §42 of the federal constitution requires the consent not only of two-thirds of the members of both federal houses but also that of three of the four regional legislatures.[72] The procedures for amending regional constitutions are included in the federal constitution,[73] and amendment requires the support of two-thirds of the members of both regional houses. Furthermore, the procedure for amending regional constitutions cannot itself be amended without the consent of at least three regional legislatures. Since the elimination of chiefs at the regional and federal levels, therefore, requires the assent of one or more houses of chiefs, respectively, their survival appears constitutionally assured.

This rigidity may be argued as desirable when one considers the entrenchment of civil liberties in the chapter on fundamental rights.[74] But if, as many Nigerians in the south assume, chiefly prerogatives are ultimately to be sacrificed to egalitarianism or democratic progress, it is not easy to see how this will ever be accomplished without a severe constitutional wrench. That the British expert draftsmen participating in the evolution of the 1960 Constitution should have permitted this entrenchment of chiefs, when their own upper house is but an interesting remnant of the past, is rather curious.

Of course, chiefs are a conservative and, for the time being, stabilizing influence, as is the customary law. Indeed, at this point, both are essential to the governing process since the administrative apparatus of regional governments would be inadequate without them. But their entrenched constitutional position will delay the modernizing process; it will, at least, delay the unification and integration of customary law and will preserve the customary courts as particularistic tribunals where partisan and highly subjective norms are often applied.[75] In a very real sense, the regional governments are perpetuating the principle of "indirect rule" inherited from the British, using chiefs and elders as supplements to their own as yet imperfect administrative and compulsive apparatus.

The foreign investor may assume that the retention of chiefs in the governmental system is indicative of conservatism, an assurance against the radical change that he usually fears. In the Northern Region, this is so. In Southern Nigeria, the chiefs owe more to the British and to a sense of expediency on the part of the nationalists who worked for and secured Nigeria's freedom. This is not to suggest that the elimination of chiefs is an issue in the south, nor is it soon likely to become one. It is simply that their presence in legislatures should not be misconstrued.

THE JUDICIAL SYSTEM

The federal Supreme Court[76] stands at the apex of the Nigerian judicial system, a position occupied until October 1, 1963, by the Judicial Committee of the Privy Council.[77] Its jurisdiction extends throughout the federation. While primarily an appellate court, the Supreme Court has original and exclusive jurisdiction "in any dispute between the Federation and a region or between regions if and in so far as that dispute involves any question (whether of law or fact) on which the existence or extent of a legal right depends."[78] Additionally, Parliament may confer original jurisdiction in matters other than criminal[79] and may confer jurisdiction to advise the president[80] on the exercise of the prerogative of mercy or similarly to advise the governor of a region.[81] "Substantial questions of law" involving the interpretation of the federal constitution or a regional constitution are referred to the Supreme Court by high courts.[82]

Appeals lie from high courts to the Supreme Court, as of right, in seven specific categories of cases[83] and, by leave of the court, in three specific categories.[84] In both instances, appeals may lie in "such other cases as may be prescribed by any law in force in the territory."[85] The appeal by right from a final decision in any civil proceedings initiated before a high court[86] does not include ex parte orders, orders relating to costs, consent decrees, or a decree absolute in a divorce or annulment proceeding founded upon a decree *nisi* that the party failed to appeal.[87] Appeals may also reach the Supreme Court, as of right, from the Sharia Court of Appeals (the highest Muslim court of the Northern Region) when a constitutional question is at stake, including the provisions of the chapter on fundamental rights, and where prescribed by law in force.[88] Similarly, such questions may come up from the Court of Resolution, the court established to resolve differences between the High Court of the Northern Region and the Sharia Court of Appeals; but the appeal from the Sharia Court of Appeals must go to the Court of Resolution, rather than directly to the Supreme Court, if the Court of Resolution "is competent to determine" it.[89]

The high courts are established in Lagos and in the capitals of each of the regions.[90] Subject-matter jurisdiction is strictly territorial. A high court applies only federal law or that of the particular region. The law of other regions is treated as foreign law.[91] High courts exercise general jurisdiction in both civil and criminal matters, within their respective regions, and are precluded only from those matters in which the Supreme Court has original and exclusive jurisdiction. Since the constitution provides that service and execution of process are subjects of both federal and regional power,[92] it has been possible for the federal Parliament to enact legislation,[93] which, in effect, permits the writs and processes of high courts and magistrates' courts to be served anywhere in Nigeria,[94] including provision for service to compel the attendance of witnesses.[95] Under the same power, the judgment of a high court or magistrates' court is enforceable anywhere in Nigeria.[96]

The high courts consist of six to twelve judges in addition to the chief justice, who is the head of the regional judiciary. Except for the High Court of Lagos, the regional high courts are divided territorially into judicial divisions. One or more judges are assigned to divisions and constitute the divisional court, which holds court both at its headquarters and on circuit.

Nwabueze describes the mode of operation of the high court thus:

For the exercise of both its original and appellate jurisdiction the High Court is constituted by a single judge, except in the Northern Region where the court must sit with two judges on appeals—three on appeals from native courts—with the Chief Justice or the senior puisne judge as president. The court acts by a majority in civil appeals and by unanimity in criminal appeals, unless in the opinion of the court in any particular case separate judgments may conveniently be delivered. Where the court is constituted by two judges who disagree... the decision appealed against is deemed to be the decision of the court if it is supported by one of the judges, otherwise the appeal must be reserved for hearing before an uneven number of judges not being less than three.[97]

The question of whether a system of federal courts should be established within the regions is still being argued.[98] There appears to be neither need nor a strong desire for "splitting off" the present "federal" function of the regional high courts. Two sets of superior courts would complicate litigation and bring on staffing problems without any concomitant benefits, at least for the present. Perhaps, as legislation becomes more complex and specialized, if federal and regional interests tend to diverge, and as litigation between citizens of different regions increases, the need for a separate system of federal courts may arise, as it has in other federal systems.

The British heritage extends down the judicial hierarchy to provide a variety of tribunals that were transplanted to Nigeria: magistrates' courts,[99] justices of the peace, juvenile courts, and coroners' courts. The process of arbitration, too, has been known in Nigeria since a relatively early date and is provided for by statute.[100]

Magistrates' courts are courts of record, presided over by legally-trained judges who, as Nwabueze says, "act as a bridge between the two extreme positions occupied by the High Court and the native or customary courts."[101] While the bulk of Nigerian litigation takes place in customary courts, the number of cases heard by magistrates is very large, generally exceeding the number of cases heard in the high courts by thirty to sixty times.[102] There are grades of magistrates, varying in Lagos and the regions, and their respective jurisdictions are gradually circumscribed from that of chief magistrate to the lowest grade. In Lagos and the Northern Region, there are four grades (chief magistrates, and grades I, II, and III); in the Western Region, three grades (chief magistrates, senior magistrates, and magistrates); in the Eastern, there are only two grades (chief magistrates and magistrates). The maximum civil jurisdiction is £500, in the case of a chief magistrate, who has jurisdiction in criminal cases to try non-indictable offenses by summary procedure (imprisonment up to two years or fine up to £200) or indictable offenses if the accused consents thereto (rather than requesting trial in the high court) and the prosecutor agrees. Magistrates also conduct preliminary hearings in criminal cases over which they have no trial jurisdiction but where, if a prima-facie case is made out, the accused is bound over to the high court for trial.

Beyond their adjudicatory functions, magistrates may exercise certain powers as "peace officers," as described by Nwabueze:

Magistrates also have important functions in regard to the maintenance of law and order, which is probably a legacy from the days when the local authority for most townships in the country was the station magistrate. Under the Criminal Code, every magistrate is made a "peace officer," with power to prevent breaches of the peace, to suppress unlawful societies, processions and assemblies, and also riots. A magistrate in whose view a riot is being committed by persons assembled within his view, may make a Proclamation in the Queen's name, commanding the rioters, or persons so assembled, to disperse peaceably on pain of imprisonment for five years.[103]

Justices of the peace have similar powers and responsibilities in keeping the peace. Unless he is given judicial powers, as he has in the Western and Eastern Regions in minor civil and criminal cases, a justice of the peace is concerned with the issuance of warrants, summonses, and search warrants; administering oaths; conducting arraignments of accused and binding them over for trial before a magistrate, and setting bail.

Juvenile courts may be constituted in Lagos and all of the regions, under the chairmanship of a magistrate who is assisted by two lay judges, "one of whom should, as far as practicable, be a woman."[104] Coroner's inquests are conducted along lines similar to those in the United States. The coroner is generally a magistrate, although others may be appointed by the regional governor.

Under the Arbitration Act, 1955,[105] an agreement to arbitrate future disputes is binding. The high court may assist the process of arbitration by naming the arbitrator if, under any circumstances, the terms of the agreement, with respect to the appointment of an arbitrator, cannot be carried out by furnishing subpoenas and by enforcing the award. As might be expected in a country that is still developing commercially and industrially, arbitration has been little used, but its availability, under procedures generally familiar to American businessmen, is a favorable factor for the investor to note.

THE PRIVY COUNCIL AND THE STATUS OF THE JUDICIARY

When the Judicial Committee of the Privy Council, on May 27, 1963, reversed the judgment of the Supreme Court of Nigeria in the case of *Adegbenro v. Akintola*,[106] Nigerian government leaders feared that political chaos threatened if the Privy Council decision were followed. It would have meant that the dismissal of Chief Akintola in May, 1962, as premier of the Western Region by the governor general of the Western Region was a constitutional exercise of the latter's power, which the federal Supreme Court had held it was not. Relying on the Supreme Court decision, Chief Akintola had resumed the premiership on January 1, 1963, at the end of the emergency that had existed in the west since the previous May. Now the Privy Council decision questioned the legitimacy of the Akintola government and all its acts over a five-month period. Also, the political foes of Akintola, and of the federal coalition government, would have won a great victory. Perhaps most important, it reminded Nigerians that, despite political independence, a tribunal sitting in London to which a Nigerian had only recently been appointed[107] had the final word on Nigerian legal questions of the most far-reaching consequences. A highly placed Nigerian official, in discussing the dilemma with an American visitor, threw up his hands and said, "We would like to follow the rule of law, but how can we?"[108]

The "rule of law" was ultimately served, although the Privy Council's decision was not followed. The solution was highly unorthodox; the Constitution of Western Nigeria was retroactively amended,[109] disposing of the problem of how the original language should be interpreted, which the two tribunals had answered with contrary conclusions.[110] The bill, it was explained, was "designed to amend the Constitution of Western Nigeria to make it abundantly clear that the Premier cannot be removed from office unless it appears to the Governor, in consequence of the passing of a resolution in the House of Assembly by a majority of the members of that House, that the Premier no longer commands the support of a majority of the members thereof."[111] It was made retroactive to October 2, 1960, the day on which the Western Region Constitution came into force. In presenting the bill to amend, the deputy premier of the Western Region (who, of course, derived his power and position from Chief Akintola) condemned the Privy Council decision in scathing language and said frankly: "The objects and reasons of the Bill are clear. Its purpose also is clearer. And that is to retain law and order in the Region and make impossible a state of affairs which might cause fresh discord in this Region. . . . What more can a lover of democracy ask for?"[112]

In the week following the arguments in the *Adegbenro* case, the Privy Council heard the appeal from the Supreme Court of Nigeria in *Balewa v. Doherty*.[113] Here, while the Privy Council affirmed (with some slight variations) the decision of the Supreme Court of Nigeria, the judgment went against the Prime Minister of Nigeria. Suffice it to say that, like the earlier decision, this one, also, found little favor among Nigerian leadership. While, at this point, the decision had already been taken to make Nigeria a republic on October 1, 1963,[114] it was not so clear that agreement existed that appeal to the Privy Council should also be abandoned on that date. It is believed that the *Adegbenro* and *Doherty* decisions, however, led to such a consensus. Certainly, thereafter, no one spoke for retention of the appeal, and, with the coming into force of the Republican Constitution, the Supreme Court of Nigeria became the final court of appeal for Nigeria.[115]

The Privy Council had been the final court of appeal for Lagos since 1867 and for the remainder of Nigeria since 1909.[116] Between 1933 and 1955, appeals moved from the Nigerian Supreme Court (created in 1914) to the Privy Council via the West African Court of Appeals, which, during that span of time, served Nigeria as an intermediate court of appeal. Since 1955, appeals lay only from the Supreme Court of Nigeria to the Privy Council and did so in three categories of cases: (1) appeals as of right, in civil proceedings involving property worth £500 or more, for dissolution or nullity of a marriage, for the interpretation of the federal or a regional constitution, and in such cases as prescribed by parliament;[117] (2) by leave of the Supreme Court, where in its opinion "the question involved in the appeal is one that, by reason of its great general or public importance, ought to be submitted to Her Majesty in Council," decisions in any civil proceedings, and as prescribed by parliament;[118] (3) by special leave of the Privy Council.[119]

It has been suggested that the Judicial Committee could, with its "Olympian aloofness, free from political pressures... in times of acute political controversy... bring a calm judicial air to constitutional problems."[120] Did not resort to the Privy Council and its decisions of the committee contribute to Nigerian legal and constitutional development, and might not preservation of the appeal have served Nigeria well in the future? A Nigerian barrister and scholar answers the question as follows:

There can be no doubt that it has been [beneficial]. The Committee had not only acted as a watchdog over the constitutional rights and liberties of the inhabitants of Nigeria against the autocratic methods of the Colonial Governors, it had also offered a rather liberal interpretation of the law in the country.... As Independence drew near it was feared that all sorts of things might happen; nobody could, with any certainty, predict the course which politics in the country was going to take. One of the ways in which the framers of the Nigerian Constitution sought to provide against these possible contingencies is to retain appeals to the Privy Council, which could be relied upon to safeguard the constitutional rights and liberties of the citizen against the Executive; at times when the local judiciary might possibly come under political influence.[121]

The Privy Council could not only bring its Olympian detachment to difficult political constitutional problems fraught with regional and tribal jealousies but, under the 1960 Constitution, it was also the final arbiter on the question of whether the judge of a constitutional court, *i.e.*, the Supreme Court or a high court, should be removed from office,[122] a matter that could obviously have profound political implications.[123] The Privy Council was, therefore, viewed as a guarantor of an independent Nigerian judiciary.

But the provision of the 1960 Constitution for a federal Judicial Service Commission appeared sufficient to insure the independence of the courts.[124] Similar bodies were established by the regional constitutions.[125] These were to have substantial roles in shaping the character of the Nigerian judiciary over the critical years of growth ahead, particularly to keep them free of regional and tribal influences. But when Nigeria became a republic in 1963, not only was the Privy Council eliminated entirely from the Nigerian court structure but the judicial service commissions were also abolished.

The functions of the judicial service commissions were to appoint and promote judges of lower courts and court officials at all levels: magistrates, district judges, chief registrars, registrars, and other officials of the federal Supreme Court, high courts, district courts, and magistrates' courts. The commission could, with the approval of the prime minister or premier, as the case might be, delegate its powers in this behalf to any of its members, to any judge, or to any other court official. Under the 1960 Constitution, the role of the federal Judicial Service Commission, with respect to the appointment of judges of the federal Supreme Court and the High Court of Lagos, was purely advisory,[126] and it had no role in the appointment of either the chief justice of the federation[127] or the chief justice of

Lagos,[128] both of whom were to be appointed by the governor general solely on the advice of the prime minister.

How, then, did provision for judicial service commissions result in a "self-perpetuating judiciary," as the attorney general of Nigeria described it? While this term is too broad to describe accurately the role of the federal Judicial Service Commission, the fact is that it was far more instrumental in the choice of judges than was the executive. The advice of the commission could not easily be ignored with respect to the appointment of judges. Even where its function was purely advisory, an inexperienced justice could not easily be foisted on the other members of the Supreme Court or of a high court; and the Judicial Service Commission, by controlling the appointment of magistrates and other lower-court officials, determined the kind and quality of experienced men who would eventually be available for promotion to the high courts and then to the Supreme Court. Except for the raw exercise of power by the governor general and the prime minister acting in concert, the Supreme Court and the High Court of Lagos would, in effect, be picked and trained by the judiciary. The same was true of the governor and the premier at the regional level, with respect to the regional high court.

The dismissal and disciplinary control of magistrates and lower judges and officials was also vested in appropriate judicial service commissions in the regions and at the federal level. The removal of a judge of the Supreme Court or of a high court, under the 1960 federal and regional constitutions, was a purposely complex matter, involving an investigatory tribunal appointed by the governor general (or governor) at the request of the prime minister (or premier) and composed of present or past judges of superior courts in the Commonwealth. The tribunal then decided whether or not to refer the matter to the Judicial Committee of the Privy Council. If it decided not to refer it, the question was closed; otherwise, the final decision was up to the Privy Council. The Privy Council is, of course, no longer the final arbiter on the dismissal of judges; instead, judges of the Supreme Court and of the various high courts may now be removed by a two-thirds vote of both legislative houses. Control of the judiciary now rests entirely in the executive and the legislatures. How did this come about? How was Nigeria's enlightened experiment in the neutral choice of judges, based on qualification, scrapped?

Among Nigerian leaders who are not trained in the law, there is a basic distrust of a judiciary that is not responsive to political change. In some cases, especially among the northerners, who essentially are in control of federal power, it goes even further; the courts are viewed as the handmaidens of the ruling oligarchy and judges must be responsive to political necessity. The contrary strain of feeling is that the courts, the most British of the institutions that survived the transition to independence and then to republicanism, are, indeed, bastions of privilege, formerly of the Crown and the colonial administration and now of the expatriates and wealthy class, and that they tend to impede the new dynamism and pragmatism of national development with norms developed for another culture, another era, another economic system. On the other hand, there are those who are more accustomed to the British concept of the supremacy of Parliament and the lack of judicial power of review than they are to operating under a written constitution; they quite honestly question the role of a handful of judges as the arbiters of a nation's destiny through their power to set at naught the decisions of the elected representatives of the people and their duly appointed executive.

The complete politicization of the higher Nigerian judicial system through the abolition of the judicial service commissions, therefore, represents a constitutional reorientation of substantial importance, but one not widely appreciated at the time nor since. This cannot solely be attributed to public misapprehension. Clever politics was also responsible, it is believed.

In late July, 1963, the regional premiers descended on Lagos for the all-party "Constitutional Conference" that was to consider the alterations to be made in the 1960 Constitution for the change-over to a republic. With surprising unanimity, all spoke of the desirability, and even necessity, of including a provision for preventive detention in the new constitution. Such a proposal was not even on the conference agenda. What was involved was this: under present law, a person may be detained by the Nigerian police only twenty-four hours on suspicion without formal charges being brought against him before a magistrate. Under a Preventive Detention Act, which would have to be authorized by the constitution, persons could be held for longer periods, as up to three months in India[129] or for indeterminate periods in Ghana.[130] The public uproar against this proposal was loud and sustained until the idea was dropped.[131]

West Africa pointed out in an editorial that "the only justification for such an Act is that the ordinary machinery of justice is proving inadequate to protect the State's security. To introduce such an Act now in Nigeria, while a large-scale treason trial is in progress, might be considered a grave reflection on the conduct of the courts."[132] Its mere proposal at that juncture was, in fact, such a reflection; certainly the proposal to abolish the judicial service commissions confirms this. But in the storm of criticism that discarded the detention act proposal, the "relatively harmless" proposal to abolish the commission was accepted—not without objection, to be sure—but as a concession, as it were, for the other.[133] The more dangerous threat, or so it seemed, which may well have been a straw man, had been defeated, after all. While lawyers, judges, and the opposition newspaper, the *Daily Express,* appreciated the significance of the commission's demise and opposed it, the decision to abolish it evoked no public objection.[134] The relative assurance of a judiciary free from the pressures and vicissitudes of Nigerian politics, providing a bench mark of stability and predictability in an era of vast change, was surrendered without a struggle.

If the judiciary of any new African nation less deserved the rebuke handed it by withdrawing control over its own membership, it was surely that of Nigeria. No other African nation—indeed, perhaps no other developing nation—can boast the uniformly high quality that characterizes the Nigerian higher judiciary. This is true not only of the Supreme Court of Nigeria but also of the High Court of Lagos and the regional high courts. Of all the liberal accusations of corruption and bribery that have been bruited about in Nigeria over the last four years, none, to the writer's knowledge, has even remotely touched any judge of any of the higher courts of Nigeria.

PROTECTION OF FUNDAMENTAL RIGHTS

A survey of the work of these courts would be interesting and helpful, but it is a study of such a scale, even within one area of the law and within the bounds of the reported cases, that it cannot be made here. Of particular interest to us is the manner in which individual rights, the regulation of tensions between the competing needs of state and citizen, have been considered by the courts since we may find some indication of how vigorously the courts will protect the rights of aliens against incursions by government.

David Grove, writing in the *Journal of African Law,*[135] has provided a valuable insight by evaluating the litigation that has arisen under the chapter on fundamental rights of the 1960 Constitution.

Citing the statement of Justice Brett of the federal Superior Court, "The courts throughout the British Commonwealth have traditionally regarded questions of policy as outside their scope,"[136] Grove concludes that the Nigerian courts, while "[d]iligent in safeguarding the rights of individuals in those cases where they do not conflict with any major interest of society, as in the 'fair hearing' cases ... nevertheless generally leave to Parliament the task of striking the balance between the state and the individual."[137] Thus, in interpreting the phrase "reasonably justifiable in a democratic society,"[138] which is a criterion that permits state action in derogation of five of the fundamental civil rights set forth in the Nigerian Constitution,[139] the Supreme Court has not given the phrase the narrow interpretation one would hope for,[140] under which the court could better have restrained legislative and executive excesses.[141] It is believed that such control was specifically intended: "It is significant that the Fundamental Rights chapter was included in the Constitution in large measure to guard against the actions of the majorities that were expected to dominate the political life of the various regions."[142] These provisions only have meaning if they are construed and applied by courts as the supreme law of the land, which the Nigerian Constitution, in fact, is.[143] Only the courts can say what is "justifiable in a democratic society." This task, Grove concludes, the Nigerian judiciary has not yet taken up, and "it remains to be seen if the Nigerian judiciary will be 'sentinels' of liberty."[144] One may, indeed, question, as Dr. Holland does, the concurring opinion of Justice Brett in *Director of Public Prosecutions v. Obi*,[145] which stresses "the role of the legislature as the guardians of a democratic society."[146] Thus, in judging whether the "colonial" enactment[147] against sedition contravenes the Nigerian constitutional guarantee of free speech, Justice Brett suggests that, since a similar provision has been enacted by the federal legislature in the Northern Penal Code of 1960,[148] it has been demonstrated that the legislature considers such a law is "reasonably justifiable in a democratic society." While perhaps true, it is hardly relevant, as Justice Brett says it is: "This does not in any way relieve the Court of the duty to judge for itself, but it [the legislature's action] is among the matters to be taken into consideration."[149]

Certainly, the Supreme Court's decision in *Doherty v. Balewa*[150] was reassuring. There, the Supreme Court held unconstitutional the legislature's effort to attenuate the power of judicial review in its enactment of the Commissions and Tribunals of Inquiry Act, 1961.[151]

That act provided, in §3(4), that "neither the Commission itself, nor any action of the Prime Minister, in relation thereto shall be inquired into in any court of law." The Supreme Court held this to be in contravention of §31 and §108 of the 1960 Constitution.[152]

In a case growing out of the Western Region crisis of 1962, *Williams v. Majekodunmi*,[153] the question was whether a restriction on the movement of Chief Rotimi Williams was "reasonably justifiable in a democratic society." There, Justice Bairamian asserted the court's right and responsibility to judge the content of this phrase more liberally:

"Those words . . . must be read in the context of the Constitution, and more particularly in the context of Chapter III in which they occur. The Chapter confers certain fundamental rights which are regarded as essential and which are to be maintained and preserved; and they are to serve as a norm of legislation under majority rule, which is the form of rule pervading the Constitution. If they are to be invaded at all, it must be only to the extent that is essential for the sake of some recognized public interest, and may not be farther."[154]

Standing to question the constitutionality of an act and the power of the courts to hand down an advisory opinion (or declaratory judgment) were passed upon in *Olawoyin v. Attorney General of the Northern Region*.[155] The plaintiff sought to determine the validity of the Children and Young Persons' Law[156] of the Northern Region, which makes it a crime to induce young persons and children to engage in political activities. The plaintiff claimed the act infringed his freedom of private and family life, as well as his right of free expression, for he could not instruct his children in civic and political affairs without fear of violating the act. The Supreme Court, reversing the Northern Region High Court, held that the high court, indeed, "has power to make a declaration, whether there is a cause of action or not, at the instance of a party interested in the subject matter."[157] Here, however, the plaintiff had failed to show a sufficient interest: "There was no suggestion that the appellant was in imminent danger of coming into conflict with the law or that there had been any real or direct interference with his normal business or other activities."[158] The matter of plaintiff's standing would seem to have been capable of more liberal treatment, especially after the principle of the advisory principle had been allowed.

As most commentators agree, as they surely must, it is premature to judge Nigeria and its judiciary on the record thus far established, with respect to the protection of fundamental rights. The nation and its constitution are young, and there has been little experience with the interpretation of a written constitution—indeed, the experience has been the observation of the English unwritten constitution and parliamentary supremacy in action. Additionally, the dynamics of nation-building, no doubt, cause the vindication of individual rights to be somewhat undervalued. A stabilized, mature political society can better afford the luxury of litigation and the preoccupation of limited judicial facilities with issues that, if resolved against the state, tend only to hamper its campaign for the more tangible and prestigious accoutrements of nationhood.[159] It may well be argued that, during the period of rapid development and limited resources, the courts should take cognizance of the impatience of political leaders with constitutional and judicial processes and adjust themselves to it. They can thus preserve their place in the order of things, in the expectation that, as the society matures, social and political interests will permit greater latitude and attention to individual rights.

On the other hand, what is surrendered initially may never be regained. While compromises of individual freedom for the sake of social interests must, at times, be made, the burden of proof must rest on those who would compromise freedom.[160] Certainly, the courts should make it clear that they have a lively interest in protecting the individual;[161] that, while circumstances may for the time being dictate a circumscription of rights, they are aware of the full implications of the guarantees contained in their constitutions; and that they await only the conditions under which they can be fully implemented.

For the time being, caution and strict construction would seem to be the watchwords in fundamental rights cases. The guiding principle is to be found in *Citizens Insurance Company of Canada v. Parsons*,[162] a decision of the Privy Council quoted by Justice Brett in *Olawoyin v. Commissioner of Police*:[163] "In performing this difficult duty, it will be a wise course for those on whom it is thrown to decide each case which arises as best they can, without entering more largely upon an interpretation of the statute than is necessary for the decision of the particular question in hand."

Nevertheless, it may be an excess of caution that has led the Supreme Court to express the right of free speech in rather negative terms on two occasions. In the *Obi* case,[164] §50(2) of the Criminal Code[165] was described as containing exceptions that "form *enough protection* to a charge of sedition and . . . offer *enough freedom of expression* to anybody in our democratic society."[166] In *The Queen v. Amalgamated Press, Ltd.,*[167] §24 of the Independence Constitution, providing for freedom of expression, was held to guarantee "*nothing but* ordered freedom."[168] One may, perhaps, be justified in expressing concern for this approach in prosecutions for sedition, where the line between fair and frank criticism and a criminal act is very thin at best.[169]

THE PROFESSION OF LAW AND LEGAL EDUCATION

There are estimated to be more than 1600 lawyers in Nigeria, more than in all the rest of tropical Africa combined. "As a group," says Bretton, "lawyers in African society occupy a key position. They are an aristocracy, privileged, prestigious, and valued by the rulers as a support group."[170] All of them have received their basic legal training in the United Kingdom and Ireland, and hundreds more are engaged in law studies there at the present time.[171] The first graduates of Nigerian law schools, only recently established, will not be admitted to the bar before 1966. A small number of Nigerian lawyers have pursued postgraduate work, both in England and, on an increasing scale in the last few years, in the United States.

Although the Nigerian lawyer practices as both barrister and solicitor, English legal education equipped the Nigerian only to act as barrister. Few were ever articled to solicitors for the extended training period in solicitors' offices.[172] Furthermore, admission to the bar in England has not required attendance at a university; normal practice was for a student to take courses under the program of the Council of Legal Education, preparatory to taking the council's examination. If he passed and fulfilled the formal requirements of the Inns of Court, he was called to the bar. Some, also, took degrees at universities as well as the examination, fewer still took the council's post-final course or read in chambers, either in England or Nigeria.

The Nigerian barrister returns to Nigeria with, at most, a classical, general legal education of three years' duration or less, superimposed on the secondary education he underwent in Nigeria. He knows little beyond the theory of the law and nothing about Nigerian law. He is educated, but he is not trained to meet the problems of the Nigerian litigant, businessman, or landowner.

To remedy this defect in the preparation of barristers educated abroad, and to supplement the basically English curricula of the new Nigerian law schools, the Nigerian Law School was established, in 1962, to provide a three-month postgraduate course in Nigerian law and the work of solicitors. The course was designed for Nigerians who had passed the final examination qualifying for a degree in law at an approved university in the United Kingdom or Ireland before August 31, 1963. As of October, 1963, the course was to have been extended to one year, to provide for those who have done their work as non-university or "external" students. The imposition of this requirement by the Council of Legal Education, which regulates legal-training requirements in Nigeria,[173] was protested by overseas students. It adds considerably to the already heavy financial burden (usually met out of family funds) and is viewed by many as an unwarranted qualification on the competence attested to by being called to the English bar. The council capitulated and postponed the deadline one year, despite its recognition that existing deficiencies have seriously hampered the effective role of the bar in Nigeria. These have appeared in several ways and in numerous instances: the preference of the lawyer trained as barrister for litigation work and his shunning of, and inadequacy in, the role of counselor, which has resulted in the "underemployment" of Nigerian lawyers, particularly in Lagos. Ineptness in handling land cases and unfamiliarity with such rudimentary tasks as conveyancing and the registration of mortgages have caused serious problems.

In addition to the postgraduate Nigerian Law School, housed in Lagos near the Supreme Court Building, there are four law schools proper in Nigeria:[174] at the University of Lagos located at Yaba, a suburb of Lagos; at the University of Ife, the law school of the Western Region, temporarily located at Ibadan; at the University of Nigeria, located in the Eastern Region at Nsukka; and at Ahmadu Bello University, located at Zaria in the Northern Region.[175] These schools offer a three-year curriculum following completion of secondary education. Students are thrust into law school at the age of eighteen or nineteen and pursue a course devoted almost entirely to a theoretical study of the law before entering the professional "finishing school" at Lagos. The end product must necessarily be a man of limited depth and perspective. The multiplicity of law schools has necessitated spreading available resources very thinly—particularly teachers, so that, at best, even this brief and specialized training cannot be described as satisfactory.

Regionalism is, of course, responsible for the proliferation of universities and law schools. Nigeria does not need four law schools at this stage, nor can it afford to staff and equip all of them adequately. Of greater concern is the employment of all the graduates these schools will produce. There are at present, as noted above, some 1600 lawyers in Nigeria, most of them youthful, since most have been trained in the United Kingdom since 1945. There are estimated to be approximately 425 lawyers practicing in Lagos, 375 in the Western Region, 375 in the Eastern Region, and 150 in the Northern Region (of which only one is a native Northerner, the remainder having come up from the south). Some 275 are employed by government and by companies. A very small proportion of Nigerian lawyers are women—probably not over 1 per cent, although one or two have risen to posts of considerable importance. A woman is general counsel of Mobil Oil Nigeria Limited and sits on its board of directors.

Many of these lawyers are underemployed, in the sense that their time is not fully occupied in the use of their professional skills. Many drift off into business ventures, often on a part-time basis, although, of course, here they serve a useful function in economic development, particularly when they act as members of boards of new corporations. On the whole, however, the employment possibilities for large numbers of law graduates are distinctly limited. Government will continue to be a large employer of law graduates, and the enlargement of the judiciary will absorb more in the future. But it is difficult not to see the training of lawyers in Nigeria at four law schools as a basic misallocation of resources.

Nigeria does not need additional lawyers as badly as it needs scientists and technologists, and the law schools, in the near future, will make a disproportionate demand on able secondary graduates to the disadvantage of more critical disciplines. Training in the law is more attractive for several reasons: as presently established, legal training is easier, briefer, and less costly; its "status rating" is high, and the income of lawyers on whom ambitions are modeled is very good; law and lawyering are the most direct route to politics and power, as well as providing access to participation in business enterprise with little or no capital. The legal profession also makes small demands on its practitioners relative to the monetary gain, status, and power it returns. Law as practiced in Nigeria is not complex and is relatively unsophisticated. Reference materials are scarce, few cases are reported in Nigeria, and sets of English reports and annotated laws are mostly to be found in a few libraries. Little reading of, or writing for, law journals is done. Only a handful contribute to the serious study and growth of Nigerian law. Hornbooks and treatises are heavily relied upon in court and out. It is not an exacting profession and is one where a man with a modicum of intelligence can do well. This is not to condemn the profession as a whole; it is merely to explain why it attracts so many young Nigerians.

An important historical factor is also at work here. During the colonial days, the educated Nigerian had entry only into the learned professions, and, consequently, the Nigerian who went abroad usually trained in theology, medicine, law, or in the liberal arts as preparation for a teaching career. Education in the sciences and in technology was inhibited by the deficiencies of secondary education, the low level of demand in Nigeria for such graduates, and the fact that such positions as existed were usually closed to Nigerians, as were positions in business management. Furthermore, the level of society from which the Nigerian student came encouraged professionalism and its attendant status. Of significance, also, was the fact that training in the law and admission to the bar offered the Nigerian the best opportunity to meet the Englishman on equal footing. But the situation is different now, and a reassessment of the employment of critical human resources at the top levels is urgently required.

THE BAR AS A FORCE IN NIGERIAN LIFE

Upon the enactment of the Legal Practitioners' Act, 1962, the Nigerian Bar Association, until then a private and voluntary association, became a statutory body. This should have important consequences, but not necessarily salutary, for the future role of the organized bar in Nigerian life.

On the positive side, it may be said that the act has firmly institutionalized what was formerly a diffuse and haphazard organization that lacked a program and, although it had good leadership at the top, suffered from the absence of broad support. Under the statute, the Bar Association is now "integrated." To practice law in Nigeria one must now pay an annual fee to the association, although a modest one: lawyers who have practiced more than five years pay five guineas ($14.70); and all others, three guineas ($8.82). Of the fees collected, the Bar Association receives 75 per cent.

The association has eleven branches in the principal cities of Nigeria and publishes the *Nigerian Bar Journal*, edited by Aliyi Ekineh, a Lagos barrister who has studied law in the United States, but the journal has appeared sporadically, owing to lack of written contributions and funds. The Law School of the University of Lagos is training its students in analytical and critical writing on the law. It is to be hoped that, if this pattern is repeated at other schools, the increase of thoughtful writers, together with the funds made available under the new act, will remedy both deficiencies. The association has plans to move into larger quarters (it now occupies one small room in the High Court Building in Lagos) and to employ a full-time executive secretary. The latter appointment, perhaps more than any other, will signal the beginning of meaningful activity. A Continuing Education of the Bar Program is under active consideration.

It is unfortunate that the Bar Association, to be in the position to secure necessary funds, had to submit to legislation making it a government-sponsored body.[176] Under the act, the General Council of the bar was created, "charged with the general management of the affairs of the Nigerian Bar Association," and this consists of the federal attorney general, the attorneys general of the three regions, and twenty members of the Bar Association. The required fees are paid to the registrar of courts, a government official. It is doubtful if the new Bar Association can in any real sense remain independent of government. It is meaningful that executive officers, rather than judges, were chosen as the ex-officio, government members of the council. This factor, together with the abolition of the federal Judicial Service Commission, in October, 1963, has deprived the judiciary and the independent bar of any institutions through which they could effectively challenge inroads on the rule of law by the executive. The judiciary, members of the bar and heads of Nigerian law schools maintain a majority in the Council of Legal Education, established in 1962,[177] which supervises all legal education in Nigeria. This body, however, also has all attorneys general as members and is obviously not one that can effectively serve the important purpose of giving voice to the political hopes and fears (in the larger, non-partisan sense, of course) of judges and lawyers. Dissent, it is feared, must henceforth come from individuals and will, consequently, be inhibited.

The pre-1963 Bar Association unfortunately did not have a reputation as a "watchdog" of constitutional rights. It failed utterly during the Western Region crisis of 1962 to protest the restrictions placed on the movements of its distinguished president, Chief F. R. A. Williams. By contrast, the Nigerian organization of newspaper editors raised a hue and cry when several of their members were similarly restricted, and it is reported that a high official of the government expressed puzzlement as to why the journalists objected since the lawyers had not. This was an unconscious and unintended rebuke of the Bar Association but one that was well deserved. The lawyers had permitted their leading member, a man who had, in fact, played a vital part in attempting to "keep the peace" in the Western Region, to be isolated under police surveillance in a small village away from his home. Chief Williams' detention was subsequently declared to have been unconstitutional and the bar again was silent when, immediately after the Supreme Court voided the old detention order, a new restriction order was served on Williams.[178]

After the crisis had passed, in 1963, the Bar Association was reported as having passed a resolution condemning proposals made in July, 1963, that the new constitution contain authority for a detention act similar to that authorized under the Indian Constitution. However, the Bar Association found itself joining a popular wave of protest, which included all newspapers, the trade unions, and the Nigerian Federation of Women's Clubs, among others. Also, the attorney general of the federation disapproved of a detention act. The proposal was sprung in such a hasty fashion that there is reason to believe it was used as a device to gain support—by way of "trade-off"—for the proposal to abolish the federal Judicial Service Commission, which was in fact done. The Bar Association did not protest this move, which may be viewed as far more serious: the power to detain under an emergency situation, which may be declared by Parliament under §70 of the Republican Constitution (§65 of the Independence Constitution), already exists, as the *Williams* case demonstrated. Furthermore, it is doubtful whether the four premiers, who spoke in favor of a detention act, seriously intended to emulate Ghana in this respect. But to abolish the Judicial Service Commission was an alteration of profound, but apparently unappreciated, significance for Nigeria and for its legal institutions. Note was not taken by the Bar Association of the fact that this drastic proposal to alter the condition of tenure of judges was made at a time when the two high-court judges in Lagos were weighing the evidence and reaching their verdicts in the treason trials against the former leaders of the Western Region and of the opposition Action Group party. This is not, in any way, to be construed that the judges were influenced thereby or that it was intended to influence the judiciary, but it was a thoughtless and a callous move to make at this particular time, and it should have been vigorously protested by the bar.

IV

Entrepreneurship, Forms of Establishment, and Protection of Intangible Property

But economic development does not consist only of projects and budgets.... It consists also of motivations of the population and the incentives to which they respond ... conditioned by the social and economic environment. Our attitudes toward work, accumulation and taking risks ... differ from those in the developed countries. The "captains of industry" who promoted industrial development in Europe in the 19th century were not men whose motive in going into business was a desire to make a mere living but who wanted to make a fortune. Their chief interest in life was in risk-taking and profit-making. There must be a change in the attitudes and motivations of a large number of people to bring about the emergence of a Nigerian entrepreneurial class. Their present number is ridiculously low and it is politically undesirable and economically unwise to leave the field in the hands of foreigners.
       N. A. A. Okuboyejo in Seminar on
       Manpower Problems in Economic
       Development with Special
       Reference to Nigeria, 1964.

ENTREPRENEURSHIP

The Nigerian appears to be an instinctive entrepreneur: the numbers of small traders and peddlers who operate in shops, in market stalls, and on the streets and sidewalks of Nigerian communities are countless. In Nigeria, says Nyhart, "The entrepreneur, the accomplished trader, the economic man is to be seen everywhere."[1] The role of the "mammy traders," in the distributive apparatus of the Nigerian economy, is well known, and the stories of their wealth and influence in the social structure of their families and communities are legendary.

The chief characteristic of this group of entrepreneurs is their individualism. They operate as sole proprietors, presiding over a stock that can range from a few shillings' worth of peanuts to a store banked with thousands of pounds' worth of colorful bolts of fabrics. They may be assisted by family members, but control rests with the owner. The only nexus between governmental regulation and this form of enterprise may be the Registration of Business Names Act[2] that requires registration if the business is conducted under a name other than that of the sole owner or the partners. Quite often, the act has served a purpose contrary to its intention. It has been used to give the color of legal organization and government approval and control to enterprise that is not organized and is subject to no control whatsoever.[3] The owner himself, in some cases, appears to believe that his certificate of registration, for which he pays a small fee, is evidence of such approval. Nyhart cites instances of businessmen who believed that registration actually limited their personal liability for business debts.

Beyond sole proprietorship, the range of business associations known to Anglo-American jurisprudence are open to the Nigerian. There is an aversion among Nigerians to forming business associations among themselves, and even partnerships are rare. This is based not merely on dislike of sharing control but also on lack of trust.[4] This is said to stem from the prevailing low level of business ethics. While this appears, indeed, to be a substantial factor, the prevalence of sole proprietorship may also have a rational explanation in the closeness of family in Nigeria. Loyalties are not split—one running to the family and another to the business—and demands made by the extended family on a businessman do not distinguish between his personal wealth and the assets of his business. In fact, family demands tend to be proportionate to his success in business. Thus, Nigerian partners find it difficult to develop loyalties to each other that are not necessarily higher than, but are distinct from, those to their respective families and that can isolate the business from the families and their demands.

Hunter has described the African trader's hardships thus:

The trader is attempting to build up an individual business in a rough sea of social change in which his obligations to an extended family are felt as binding, and in which he must help at many launches and many rescues. The general flux and instability around him strain his business in other ways. Customers, themselves under strain, default on credit; employees steal; inefficient relatives have to be kept on the staff; customs officials or police may suddenly become difficult or demand bribes.[5]

Furthermore, profit margins are very narrow (many traders do business on a 5 per cent margin), competition is extremely keen and sometimes bitter, and the keeping of proper accounts is almost entirely unknown.[6] The shared control of a partnership does not facilitate meeting any of these problems; in fact, it compounds them since few of them are capable of an objective solution on which agreement between the partners might perhaps more readily be expected. Furthermore, if accounts are properly kept, as they must be in a partnership if disputes are to be avoided, they are available also to the taxing authorities, an exposure unwillingly risked.

The sole proprietorship, therefore, continues as the major form of doing business, with consequent inhibitions on consolidation and growth during the owner's lifetime and its inevitable breakup when he dies. Upon the death of the proprietor, the claims of heirs to the estate very often result in the dispersal or sale of the assets of the business. This, possibly, can be prevented if there is someone in the immediate family capable of carrying on the business and more certainly if a will is made leaving the business to him, although wills are said to be ignored upon occasion.[7] In the absence of a will, the estate of a person married under customary law passes under customary rules, and these may range from primogeniture to ultimogeniture, including division "into equal shares between the respective branches"[8] of the family.[9] If the decedent was married under English law, as provided by statute,[10] or was the issue of such a marriage, his property should pass according to the principles of English law if he dies intestate, but this fact is often conveniently forgotten. Marriages under "English law" and the making of wills are becoming more common among urban and educated persons, but customary marriage and customary rules of inheritance prevail among the vast majority of Nigerians. Land that the decedent used or occupied, as a family or tribal member, continues to be governed by customary law. The decedent's will or his English marriage, in case of intestacy, can affect only property rights that he held individually.

The partnership[11] might be said to offer insufficient advantage to overcome the lack of confidence in forming a business association outside the family: liability is joint and several for all the debts of the partnership, and it is unlimited; the partnership cannot sue or be sued as an entity; and it comes to an end upon the death of a partner. The Nigerian entrepreneur may then go the next step and form a private corporation with one other, or up to fifty other, Nigerians,[12] but only one director is required. This creates a legal entity that can sue or be sued, and it can own property separate and distinct from that of its shareholders. Or, if he joins with six other subscribers and wishes to have access to the capital market through the sale of shares, he may incorporate as a public company, which must have at least two directors. A private company is defined as one that restricts the right to transfer its shares, limits the number of its members to fifty (exclusive of employees), and prohibits any invitation to the public to subscribe for shares or debentures.[13] Since the characteristics of a private company are all (except as to the number of stockholders) by way of exceptions to the general rule, a company is public unless it qualifies as private under the stated provisions. To turn itself into a public company, a private company need simply pass a resolution and file certain statements with the registrar.[14] By contradistinction, then, a public company is one that does not restrict the right to transfer shares, has no limit on the number of members (but has at least seven), and whose articles do not prohibit the solicitation of public subscriptions.[15]

Neither public nor private companies are required to publish balance sheets, except limited insurance companies, and deposit, provident, and benefit societies;[16] banks are regulated by a separate statute.[17] However, both public and private companies must file balance sheets annually with the registrar of companies, although a profit and loss statement need not be included.[18] Both private and public companies may take three forms with respect to liability: (1)

companies limited by shares;[19] (2) companies limited by guarantee;[20] and (3) unlimited companies.[21] Trade associations, chambers of commerce, and other "not-for-profit" corporations generally take the form of companies limited by guarantee. The third, needless to say, is little used.

In the introduction to his final report as commissioner on the Working and Administration of Company Law in Ghana,[22] Professor L. C. B. Gower conceded that his proposed company law draft was "too complicated for the average small African business in its present state of development."[23] But he went on to say that the average small African business is not yet ready to operate as a corporation whose limited liability poses dangers to outsiders dealing with the business and where separation of ownership and control creates a hazard for the shareholders. Nevertheless, the lack of business continuity, resulting from the death of the sole owner, or the dissolution of partnership, by the death or retirement of a member,[24] demanded a solution.

Professor Gower's suggestion was the creation of a new form, the "incorporated private partnership":

What [is needed] is a fundamentally different type of organization analogous to the partnership, with unlimited liability and without any separation of ownership and control. This, and this alone, can provide the needed simplicity without sacrifice of essential safeguards. But, and this is where the English conception of partnership does not meet the need, the business itself must be personified (i.e., incorporated) so as to afford a better possibility of survival from one generation to another, and a clearer separation between business and private assets. This is vital if African businesses are to expand.... Unless the business can be clearly distinguished from the family, there is little chance of profits being ploughed back sufficiently to allow for expansion or of the business escaping from dispersal on the death of the founder.[25]

This unique association, Professor Gower suggested, could be formed by two to twenty individuals by registration. It would, thus, become a separate legal entity like a company, but the members would retain personal liability for the firm's debts. The entity would survive the death or withdrawal of a member, but, within six months, the remaining partners must do one of three things:

1. Admit the successor to the deceased's share, or a nominee of the retired partner if he has found a buyer for his share;

2. Buy out the share of the former partner at an agreed price; failing agreement on price, to have an arbitration to settle price;

3. Wind up the firm, selling it as a going concern if possible.

This form of association is now possible in Ghana under the Incorporated Private Partnerships Bill of 1962.

While the new Ghana Company Code Bill,[26] following another of Gower's drafts, permits formation of a one-man corporation, two directors are required to be named, so that someone will be available to take over the running of the business in the event of the sole shareholder's death. As in the case of the incorporated partnership, the surviving director is expected to resist efforts of the heirs of the owner to divide the stock in trade, thus destroying the business.[27] In both forms of business, continuity is to be accomplished by separating, or dividing, ownership and control, and therefore each stipulates a minimum of two member-controllers.[28]

While limited liability is attractive, Gower doubts that it is a prime consideration in forming business associations. It is of importance, rather, for the investor who does not himself wish to engage in business, and it assumes importance only at later stages of development. Rather than limited liability, the incorporated private partnership provides instead "... [A]ll the other advantages of incorporation ... and ... these are considerable. The firm's property can be clearly distinguished from that of the members (a particularly important point in a country with a system of family ownership); difficulties regarding rights and obligations on a change of membership of the firm are avoided; borrowings can be effectively secured by floating charges ... ; and, above all, the business is given a far better chance of survival...."[29]

Simply because a companies act—or any other legislation, for that matter—was derived from a colonial power does not mean that it is outmoded when independence comes. But the passage of time and changed conditions require the re-examination of statutes transported from another culture in another era. The former Ghana Companies Act, introduced there in 1907, was essentially the English Companies Act of 1862. Nigeria's present Companies Act is the English Act of 1908.

In the National Development Plan, 1962-68, it is stated, "Legislation in relation to company law in Nigeria remains related to practice of a bygone era...."[30] Gower's study preparatory to the drafting of the new Ghanaian Company Code Bill and the code itself reveal that (apart from the resulting Incorporated Private Partnerships Bill, which is a separate statute) what was required was really a revision of company law concepts applicable anywhere, not one specially designed for "Ghanaian" or "African needs." Thus, there are provisions in §40 for "no par" shares, to avoid confusion between par and market values; §50 forbids the issuance of non-voting stock and provides that each share is entitled to one vote;[31] §59 permits a company to purchase its own shares; while §63 safeguards against insider transactions.

One commentator says of the new act:

The new code has the dual object of simplifying the regulations for foreign investment[32] and of encouraging and facilitating the formation of Ghanaian companies, and the participation of the Ghanaian public in the share market. Anyone looking to the code for evidence of Ghanaian Socialism will hardly find it....

However, there are important clues to the Ghanaian climate of thought. Article 203 ... stipulates that "in considering whether a particular transaction or course of action is in the best interests of a company as a whole, a director may have regard to the interests of the employees, as well as the members, of the company"....[33]

In fact, §203 enjoins far less than is commanded by labor's rights under co-determination in the Federal Republic of Germany.[34] For that matter, §203 merely suggests what any fair-minded employer will consider, in any event. All of the other new provisions cited have been commended by authorities as desirable modifications of corporate organization and operation.

The Nigerian government recognizes the need for a revision of its Companies Act, and a Commission on Company Law Revision was constituted in June, 1962. A London firm of chartered accountants, in a report to the commission, made in August, 1962, stated its opinion that "the present legislation, subject to certain amendments, [was] quite satisfactory for some time to come."[35] This opinion was based on the relative number of companies in Nigeria today, compared to those in England in 1908, and the few Nigerian stocks listed on the Lagos Stock Exchange, in 1962, compared with "hundreds in the United Kingdom in 1908." Further, the report stated, "no shareholder in, or creditor of, a limited liability company has suffered, to the best of our knowledge, as a result of the existing legislation and we see no likelihood of them suffering in the foreseeable future." Hundreds of small Nigerian companies operating satisfactorily under a statute with which they are "reasonably familiar" would be handicapped by the introduction of "complicated and sophisticated legislation," and newcomers would be discouraged from incorporating by such legislation. Lastly, "chaos" would result among government officials administering a new company law.

As the result of this rather peculiar view, the ensuing suggestions for amendments mainly skimmed the surface of the act. They dealt with such matters as simplification of fee payments, numbering of shares, the register of members, and exempting private companies from holding required statutory meetings. Several portions of the 1948 English Companies Act were recommended for adoption: those concerning the prospectus, auditors, rights of creditors in a voluntary winding up, and striking defunct companies from the register. Despite the fact that the reporters had Professor Gower's proposals and reports available, they apparently ignored his suggestion for incorporated private partnership, perhaps believing it to be outside the scope of their responsibility. However, with respect to company law, while they did propose reducing the required number of directors in a public company to two, they held that one is sufficient in a private company. They, thus, ignored the principle of divided control that Gower views as essential to business continuity in Africa.

The commission appointed in 1962 contributed nothing original either to the work of revision. It started out without clear criteria, only a mandate to review and revise. Lawyers appointed to the commission, apparently viewing the task as too time-consuming under these circumstances and too uncertain as to its results, fell away from the commission, and further sessions were shortly abandoned. A new commission was subsequently constituted that was to report its findings during 1964. A draft, closely following the 1948 United Kingdom Companies Act,[36] with modifications suggested by the Jenkins Commission,[37] was being circulated for comment in late 1964.

SMALL BUSINESS AND INDUSTRY

Not all Nigerian businessmen and women are engaged in the retail trade, of course. Small industry abounds in the cities, homes, and villages, each establishment employing very few workers but together accounting for approximately three or more times the total number of workers employed in large-scale manufacturing. Small industry includes the service industries (such as tailoring, dry cleaning, shoe-repairing) and small manufacturing establishments (such as mattress-making, baking, goldsmithing). It is typically labor-intensive, with an average capital investment per worker of about £100, compared with approximately £1,000 to £3,000 per worker in large-scale industry.

The best picture of small industry in Nigeria is that delineated by Peter Kilby in *The Development of Small Industry in Eastern Nigeria*.[38] Kilby describes small industry, which exists in an "almost staggering number of very small firms ... [as] an incubator for the skills of the artisan and the manager ... [and] given the proper environment ... capable of greatly increasing its contribution to ... development."[39] But, Kilby says, small industry has received very little government attention or assistance.[40] (Schatz and Edokpayi, in their survey, conducted in the Western Region, found that many businessmen were ignorant of those government aids that existed.)[41]

Kilby canvassed 14 towns in Eastern Nigeria and recorded 10,728 firms, employing 28,721 workers—an average of 2.7 workers per firm but distributed as follows: one-man business, 38 per cent, 2 to 5 employees, 54 per cent; 6 to 9 employees, 5 per cent; 10 or more employees, 3 per cent. Most were workshops crudely housed: only 37 per cent operated in concrete buildings or rooms. One or more machines were found in 42 per cent of the establishments, but, when tailors and sewing machines were excluded, this figure dropped to 15 per cent, and, if powered machines only were counted, to 7 per cent.

Kilby analyzed the situation of small industry as follows:

A low level of *per capita* income, a surplus of labour and little technical knowledge are the salient features of the small industry landscape, low incomes mean that the consumer has little to spend ... and savings available for investing in tools and equipment are very slight. Rudimentary technical knowledge means that production techniques are simple, allowing practically anyone to establish a firm ... [and] that tools and machinery in use are seldom employed in the most productive manner ... [A]n abundance of labour works in conjunction with the low capital and technical entry requirements to produce a multitude of small firms.[42]

Thus, of the sole entrepreneurs interviewed who used their own savings to begin a business, only 7 per cent started out with £500 or more, and 61 per cent began with less than £50.

Kilby found that of 160 enterprises, 24 per cent were partnerships, and one-third of these began business with £500 or more—almost five times as large a number as the sole proprietors who commanded that amount of launching capital. But these figures must be qualified, and the result is that the observations made earlier about the reluctance to form partnerships appear to be borne out. "If all carpenters and motor mechanics whose partnerships consist only in sharing shed rent and dividing up large contracts (i.e., no combining of capital) are deleted, the percentage of partnerships drops to 20. And if all (extended) family joint enterprises are put aside, the residual of non-relative capital-pooling partnerships is 9 per cent. It is estimated that a representative sampling would yield only 1 or 2 per cent of such partnerships in the small industry sector."[43] One must reluctantly conclude that one of the principal barriers to industrialization and economic progress in Nigeria is the Nigerian entrepreneurs themselves.

THE ALIEN ENTREPRENEUR

The foreign investor who wishes to establish a business in Nigeria requires first the consent of the Nigerian government, whether he seeks to set up a new enterprise or wishes to buy into an existing one. Even before he arrives, he will have had to offer evidence of his *bona fides* in order to get a visa to visit Nigeria—usually for no longer than twenty-eight days on the first occasion—and, of course, his right to stay in Nigeria, even if he is admitted as a resident alien, is subject to revocation.[44]

Permission to go into business is by no means granted automatically; if anything, quite the reverse is true. For all that has been said about enticing foreign capital into Nigeria, permission seems to be granted almost reluctantly. Permission to enter the retail trade will no longer be granted; this is an area of economic activity reserved for Nigerians as far as new entrants are concerned. This was already apparent in 1961, as reflected in the statement of the Minister of Economic Development in the House of Representatives, "reserving" the distributive trades and road transport to Nigerians.[45] In 1962, the director of the Rockefeller Brothers Fund in West Africa said: "I know of at least two well-intentioned American firms which have been turned down in their applications for permission to establish agency companies with expatriate management. This sort of activity, the Nigerians feel, is within their current capacity and, therefore, should be left to them."[46]

Control can be exercised over the businessman and his establishment in a variety of ways, apart from the control of the alien person. Since the passage of the new Immigration Act of 1963, there is a general "license" that must be sought by the alien from the Minister of Internal Affairs, before he may "on his own account or in partnership with any other person, practise a profession or establish or take over any trade or business whatsoever or register or take over any company with limited liability."[47] Furthermore, all foreign investment is subject to the control of the Minister of Finance by virtue of the Exchange Control Act of 1962.[48] If one wishes to establish a branch of an American parent firm in Nigeria, one is required to register under the Companies Act,[49] and one may incur penalties for not doing so, but the act does not authorize the rejection by the registrar of companies of properly submitted documents. However, even if the branch is staffed entirely by Nigerian personnel, as a sales branch-office might be, "approved status," or a specific license, will be required from the Minister of Finance when the branch desires to remit earnings to the United States. If, as is most common, it is contemplated to set up a Nigerian subsidiary, control can also be exercised in passing on the application for incorporation. In order to get the tax benefits of a "pioneer industry," the enterprise must not only be incorporated as a public, limited-liability company in Nigeria but its application for "pioneer status" must be approved at Cabinet level. Finally, continuing "selective" control can be exercised, once the foreigner is established, by regulating the number of expatriate employees the foreign entrepreneur is permitted to bring into Nigeria. The allocation of an expatriate quota is a matter within administrative discretion that would probably not be considered reviewable by a Nigerian court.

Thus, through the control of the entry and the stay of personnel, the repatriation of his money, the act of incorporation, and tax benefits, the federal government can effectively channel, encourage, inhibit, or forestall the initiation and, to a lesser degree, the continuation of economic activity by the alien. The regional governments have no similar direct powers. Beyond the "police" powers regulating activity for the benefit of public health, safety, and morals, the only effective legal control the regions have is the disposition of land required for a business or industry, since outside Lagos and the Colony Province of Western Nigeria, the alien, or a corporation controlled by aliens, cannot acquire any interest in land without governmental permission.[50]

There is, then, no possibility of the alien's avoiding a direct confrontation with the Nigerian federal authorities if he expects to do business there. Nevertheless, if the decision has been made as to the location of the business, a prior approach to regional authorities may be desirable, in order to secure support for the approach to the federal authorities and, perhaps, to forestall regional competition for the business that may otherwise considerably delay approval by federal authorities.

Selling from abroad to Nigerian importers or through brokers—in short, under any circumstances where commonly the alien is not "doing business" and has no "establishment" in Nigeria—does not, as elsewhere, raise the problem of securing governmental permission for the seller. Also, buying does not require permission from the state,[51] except that, if the purchasing agent is an alien, he will require permission to enter Nigeria and to remain there.

Theoretically, all the forms of establishment available to the Nigerian and discussed previously are also open to the alien. As a matter of practice, however, the foreign investor generally chooses the form of public limited-liability corporation in order to qualify for pioneer status. Or, more commonly, having secured pioneer status, the investor then incorporates as a public limited-liability company. The consequences that follow this are not only tax benefits but also access to the local capital market, through the sale of shares (which is of little help at present), and the necessity of constituting a membership of at least seven stockholders. None of the stockholders need be Nigerian, nor, indeed, need the stockholder meetings be held in Nigeria. There may be advantages in having knowledgeable and prominent Nigerians on the board, but these need not be stockholders, unless qualification shares are specified in the corporate articles.

The policy of Nigerianization encourages, but does not require, more than nominal Nigerian participation. One condition of pioneer status, for example, is that the articles of incorporation not prohibit the acquisition of stock by Nigerian governments and citizens, but it is not required that shares be made available for purchase.

Nigeria has no restrictive business-practices act, but the attorney general has indicated to the writer that such legislation is under consideration. Common-law remedies are of course available.

LICENSING AND THE PROTECTION OF INTANGIBLE PROPERTY

The licensing of patents, trademarks, know-how, copyrights, and designs is often an "intermediate" form of doing business abroad. It follows the experience of exporting finished goods to a country and precedes direct investment that results in a manufacturing establishment in the foreign land. But, if the technology and industrial capacity of the host country are not developed, the foreign businessman must generally move from export to direct investment. This is simply because there is usually no one who can be licensed who can assure that production of the licensed article will be carried out as intended. Thus, in Nigeria, trademarks originating abroad are generally employed by a producer affiliated with, or owned by, the overseas originator, and the Nigerian rights to the mark are held by the Nigerian producer. But there is an additional reason: the licensing of a bare trademark is not recognized in Nigeria.[52] Consequently, to exploit a trademark there, it is said that equity investment is necessary, although any other form of license can be granted by way of a contract.

However, the licensing of trademarks, without investment and production, is, in fact, accomplished by an arrangement under which the local producer acts as agent for the foreign, registered, trademark owner in the manufacturing process and then sells the goods to himself, as an independent distributor. Although it does not seem to have arisen, this procedure would appear to raise the question of whether the trademark owner is not, in fact, doing business in Nigeria, as well as the question of his tax liabilities that must follow. It is hoped that the problem will be overtaken by the reform in Nigerian trademark law that was under way in 1964.[53]

Remission of licensing fees abroad is subject to control, and approval of such remission should be sought from the Ministry of Finance before making a licensing agreement. Although there are no formal limitations on fees, as a percentage of sales price or per unit of manufacture, the government employs the criterion of reasonableness in passing on applications. No tax is imposed on licensing fees and royalties.

Nigeria is a party to two multilateral conventions pertaining to the protection of intangible property: the International Convention for the Protection of Industrial Property[54] and the Universal Copyright Convention.[55]

PATENTS

Nigeria does not yet provide for the original registration of patents or for their renewal in Nigeria. Under the Registration of United Kingdom Patents Ordinance, 1925,[56] patents granted in the United Kingdom may be registered, within three years of such grant, with the Nigerian Registrar of Patents, through an agent in Nigeria who is authorized to accept service of process for the grantee.

Once granted, the Nigerian patent, aside from extending the patent right to Nigeria, becomes coextensive with that in the United Kingdom. It relates back to the date of the grant there;[57] it continues in force only as long as it remains valid in the United Kingdom; and, if it is renewed in the United Kingdom, production of the certificate of renewal in Nigeria will similarly extend the life of the patent there, as will an order of a United Kingdom court of competent jurisdiction extending the term of a patent.

It was reported, in 1961, that legislation was being prepared to permit registration of patents taken out in countries other than the United Kingdom, but, to date, this has not been accomplished.

It is not surprising that neither the reports of selected cases of the Supreme Court of Nigeria nor the old West African Court of Appeal reveal any cases in which patent rights were litigated.

DESIGN PROTECTION

While there is, as yet, no provision for the registration of designs in Nigeria, protection is afforded if the design has been registered in the United Kingdom under the Patents and Designs Acts, 1907 to 1932.[58] This is provided for by the United Kingdom Designs (Protection) Ordinance, 1936,[59] and the registrant enjoys "in Nigeria the like privileges and rights as though the certificate of registration in the United Kingdom had been issued with an extension to Nigeria."[60] However, damages for infringement may not be recovered against a showing by the defendant that "at the date of the infringement he was not aware nor had any reasonable means of making himself aware of the existence of the registration of the design."[61] This defense cannot be set up against a prayer for an injunction.[62]

Publication of the design in Nigeria before its registration in the United Kingdom, if proven, vitiates the registration,[63] and puts the design in the public domain.

TRADEMARKS

The increased tempo of Nigerian business activity since independence and the high expectations it has generated are dramatically indicated by the increase of registered trademarks from three thousand, in 1961, to over thirteen thousand, in 1963. The majority of these are foreign, and, of course, many have been registered in anticipation of use and the expectation that new trademark legislation will shortly permit licensing. If all are successfully brought into use in Nigeria before five years elapse, after which "non-working" trademarks are struck from the register, Nigerian consumers will apparently have as rich a choice of brand-name goods as many highly developed nations.

Trademark rights, in sharp contrast to patent rights, have been the subject of litigation in Nigeria since at least 1901, when *Lagos Stores, Ltd. v. Blackstock & Co.*[64] was decided. At that time, trademarks were registered and protected under the Trade Marks Proclamation, 1900, enacted by the high commissioner of the Protectorate of Southern Nigeria (Northern Nigeria became a part of the Protectorate of Nigeria in 1914). Subsequently, trademarks ordinances were promulgated in 1910, 1914, 1923, and 1954, and these were finally consolidated in a comprehensive ordinance in 1955, which is the present law.[65] The substantive language of Nigerian trademark law has changed very little over that span of time. The most significant change took place in 1914, when it was provided that trademarks of cotton goods must first be registered in England, in order to be registered in Nigeria.[66]

Lagos Stores was an infringement case, and the issue stated by the judge was "whether... two labels were so similar as to be likely to be mistaken by 'an ordinary native.' "[67] A 1903 case employed the criterion of "ordinary purchasers" developed in two English cases, of which one[68] had arisen in Nigeria and had used the standard of "the intelligence and experience of... the native population of Ibadan."[69]

Where registration has not been effected, and infringement cannot be shown, relief may, nevertheless, be available by way of an injunction, if use over a period of years has established a reputation. The language of §49,[70] prohibiting the granting of an injunction to restrain infringement of an unregistered mark, unless a certificate of refusal to register were produced,[71] does not preclude equitable relief against palming off.[72] This reflects the English common law, as set forth earlier by the Privy Council.[73]

In recent years, few trademark cases have been reported in Nigeria. This may be attributable to the strict rulings of the early cases, or to the fact that trademark cases have not been included in the cases selected for the reports. Where the standard of the illiterate purchaser was applied, a finding of confusion between trademarks followed more often than not. These cases, undoubtedly, had a deterrent effect. In his discussion of Nigerian trademark law, Dr. Elias says: "Nowadays, it is reasonable to expect a less generous concession to illiteracy than has hitherto been the practice of the courts."[74]

Application for registration of a trademark is made to the Registrar of Trade Marks in Lagos.[75] The trademark must consist of at least one of the following "essential particulars":[76]

1. the name of the company, individual, or firm represented in a special or particular manner;

2. the signature of the applicant or that of some predecessor in his business;

3. an invented word or invented words;

4. a word or words having no direct reference to the character or quality of the goods (a geographical name or surname "according to its ordinary signification" may not be registered); and

5. any other distinctive mark.

The strict provisions of the first four categories may be relaxed by a court, and a name, signature, and a word or words may be, then, characterized as "distinctive marks" under the fifth category. "Distinctive" is defined to mean "adopted to distinguish the goods of the proprietor of the trademark from those of other persons."[77] The law deems any mark registered in England, under the Trademarks Act of 1905, to be distinctive in Nigeria.[78]

Trademarks are registered with respect to classifications of goods, and a mark that is intended for use on more than one class of goods must be separately registered, with respect to each. Trademarks may not be registered if they are "calculated to deceive," are "contrary to law or morality," or contain a "scandalous design."[79] No cases interpreting this language have been found, but it is well to remember that what is acceptable in one culture may be anathema in another.

If the trademark is regularly used in a certain color or colors, broader protection may be secured by registering the mark in black and white, or "without limitation to colour," as the law puts it, since the trademark, then, "shall be deemed to be registered for all colours."[80] Trademarks are registered for periods of fourteen years but may be renewed for further like periods. A trademark that is not used within five years of registration may be struck from the register,[81] and a registered trademark may not be assigned without the business goodwill associated with the class of goods to which it pertains.[82]

Trademarks registered in Great Britain have priority in registration under the Nigerian ordinance, the date of registration in Nigeria being carried back to the date of *application* for registration in Great Britain. However, no relief is available for alleged infringement occurring earlier than the actual registration in Nigeria.[83]

Remedies available under trademark law include an appeal from the registrar's refusal to register;[84] opposition to registration, which is accomplished by filing an objecting statement and then furnishing security if a counterstatement is filed (the burden of taking the matter to court lies with the applicant);[85] and an action for infringement, either of a registered trademark or an unregistered trademark, if the latter has been in use at least three years before the action and has been refused registration under the ordinance.[86] As noted above, the statute does not preclude an equitable action to protect an unregistered trademark against palming off.

V
Labor

In the end, the crucial question is whether the machinery works. The precise location of a planning unit in an organization chart is not a matter of major consequence; it is far more important to link the planning function to clearly identified centers of power wherever they may be. Particularly in the human resources area, the planning process needs to involve local and regional as well as national government bodies and influential private groups. This is important to create "systems of consent-building" which are essential if plans and strategies are to be implemented effectively.

Frederick H. Harbison in Seminar on
Manpower Problems in Economic
Development with Special
Reference to Nigeria, 1964.

THE WORK FORCE

There are only two generalizations about labor in Nigeria that can be put forward with any certainty: unskilled workers are in plentiful supply, and skilled workers are in short supply. All others —that the Nigerian laborer's productivity is low, that he is a slow learner, or that turnover and absenteeism are high—must be sharply scrutinized and either qualified or rejected.[1]

Nigeria, it must be remembered, is predominantly a rural, agricultural economy, still only slightly above the subsistence level. The per capita annual income is only £30 ($84.00). Wage earning, of any scale, is a comparatively recent phenomenon in Nigeria. Following the end of the West African slave trade, a de-urbanization took place as the countryside became safe again, and, during the first thirty years of the twentieth century, such a shortage of voluntary workers existed that the colonial administration deemed it necessary to resort to forced labor for public works.[2] This practice persisted, in fact, until the 1930's and was permissible under law until 1956.[3]

One commentator has said, "Nigeria is too close to the primary stages of social development to have already produced the foundation for the production of an adequate body of technicians."[4] One must add "social development in the Western sense" or, perhaps even better, substitute "modern economic" for "social." In a real sense, difficult for Westerners to comprehend and appreciate, Nigeria and its people have long enjoyed a high degree of "social development." Today, it is true, the West provides the economic, as well as the political, model. As a result, the movement is away from the historic center of Nigerian social and economic life, the tribe, to the modern center of social and economic life, the city. Cities and city life are sustained by commerce and industry, which pay a premium for learning, and the Nigerian school-leaver, equipped with six years of elementary education, moves to the urban center to seek employment. He is among an estimated 800,000 young Nigerians who enter the labor force each year.

If he is fortunate, has a tribal or family connection that he can exploit, or is very bright and persistent, he may find a job in a commercial enterprise. Unless he is willing to apprentice himself (for which he must usually pay a fee), he is unlikely to find a job in industry, and, if he does, it will most likely be in a very small shop employing only simple tools. While the Nigerian industrial sector is growing, it employs only a miniscule portion of the work force.[5] In terms of volume, it does not yet contribute significantly to total production; certainly, manufactured goods account for less than 3 per cent of the gross domestic product. Psychologically, however, the emphasis on industry is of great importance. Like the leadership of most other less-developed nations, that of Nigeria is convinced that the country's future depends on increased industrial strength. And, as in other less-developed nations, one cannot press too closely for the reasons; the equation of modernity and economic strength with industrialization is everywhere taken for granted. Nigeria could, at any rate, present a better case for industrialization than most of the new nations, with her large area, her large population (roughly one-fifth the population of all Africa), her resources, and her level of development at independence. Furthermore, Nigerian leaders do not view industrialization as a panacea. Probably the chief economic reason that spurs the Nigerians to industrialize is the wish to diversify production, so that, ultimately, Nigeria will be relieved of complete dependence on the sale of agricultural commodities and purchases from foreign suppliers for essential manufactured goods. The greatest obstacle to Nigeria's achievement of this goal is the lack of skilled labor, a lack even greater than that of capital. It is a lack that also plagues agriculture, which Nigerian leaders know will remain the predominant sector of the economy and on which the general well-being of Nigeria will always rest.

Until the 1963 census figures are available and analyzed,[6] one must work with the census figures of 1952-53 and such special surveys and estimates that have been made since.

In 1952, the total work force of Nigeria was 14.5 million, out of a population of 31.5 million; 8,069,000 of these were male, and 6,427,000, female. The labor force comprised those who were "economically active," and this was said to be 54.4 per cent of the male population and 41.7 per cent of the female. The inclusion of children, between the ages of seven and fourteen, who were unpaid family workers, mainly in agriculture, would have added 2 million to the total. Of the 14.5 million, over 11.5 million were engaged in agriculture and fishing.[7] The census did not even include an industrial labor category, and, apparently, no effort was made to segregate wage earners. Over 0.5 million were identified as "craftsmen," and a slightly larger group were lumped as "other occupations." Administrative, professional, and technical personnel numbered 231,000. Trading and clerical occupations claimed 492,000 males and 1,439,000 females—most of the latter being petty traders.

By December, 1961, when the work force was estimated to be about 18 million, five successive annual surveys, in establishments having ten or more workers, showed the following wage earners employed:[8]

Estimated Number of Persons Employed by Type of Employer, 1957-1961

Employer	September 1957*	September 1958*	September 1959*	September 1960	December 1960**
Federal Government	45,500	47,500	51,200	54,700	48,000
Regional Governments	70,600	73,400	77,400	83,900	80,000
Local Governments	100,600	92,200	97,700	95,100	88,000
Public Corporations	93,300	96,600	84,900	73,800	80,000
Commercial Firms and Voluntary Agencies***			197,200	212,200	182,000
	217,600	206,300	10,900	34,500	35,000
TOTAL	527,600	516,000	519,300	554,200	513,000

* Includes Southern Cameroons, estimated 40,000 of total.
** The 1960 figure is said to have been greatly overestimated; the drop from 1960 shown here is, therefore, in part a correction.
*** Figures for Commercial Firms and Voluntary Agencies were segregated after 1958.

Employment in selected industries over four years was estimated as follows:[9]

	1958*	1959*	1960	1961
Manufacturing	29,154	32,000	32,821	34,263
Construction	116,596	96,860	112,719	89,303
Electricity and Gas	9,847	16,309	8,340	11,248
Transport and Communications	46,943	45,838	39,272	42,737
Services	117,678	136,519	183,604	143,172

* Southern Cameroons not included.

All of the figures given in the above tables are to be taken only as the roughest approximations. The wide fluctuations, from year to year alone, make the figures suspect; for example, it is submitted that the electricity and gas industries are simply not susceptible to such great changes in employment from year to year. The Ministry of Labor, in presenting these tables, confessed that it had been "impossible to check the correctness and trend of the employment figures obtained as a result of the enquiry from year to year."[10]

In the 1963 survey, made by the National Manpower Board,[11] which is believed to be reliable, a total of 493,351 employees was actually counted. These were estimated to be 90 per cent of an estimated work force of 550,000 wage earners. The 1963 survey, also, included only establishments having ten or more workers. The total of 493,351 was broken down between public and private sectors as follows:

Public Employers		339,298
Government	243,344	
Teachers and Research Staff	85,954	
Private Employers		164,053

In viewing these figures, it is important to remember that probably one-half are unskilled workers. High-level manpower, counted by the National Manpower Board, comprised 20.3 per cent. Thus, approximately 30 per cent are skilled and semi-skilled workers.

The labor supply, generally, favors the individual entrepreneur in manufacturing, except for the paucity of skills. Labor is plentiful; its cost is relatively low;[12] and "the average untrained Nigerian worker is cooperative, friendly and capable of doing repetitive and routine work in which he is as productive as his European or American counterpart, providing welfare and working conditions are adequate."[13] Labor unrest does occur, however. Apart from the general strike of 1963, discussed at the close of this chapter, 93,476 man-days were lost in 1963-64 during fifty-four disputes.

There is a considerable amount of labor legislation on the statute books,[14] most of it adopted directly by colonial authorities or legislatures from English models. But the legislation is not over-restrictive and is not rigidly enforced.

Training of workers must start very near the bottom. In addition to teaching skills, it is necessary to inculcate a new attitude. The pace and continuity of Nigerian rural life is quite different from that of even the smallest industrial enterprise. A low level of demand, easily satisfied, is the heritage that the Nigerian agricultural worker brings to his new job: he has been raised on a poor diet, and he is barely literate or even illiterate. His whole background is the rural, subsistence economy, where the tempo is regulated by crops and weather and is characterized by the informal and easy ways of tribal life on the land. He has, generally, had no experience with machinery; indeed, "Unlike his foreign counterpart, the Nigerian child is not brought up with mechanical and manipulative toys and receives no early stimulus in handling mechanical and precision equipment."[15] On the farm, his family and he pursued their meager livelihood on small landholdings, using primitive methods and tools. He comes into an industry, if he is fortunate enough to find a job, that lacks tradition and, more often than not, lacks modern machinery, skilled management, and adequate training facilities. The job lifts him above the mass, but only at the end of a long and rare process does a skilled technician result. In the meantime, one of his fellows might have made it and returned to the land after earning a "stake." Some refuse to commit themselves to life in the city and the discipline of the factory or workshop; others return to assume family responsibilities. But the attraction of a regular income and the ability to buy the consumer goods for which demand is building up, even in remote villages, is overcoming the attachment to rural life.[16] The transition is increasingly being eased by the addition of educational facilities to train workers for industrial employment.

TRAINING FOR EMPLOYMENT

Vocational training in Nigeria began in earnest at the end of World War II, with the return of thousands of Nigerian war veterans. A ten-year Development Plan of Technical Education was inaugurated in 1945, financed under the Colonial Development and Welfare Act of 1940.[17] Institutes for training technicians and trade centers for training craftsmen and artisans were established. Assistance was also given to private technical and vocational schools.

The vocational schools turn out such craftsmen as bricklayers, electricians, sheet-metal workers, and welders.[18] Eight are run by the federal and regional governments, each offering three-year courses, except in the North, where they vary from three to five years. The federal center at Yaba offers students the opportunity of a further two-year program in industry.

The four government technical institutes, located in the federal territory and in each of the regional capitals (except the newly-created Midwest state), offer both senior- and junior-level courses. Senior students are given "sub-professional" engineering training (architectural, civil, electrical, and mechanical). Two years of study earn an Ordinary Certificate; four, the Higher Certificate, roughly the equivalent of completion of the course of a technical high school in the United States.

As of May, 1961, 3,600 male students were attending courses (day, evening, and part-time) in the twelve government technical institutes and trade centers.

In addition, an unknown number were attending private vocational schools, and approximately 2,700 persons were in courses offered within private industry or public corporations.[19] The United Africa Company has over five hundred employed apprentices in training at its five schools scattered through Nigeria, and seven hundred are taking refresher courses. The apprentices' course lasts five years and produces about seventy-four graduates annually for UAC. The cost per student varies between £400 and £675 per year, which includes living expenses. Shell–B. P. Petroleum Development Co., Ltd., initiated a training program, in 1960, that attracted twenty thousand applicants. The school, located at Port Harcourt, now trains 125 full-time students, as well as giving evening courses and short-term refresher training. Graduates are not assured, or committed to, employment by Shell–B. P.

Among statutory corporations and government ministries, extensive training programs are conducted by the Nigerian Railway Corporation, the Electricity Corporation of Nigeria, the Nigerian Ports Authority, the Nigerian Chamber of Mines, the Ministry of Posts and Telegraphs, and the Ministry of Works and Surveys. One such program is described as follows:

[A]t the Ports Authority Technical and Craft Training Centre at Apapa dockyard, nearly 300 indentured apprentices undergo training for as long as 5 years. The first year is spent full-time at the training centre, at the end of which time they take aptitude tests and are assigned to a trade. During the following four years they receive on-the-job training but return to the Centre once a week for theory, mathematics, engineering science, and drawing. Seventeen trades are taught....[20]

Approximately 1,200 apprentices are in training under such programs.

Other than the programs run by public corporations and larger industry, the apprenticeship system in smaller establishments is chiefly a source for "cheap and unpaid labor," and the payment by the apprentice of premiums to the employer has resulted in "a rather iniquitous system."[21]

Further facilities are to be developed under the 1962-68 Development Plan, and educational expenditures, including those for technical training, bulk large in the six-year budgets of both the federal government and the regions. Approximately £1.2 million is budgeted for technical training in Lagos alone. Long-range planning by the federal Ministry of Education has set a tentative goal of achieving, in the next decade, an annual rate of graduating 5,000 technicians and 28,000 artisans and craftsmen. The Technical High School at Port Harcourt, established with AID funds under the auspices of the Eastern Region and conducted by the University of California, is an example of the successful integration of vocational training with the social sciences. This permits the simultaneous education of highly qualified apprentices and those who have the capacity for higher education. The school, which started with 112 students in 1961, has expanded to a student body of 600. Applications far exceed available places.

The critical need for skilled secretarial, accounting, and clerical help has not been overlooked, and government, industry, and private schools (most of the latter are inadequate) provide training, but in limited numbers. The long-range goal in these categories is to produce one thousand graduates a year. The present output of qualified personnel is perhaps three hundred to four hundred per year.

MANPOWER NEEDS

Happily, although belatedly, a National Manpower Board in which the regional governments also participate was established by the federal government early in 1963. Resource inventories, assessments of needs, and manpower planning for the objectives set out in the development plan—and into the future—can now, it is hoped, proceed on a national, rational, and systematic basis. Among the board's responsibilities are the formulation of recommendations regarding training programs, including university expansion. Review and restatement of employment policies are also within the board's frame of reference.

Both Frederick Harbison[22] and Archibald Calloway,[23] two of the most knowledgeable observers of the Nigerian labor and educational scene, lay stress on Nigeria's "high-level manpower needs"[24]—that is, beyond the shortage of skilled laborers and technicians, there is as pressing a lack in all levels of management and executive skills. They, therefore, quite rightly argue that the expansion of intermediate education is now Nigeria's most pressing need.[25] There is a more than ample pool of primary-school leavers (those who have finished six years of elementary education) to feed the technical institutes, the trade centers, and the apprenticeship programs. There is not yet, however, a sufficient supply of secondary-school graduates of adequate quality who can be absorbed into business and industry as management trainees, or, more broadly put, as white-collar employees, which would include high-level clerical and supervisory personnel, capable of moving up into executive positions. The lack of adequate intermediate educational facilities not only fails to produce this kind of employee but it creates other problems, or contributes to them: (1) it is providing insufficient candidates for available university openings; (2) it fails to provide channels for the energies, ambitions, and abilities of primary-school leavers whose mounting numbers are far in excess of employment opportunities at their level, creating great dissatisfaction and social unrest; (3) it results in under-utilization of manpower, because persons capable of achieving higher skills and greater productivity level off as semi-skilled laborers or low-level technicians. This, in turn, crowds and cheapens the labor market at this stage and results in policies that often tend to favor over-hiring and labor-intensive methods and industries.[26] Beyond the secondary level, there are very few university graduates available for immediate entry into junior executive or management-trainee ranks.

Calloway argues that labor-intensive industrialization should not be favored, for industrialization is not the solution to Nigeria's unemployment problem.[27] It is difficult to disagree, for the creation of wealth in Nigeria, rather than the creation of jobs, is the proper objective of industrialization. The capital cost per job in industry is high—£1000 to £3000 per man. At this rate, modern industry absorbs relatively few workers, and it will be long before industrialization makes a significant dent in Nigerian unemployment. Doubling or tripling the number of employees, or foregoing modern machinery for the sake of preserving labor intensity, will not meaningfully diminish the pressures of unemployment. However, it will threaten the external competitive position of Nigerian industry, in the long run, and a policy of labor-intensive industry cannot be indefinitely maintained.

It is believed that the present posture of the Nigerian authorities reflects this conviction. However, the new census figures may bring about a reappraisal of the problem of unemployment. This may alter the present position, generally, favoring efficient rather than intensive employment of labor. This is, perhaps, best demonstrated by the program for dieselization of the Nigerian Railway, in the face of a declining market for Nigerian coal and persistent operating losses for the mines, which employ several hundred Eastern Nigerians.

The great shortage of management personnel has required the retention of large numbers of expatriate employees in established firms, and the importation of such personnel for new foreign-owned enterprise is an absolute necessity. This need is filled within the framework of a pervasive campaign to "Nigerianize" employment, and "quotas" of expatriate employees are established by government under the authority of the Immigration Act of 1963.[28] The quota system has been, and continues to be, highly restrictive and, in the view of many, counter-productive. It is, after all, simply another facet of the attitude favoring labor-intensive industry. If the creation of wealth in Nigeria, rather than the employment of Nigerians, is the objective of industrialization, who creates the wealth is of secondary importance. The restrictions on immigration are open to the criticism that "This policy disregards the great probability that the income-producing effect of the influx of highly-qualified immigrants would greatly outweigh any adverse substitution effect experienced by certain nations."[29] However, there are nationalistic and social factors at work here that cannot be dispelled by sheer economic argument. First, the Nigerian must assume his rightful place on the decision-making level of business and industry. Second, the higher rates of pay and the much higher standard of living enjoyed by expatriates (usually marked by separateness of the white community and conspicuous consumption by the expatriates) are a constant reminder of the old colonial status. The need for expatriate skills is recognized, but the process of obtaining or enlarging expatriate quotas, which are established for each business, is fraught with bureaucratic difficulties and delay. Most companies report needs that they cannot easily fill, although there is no question of their willingness to hire Nigerians if they were available. But, in this manner, the pressure to train Nigerians to higher jobs is maintained, and it may be argued that this might not otherwise be possible.

To date, the most thorough-going Nigerianization has taken place in government, and all ministerial posts have long since passed into Nigerian hands, except the post of attorney general of Northern Nigeria (the chief justice of Northern Nigeria is also an expatriate). In 1961, a sample survey showed 4,121 non-Nigerians employed by the federal and regional governments;[30] an actual count, in January, 1963, showed that the number had dropped to 2,334. The north continues to employ, proportionately, the greatest number of expatriates in government; in January, 1963, there were 802 serving there in senior and intermediate categories. The federal government remains the largest public employer of expatriates in absolute numbers, however; there were 658 in senior positions, in 1963, and 307 in intermediate positions. At the same time, the Nigerian governments had 1,029 vacancies in senior managerial and administrative staff positions alone, 346 for engineers, and 153 for accountants and auditors.

In the private sector, economic development has increased the number of expatriates. The rise is at the managerial level and is attributable to the increase in total economic activity. A comparison between surveys made in 1961 and 1963 demonstrates that Nigerians are effectively pushing their way up, since the number of expatriates in professional and technical positions declined.

Expatriates

	1961	1963
Administrative, Managerial, and Executive Positions	1,904	2,310
Professional and Technical Positions	2,841	2,525
TOTAL	4,745	4,835

The 1963 survey also showed the following groupings for occupations that are included in the total of 2,525 professional and technical positions:

	Expatriate	Nigerian	Vacancies*
Engineers	625	173	80
Engineering Assistants	196	873	
Accountants and Auditors	386	509	25

Accounting and Auditing Assistants	71	1,035
Foremen and Supervisors	471	1,893
Secretary Typists and Personal Secretaries	161	384

* Vacancies were not shown in all categories.

As Nigerian economic development moves ahead, it must rely on progressively higher levels of skills, which the Nigerian educational system is not yet geared to provide. The numbers of expatriates will, therefore, increase and peak sometime in the mid-1970's. By then, Nigerians should be able to begin narrowing the gap in absolute terms. It is up to foreign-owned enterprise to help the Nigerians do so, for it is both politically and economically advantageous. Expatriates cost far more than do Nigerian employees: expatriate wages are higher, housing is more expensive, travel and other fringe benefits are costly. There is no reason for management not to replace an expatriate as soon as his Nigerian equivalent shows up. Most Nigerian authorities recognize this; some Nigerian politicians do not. Manipulation of the immigrant quota system to regulate reliance on expatriates is probably slowing Nigerian development. But it is deemed politically necessary to demonstrate this kind of control, and it may serve to divert some corporate funds from expatriate salaries into training programs for Nigerian employees. The Advisory Committee on Aids to African Businessmen, in its 1959 report,[31] recommended that, in the future, foreign investors be permitted to establish themselves in Nigeria only if they bring with them technical and managerial skills which they are willing to share with Nigerians.

In this connection, it is of interest to observe that the European-owned firms have a better record of Nigerianization than do the Levantine-owned firms, those run by Syrians and Lebanese. The Advisory Committee criticized the Levantines (most of whom are in trade, but some are also in industry) for refusing to share their technical knowledge and managerial skills with Nigerians, unlike the Europeans.[32] This results, very often, from the close "family" type of enterprise that is characteristic of the Levantines. The criteria for admission suggested by the Advisory Committee would eliminate most Levantines and Asians, who, in fact, generally possess only trading skills and have little or nothing to offer in the modern technical and managerial line. Trading skills, of course, are something on which the Nigerians pride themselves, and the most determined push for Nigerianization (after government) has been in the distributive sector. There, even the European-owned firms have felt the thrust, and the movement of such giants as UAC, which still controls a very large segment of the Nigerian wholesale and retail trade, is toward greater investment in industrial production.[33] New distributive businesses that have been permitted entry are few and are tied to at least some packaging or rudimentary production in Nigeria, such as tableting in the case of pharmaceuticals. The sole known exception is the Italian oil company, Ente Nazionale di Idrocarburi, which has been permitted to start a chain of service stations in Nigeria and has no production facilities there, although it is engaged in exploration for petroleum along with a number of other foreign oil companies.

Women predominate in the Nigerian retail trade. Of the 16 million women counted in the 1952-53 census, 1,400,000 gave their occupation as traders, most of them in southern areas of the country. A larger number, to be sure—5 million—were active in agriculture; but this is to be expected from the tribal and family mode of farming the land. In the March, 1961, survey, 50 per cent of the 8,500 women counted[34] were professional and technical workers. Of the remainder, 650 were clerical, 950 were skilled and semiskilled, and 1,440 were unskilled.[35]

WAGES AND HOURS

The large number and concentration of government employees, compared to non-government wage earners scattered among a few sizable enterprises and countless small businesses,[36] means that government wage rates, by and large, set the basic pattern throughout Nigeria almost as effectively as if there were minimum-wage legislation. There are, of course, variations among regions and among metropolitan centers, towns, and villages.[37] However, wages in private employment are generally 5 to 10 per cent higher than in government, except for unskilled labor, where the pool is so large that wages in both sectors are approximately equal.

While there was no standing national minimum-wage legislation as of 1963, there is machinery for the setting of wage rates by government in specific cases under the Wages Boards Ordinance of 1957.[38] This empowers the Minister of Labor, "if he is of the opinion that wages are unreasonably low or that no adequate machinery exists for the effective regulation of wages or other conditions of employment,"[39] to direct that a wages board be established,[40] or he may appoint a commission of inquiry to determine whether a wages board shall be appointed.[41] In the absence of such action by the federal minister, the regional authority may act to the same effect. If the wages board's recommendations are accepted by the responsible minister, federal or regional, he may make an order incorporating the recommendations, with or without amendments of his own. If he wishes, he may ignore the recommendations. The power of the wages board to set scales of pay is broad, as was the former authority of the colonial administration to fix wage rates by Order in Council.[42] §11(1) of the Wages Boards Ordinance reads: "Any wages board may, subject to the provisions of this section [respecting notice and consideration of objections], recommend the remuneration to be paid either generally or for any particular work, by their employers to the workers described in the order establishing the said wages board."

Orders made under Orders in Council[43] have regulated, for some years, minimum wages and working conditions in certain industries, principally in Lagos but also in the plateau mining industry. These are found in the statute books as subsidiary legislation but, for the most part, are out of date.[44]

Wages may also be the subject of investigation by Commissions of Inquiry,[45] which have powers to make recommendations but not to bind. This mode was used in 1959 to survey the wage and salary scales of government employees,[46] resulting in recommendations that were implemented in 1960—the only general wage increase for government workers that had been given since 1954.[47] Government employees received increases ranging from 12.5 per cent to 20 per cent, and this immediately provided a pattern that the private sector could not ignore. The statutory authority is broad enough to permit the use of a commission of inquiry to survey wages and salaries generally,[48] but this has not been done.

Collective bargaining machinery exists to negotiate wages and working conditions, as a rule, in industries where minimum rates have been established by the procedures described above, for these are the areas of employment in which the workers are organized and the unions have some strength, but it is seldom used. In at least one industry not covered by statutory rates, however, the joint efforts of employers and unions, working through a common body, have resulted in setting minimum wages that are applicable throughout Nigeria.[49]

Wage rates, of course, do not reflect total wage costs. Fringe benefits are often numerous and costly: occasionally, canteens and restaurants must be provided, transportation allowances granted, special clothing supplied, housing made available at low cost, special risk and Christmas bonuses paid, and longevity and severance pay added. Where a labor health area has been proclaimed by a regional governor,[50] that is, a place where workers must "live in" and are unable to return home each day—benefits will include food, housing, and medical care. Once a labor health area has been proclaimed, the regional government has wide powers to regulate town planning, health and sanitary facilities, construction, and the supply of water, food, and fuel.[51] No criteria are provided in the ordinance for determining when a labor health area may be proclaimed, and it is doubtful whether the exercise of this power could be upheld under the subsequently adopted regional constitutions. At present, an estimated fifty thousand persons are employed in such areas.

There is constant pressure being exerted in the wage front because of the steadily rising cost of living in Nigeria, which the government was able to bring to a halt in 1963, but not before public resentment had reached the point where a general strike was mounted.[52] In Lagos, the cost of living had risen 21 per cent between 1956 and 1962. In 1962, it rose by 4.3 per cent, but, in 1963, it leveled off. Other large cities showed similar increases since 1955: Ibadan and Enugu, between 1956 and 1962, showed increases of 20 and 33 per cent; Kaduna had an increase of 18 per cent between 1958 and 1962. And rather than leveling off, the price indices of these three centers dropped significantly during 1963.

CONSUMER PRICE INDEX
1953 = 100
(Kaduna, 1957 = 100)

	Lagos	Ibadan	Enugu	Kaduna
1963*	(110)**	128	144	119
1962	145	137	149	122
1961	139	127	122	115
1960	132	117	119	108
1959	124	112	119	109
1958	119	110	115	103
1957	119	117	112	
1956	117	114	112	

* November, 1963.
** New base: 1960 = 100. In old base terms, 110 = 145.

A survey made in 1961, by the Nigerian Trade Union Confederation and based on a "minimum market basket," established the monthly cost of living for an urban Nigerian family of five at £18/6 ($50.47). The market basket included basic necessities plus extras, such as laundry, beverages, cigarettes, medical care, education, and savings, which, needless to say, many families cannot afford—certainly, not unless two or more of the family unit are working.

Since 1960, when the last major wage-revision took place, independence has come to Nigeria and, with it, ambitious economic development plans that call for increased capital investment and decreased consumption. Inflation has naturally taken its toll, and wages have steadily fallen behind the cost of living, owing to: increased customs duties; the decline in Nigeria's terms of trade (principally, the fall in cocoa prices in 1962); and rising rents and land speculation. This finally culminated, in 1963, in a demand for the revision of wage scales.

Working hours may be set by governmental authority in two ways: generally, by regulations promulgated under the Labour Code Ordinance and, for particular industries, under the Wages Boards Ordinance.[53] The present general maximum workday is ten hours, and the workweek may not exceed fifty-eight hours, including overtime. The average workweek in private employment is now forty-four hours—eight hours on weekdays and four hours on Saturdays, although many establishments have cut back to forty hours and have eliminated work on Saturday. Overtime is usually compensated as time-and-a-half, and Sunday and holiday work, as double-time.

With respect to leave and holiday policy, government again sets the pace. Government wage earners are entitled to seven to fourteen days of leave per year, salaried employees, to fifteen to thirty days. After six months' employment, seven days of sick leave are granted. Eleven public holidays are granted with pay to all government employees and to most industrial employees.

LABOR AND SOCIAL LEGISLATION

Under the constitution adopted in 1960, and as revised and readopted in 1963, "Labour, that is to say, conditions of labour, industrial relations, trade unions and welfare of labour" appear on the "Concurrent Legislative List."[54] Thus, both federal and regional parliaments may legislate regarding labor, but federal statutes take precedence. However, since independence, the regional legislatures have passed no significant labor legislation, and the federal legislature's chief contribution has been a social security statute. Nigerian labor legislation is to a considerable extent a heritage of British colonial administration, although the federal parliament, from 1954 on, actively participated in framing a number of important laws affecting workers.

Until shortly before World War II, the status and rights of workers and the contract of employment were regulated by the common law. In 1939, the Trade Unions Ordinance[55] was passed; in 1941, a Trades Disputes (Arbitration and Inquiry) Ordinance;[56] and, in 1942, the Workmen's Compensation Ordinance.[57] In 1945, Nigeria received what remains its major labor law, the Labor Code Ordinance.[58] Not until 1954, when the Minister of Labor (a position that had existed since 1951 but, until 1954, shared responsibility with the Commissioner of Labor) became fully responsible for labor policy,[59] were any new paths trod. Subsequently, there followed the Factories Ordinance, 1955,[60] the Wages Board Ordinance, 1957,[61] and important amendments to previous legislation.[62] In the regions, passage of Fatal Accidents Acts[63] contributed to the security of survivors of workers who met accidental death but not in the course of employment.

The Labor Code Ordinance principally regulates the contract of employment. It covers workers performing manual labor, clerical workers earning under £75 per year, and domestic workers in private and government employment, including local and native authorities.[64] The president may, by order, make an exception of government departments or employees, and the penal provisions of the ordinance cannot be imposed upon governmental authorities.[65] The ordinance regulates and specifies the following: oral and written employment-contract terms; mode of payment of wages; labor recruitment; minimum ages and conditions of employment for women, children, and apprentices; registration of employees; working conditions for clerical and domestic workers; and jurisdiction of magistrates' courts to settle disputes[66] other than "trade disputes,"[67] that is, a dispute that "arises as to the rights or liabilities of either party or touching any misconduct, neglect or ill-treatment or any injury to the person or property of either of the parties under any contract of employment."[68] It also provides for the creation of "labor health areas," as previously noted, and broad powers to establish satisfactory working and living conditions in such areas.[69] Regional authorities are given exclusive powers in some sections,[70] concurrent jurisdiction in others,[71] and, under still others, regional authorities may act only if the federal government has not acted or approves of action proposed by regional authorities.[72]

Yesufu has described other labor legislation in a succinct paragraph, sufficient for our purposes here:

The Factories Ordinance, 1955, is aimed at ensuring safe conditions of work; it requires that machines shall be adequately guarded, that workshops shall be kept in a sanitary and well-lighted condition, and regulates the supply of protecting clothing and equipment, the maintenance of first-aid boxes, the reporting of industrial accidents, and allied questions. The Workmen's Compensation Ordinance, 1941 (Cap. 222), provides for the payment of monetary compensation to injured workmen in respect of injuries sustained at work which result in permanent or temporary incapacity; or for payments to the dependants of a deceased workman where such injuries result in his death. The Wages Boards Ordinance, 1957, is intended to be something of a stop-gap in the process of development of trade unions and collective bargaining. It permits the state to prescribe conditions of employment (wages, hours of work, holidays, etc.), by Order, where wages are unreasonably low and workers are not sufficiently organized. It is a mark of Government's belief in collective bargaining that, so far, only one Wages Order, which is confined to Lagos, has been made under Ordinance.[73]

The National Provident Fund Act, 1961,[74] is the first major step taken by the independent Nigerian government in social legislation. Previously, statutory social security (and that limited to sick leave and retirement benefits) was almost exclusively the privilege of government employees. A number of the larger expatriate firms had set up pension schemes and, in some cases, provided sickness benefits, by way of leave. The act imposes a mandatory scheme on all but a few categories of exempt persons, is minimal in its contributions and benefits, but does cover retirement, survivorship, invalidity, and sickness. Worker and employer contribute equally, at the rate of 5 per cent of the employee's pay, up to a maximum of £2 per month.[75] Exempt categories are casual workers,[76] those covered by any scheme of pensions on terms substantially similar to those prescribed by the Pensions Ordinance;[77] workers under educational institutions' schemes; workers (Nigerian or other) employed outside Nigeria for not less than one year; and non-Nigerians employed in Nigeria for periods not exceeding six years at a time, provided, in the last two categories, that the worker shows he is under some other benefit scheme not less favorable than that of Nigeria.[78] The scheme is funded and is operated by officials appointed by the Minister of Pensions.[79] An Advisory Council, representing the federal and regional governments, employers, and workers, may make recommendations, but the minister is not bound to follow them.[80] The Investment Committee, on the other hand, consisting of the director of the fund, an officer of the Central Bank (nominated by the governor of the bank), and an officer of the Federal Ministry of Finance, has power to give general or special directions, from time to time, on the investment of moneys in the fund which are surplus to current needs.[81] The statute imposes no restrictions on the type of investments or the proportion of types of investments that are to be made,[82] and moneys in the reserve fund are subject to appropriation only by Parliament.[83] Criminal proceedings are provided for evasion of the act or fraud with respect to it,[84] as well as civil suit for the recovery of contributions due.[85] The decision of the director, with respect to liability of an employer or benefits payable, is final, and no appeal to a court is provided.[86] Persons covered under private schemes, including those antedating the Provident Fund, and not otherwise exempt, as noted above, are required to participate.[87]

Since the scheme applies only where an employer-employee relationship exists, it is limited in its scope to the wage-earning force in being, and this now amounts to approximately 500,000 persons, less those exempt. As of December, 1963, 390,646 workers were contributing to the fund and had made cumulative contributions of £4.5 million. Voluntary participation is afforded to missionaries, through the application of any missionary society;[88] to workers in minimum-sized establishments, in terms of numbers of employers and when established, that may be exempted from the mandatory provisions of the act (no such minimum has been prescribed);[89] and to persons who cease to be subject to the act by reason of change of employment or occupation.[90]

The history of twenty-five years of labor and social legislation in Nigeria is obviously, also, the history of the gradual erosion of established tribal rights and obligations. The fragmentation of familial units and the loosening of ties that inevitably follow upon urbanization and the creation of a wage-earning class have demanded remedies for social needs in a larger framework. The arrival of independence heralded, it was believed by many, an era of greatly enlarged social benefits, to be paid for out of the wealth that no longer flowed to the colonial power but now belonged to Nigerians.

But independence has made new and costly demands upon the resources of Nigeria, and economic development is making still more. It is improbable that Nigeria can extend its social welfare program significantly for some years to come, except in education, at least to the extent that it sets up schemes requiring annual recurring budget items and to which the beneficiary makes no contribution or merely a nominal, insignificant contribution. Nigeria, for example, cannot now afford free medical services. However, it would do well to broaden coverage of the Provident Fund and to open it to all self-employed Nigerians on a voluntary basis, since it is an important and attractive way of creating savings that are available for investment in economic development projects.

In the meantime, although they are being eroded, the tribal and family ties still persist. These continue to provide a considerable measure of social security for the family member who goes off to the city. There are always other family members there to whom he can turn in need. As a last resort, he can return to his native village. He maintains these rights by fulfilling his traditional obligations vis-à-vis the family; he remits money, if he is working, to his village, and, even in Lagos, members of the family descend, often in numbers and unannounced—and, perhaps, for extended stays—on the home of their city brother. The city member also maintains ties through tribal associations in the city or such organizations as traditional dance groups. These obligations and links vary in their performance and closeness, but the completely detribalized Nigerian, who has, at most, only his immediate family to turn to, is still a rarity.

Ironically, since the struggle against the external colonial master has been won and independence achieved, there has been a retreat from nationalism and a resurgence of tribal and family identification. This springs, in part, from "fashionable sentiment"; in part, from the search in the tribal tradition for a validating substructure of the concept of "Africanness" or *"négritude"*; and, in part, from sharper realities—rising unemployment and the new political hopes and fears that find internal expression in the rivalry and interaction of regions, tribes, linguistic groups, religions, and political parties. Whatever impact this partial retreat from the larger framework of Nigerian nationhood may have politically, it may work to keep the complementary processes of detribalization and the ability of government to supply social welfare needs, in place of the tribe, in more satisfactory balance than would otherwise be possible.

TRADE-UNIONISM

The tenuous position of Nigerian trade unions was epitomized by the statement made by the Minister of Labor, in 1960, upon the introduction of the Labor Code (Amendment) Act,[91] introducing the voluntary check-off system for the payment of union dues. "The Ministry," he said, "has continued to be concerned at the financial instability of many trade unions and their officials, the inability of the unions to provide welfare schemes for their members and the increasing dependence of trade unions on external financial assistance."[92] The last phrase was a reference to the subvention of the two major competing movements in Nigeria, by the western and eastern bloc international labor organizations—the International Confederation of Trade Unions (ICFTU), and the World Federation of Trade Unions (WFTU). It is this rivalry that lies behind much of the turbulent, contentious, and ineffective history of the postwar Nigerian labor movement.

Craft guilds have existed in Nigeria since the very early days, but the individualism of the self-employed craftsmen precluded any interest on their part in the idea of unions. These guilds were not later transformed, as in other countries, into unions because industry in Nigeria came from other directions, rather than from the expansion of crafts into industries.

The first Nigerian trade union was founded, in 1912, by civil servants,[93] well in advance of the establishment of any large industry. It was, in fact, an organization limited to the elite of the native civil service, and membership, during its initial years, remained small.[94] Modern Nigerian unionism began with the 1930's, when the Railway Workers' Union[95] and the Nigerian Union of Teachers were formed. Until then, the Civil Service Union had attempted to serve both groups, and, indeed, when the railwaymen struck off on their own, the railway clerical workers chose to remain with the Civil Service Union.

Despite its relatively long history, Nigerian unionism has failed to develop and maintain adequate experienced leadership,[96] and, as a result, it has also lacked systematic, well-defined programs. Low wages, disinterest in urban and industrial employment, smallness of the wage-earning class, to say nothing of the handicaps or "disincentives" imposed on unionism by a colonial administration as the major employer, combined to inhibit the growth of unions. Dues were small and infrequently paid, and a career in trade unionism, on a full- or part-time basis, was a risky and thankless job. Where it was pursued, it was within particular companies, governmental departments, or crafts employed in local industry, rather than in a national or industrial union, with the notable exceptions of the railwaymen's and teachers' unions. As a result, the Nigerian labor movement has struggled along as an unco-ordinated mass of small, overlapping, or isolated organizations, each pursuing ill-defined goals with inadequate resources and leadership in a confined area. Neither the funds nor the capacity existed to conduct programs to educate workers in the objectives and techniques of unionism. Obviously, the provision of benefits—in particular, strike benefits—[97] was entirely foreclosed.

The depression of the 1930's intensified union interest among Nigerian workers, but the British administration realized that unionism was essentially a healthy phenomenon that deserved encouragement—perhaps as a diversion from, or means of controlling, political radicalism—and this realization significantly changed the course of Nigerian trade unions. The Colonial Development and Welfare Act, 1940,[98] made financial assistance, under the act, to colonial administrations contingent upon the encouragement of the development of "healthy" trade-union movements. There immediately followed the passing of the Nigerian Trade Unions Ordinance, 1939.[99] Yesufu says of this enactment:

[T]here can be no doubt of the outstanding importance of the Ordinance to trade union growth.... In the absence of such a law Nigerian trade unions... would have had to contend with all the complications of the English common law. If the few unions which existed before 1938 did not experience serious legal difficulties, it was partly because they were sufficiently quiescent not to draw too much notice, and partly because after 1930 at any rate, it would have been impolitic, in the face of the decided views of the Colonial Office, to embark on any policy of trade union repression. Such liberalism, however, could hardly have stood the exigencies of war.[100]

Under the ordinance, trade unions were required to register,[101] and the roster in the next years demonstrates the "shaping-up" and, to some extent, the growth that the ordinance encouraged. In 1940, only seven unions registered, but the pace quickly accelerated; during 1941, twenty-seven unions were registered, and, in 1944, ninety-one unions were entered on the books. Over the 1940-44 period, eight previously registered unions became defunct. While the ordinance provided an impetus to unionism, it did not cure innate deficiencies.

The move toward amalgamation came in 1941 when five unions of government technical workers, claiming five thousand members, founded the African Civil Servants' Technical Workers' Union. Within a year, this group had grown to twelve member unions and led the way in the formation of Nigeria's first central trade-union organization, the Federated Trades Union Congress of Nigeria, known as the TUC. Its first congress, held in Lagos in 1943, was attended by two hundred delegates, representing fifty-six of the eighty-five constituent unions.

The unions were, at this time, quite naturally seeking outlets for their nationalistic feelings. In 1944, the TUC joined the political movement headed by Dr. Nnamdi Azikiwe (now President of Nigeria), which was then the National Council of Nigeria and the Cameroons (NCNC) and is now the National Council of Nigerian Citizens. This resulted in the first disruption of the TUC, and a portion of the membership withdrew to form the Committee of Trade Unionists. In 1945, a thirty-seven-day general strike created further tensions within the TUC, and leadership of the strike was taken over by a splinter group of government workers, who, with another such group, formed a separate union in 1947, the Federation of Unions of Government and Municipal Nonclerical Workers of Nigeria. In 1948, the problem of political activity was raised again. The TUC leadership declared for a stand that was free from party affiliation and placed a pragmatic emphasis on economic matters. By 1949, the Committee of Trade Unionists had rallied its anti-NCNC dissidents to form the Nigerian National Federation of Labour. Thus, in 1950, three "national unions" were on the scene. Their leaders met that year to merge into the Nigerian Labour Congress (NLC), which included all important Nigerian unions except the Nigerian Union of Teachers and the railway workers. Among its first acts, the NLC joined the communist-dominated WFTU, and, almost immediately, the NLC leadership split on this issue. The WFTU affiliation was severed, in 1951, after ICFTU leaders had visited Nigeria. This precipitated a group in the NLC, led by the NLC president, M. A. O. Imoudu, to bolt the organization and set up a rival central body, the All Nigeria Trade Union Federation (ANTUF), which the railway workers' union joined as the only really important and sizable constituent. ANTUF decided against seeking any international affiliation and proclaimed, as its goal, the establishment of a political labor party and, through it, a socialist government in Nigeria. Attempted infiltration by leftist leaders of the NLC was repulsed by ANTUF, but the voting procedure adopted by ANTUF, nevertheless, effectively delivered the organization into the hands of communist sympathizers; all union affiliates of ANTUF had equal votes, and, by 1957, this had enabled communist sympathizers, who had control of the small constituent unions, to gain a majority of the ANTUF executive. As a result, ANTUF split, and a new organization opposed to the control of ANTUF by extreme leftists was founded on April 17, 1957—the National Council of Trade Unions, Nigeria (NCTUN), headed by L. L. Borha as secretary general. Meanwhile, the NLC withered, and ANTUF and NCTUN remained as the two principal contenders. NCTUN claimed (in 1957) 24 unions with 50,000 members; ANTUF claimed 39 unions with 57,000 members; and some 270 additional unions, with 100,000 members, fell outside these two, for reasons of being either independent of either national group or for being to the left of the NLC. Both sought ICFTU affiliation, but only NCTUN was accepted. The rejection of ANTUF's application by the ICFTU must be seen as a fundamental error, the results of which should have been startlingly clear even then.

The question of government recognition of the two contenders resulted in a brief reunion. A meeting held at Enugu in March, 1959, produced the Trades Union Congress (of Nigeria), TUC(N). M. A. O. Imoudu was elected president and L. L. Borha became secretary general. All other officers came from the NCTUN and the previously independent unions that were persuaded to join the TUC(N). "In the interest of permanent unity, communism, fascism, and national political partisanship"[102] were to be kept out of the Nigerian labor movement. But, immediately, the matter of international affiliation was raised, and, although proponents succeeded in bringing the new union into the ICFTU, the move soon shattered the organization.

Less than a year later, TUC(N) split, one faction headed by Imoudu and another by Borha. Imoudu and his ANTUF supporters left to form the Nigerian Trades Union Congress (NTUC), rallying against ICFTU affiliation. Borha and his NCTUN group now had complete control of TUC(N). In 1961, efforts were made by the government to bring the two groups together by an appeal made through the All-Nigeria People's Conference. The leadership of both unions agreed to abide by the decision of a special committee that was to arbitrate differences. A conference in Ibadan followed, in May, 1962, at which the two factions formed the United Labour Congress (ULC). When a majority of the newly constituted congress then voted to affiliate with the ICFTU and the All African Trade Union Federation (AATUF),[103] the Imoudu group withdrew and established the Independent United Labour Congress (IULC), rejecting any overseas affiliation. The government, subsequently, recognized the ULC as the majority trade-union center, and its leaders have since represented Nigeria on the international labor scene. At present, the ULC claims a membership of eighty-five unions, and the IULC, sixty-five unions, but no statistics are available to determine their actual strength.

The result of all of this has been that Nigerian trade-unionism has not played as significant a role in the postwar Nigerian political, economic, or social development as it might have, and it has prevented Nigerian representatives from assuming a leading role in the growth of the Pan-African labor movement. It is not entirely labor's fault. In a very real sense, it demonstrates the debilitating effect of the extension of the cold war to an unformed and inexperienced labor movement that has not yet established itself firmly on the national scene. This compounds the problems resulting from lack of leadership and the low level of membership support both in activity and payment of dues; for when the chief issue becomes international affiliation, when both factions can depend on financial support from overseas, and when membership benefits do not exist, the unions not only lose the credence and support of the workers but they are suspect by the government and non-unionists. As a result, Nigerian trade unions carry little weight on the political scene.

Labor's gains in Nigeria, for the most part, depend on the sometime support of the British labor movement; on an apprehension of what strong unions motivated by adverse economic conditions might come to be; and on the sense of social justice that obtains in government and among the country's leadership. Tribal, racial, and national loyalties have cultivated this sense among Nigerians over a long period, during which the employer was principally white, expatriate, and protected. The economic and social position of the Nigerian wage earner is by no means a depressed one. Indeed, one might say that the Nigerian "proletariat" is a kind of sub-elite that is not feared but envied. It is a group whose critical role in economic development is honored by government because its skills and energies are required for the task ahead, because strong and probably politically radical unionism might crystallize under less favorable conditions.

RECENT DEVELOPMENTS

Since independence, three strikes of national consequence have taken place, one by a union not affiliated with either the ULC or the IULC. The second was a general strike protesting the rising cost of living, and this was followed by a similar general strike early in 1964.

The first, involving Nigerian dock-workers, began on February 3, 1963, and lasted some two weeks. Sympathy strikes by the ULC and IULC were forestalled by federal intervention, and it was reported that non-union workers unloaded ships during the strike under police protection. The strike, which sought a doubling of the rate of pay—from 6 shillings, 3 pence, per day to 12s., 6d.—collapsed after several persons had been injured in the violence and as union workers drifted back to their jobs.

Immediately before Nigeria's becoming a republic, on October 1, 1963, leaders of the railway and municipal workers' unions issued a call for a general strike to protest the government's "hold-the-line" wage policy. The strike began at midnight, on September 27, and was soon joined by other workers, including the dockers. The strike was called off on September 30, after government officials promised to appoint a "high-powered commission" to look into the workers' demands. Chief Justice Morgan of the Western Region High Court, who performed a similar duty in the 1950's, in surveying government salaries in the Western Region, was appointed as head of a commission to review the existing wage structure, to make recommendations for changes, to "suggest adequate machinery for a wage review," and to consider abolition of the daily wage system and the introduction of a national minimum wage. The commission reported in May, 1964, and made far-reaching recommendations on all these matters.

The 1963-64 general strikes and the work of the Morgan Commission must be viewed against the background of cost-of-living increases, which, since 1959, had averaged 3.5 per cent per year and now increased sharply to 10 per cent in 1962. This was followed by a decline of 3 per cent, in 1963, but the 1962 rise had already squeezed the Nigerian wage earner too much. He was still living on wages that had remained stable since 1960. In 1963, the unions formed a Joint Action Committee (JAC) to negotiate with the federal government, which is the pace-setter for wage levels. When the government showed its reluctance to engage in meaningful discussions, fearing for the impact of wage increases on economic development, the general strike was called. Only reference of the problem to the Morgan Commission ended the work stoppage.

The government's hopes of somehow holding the line on wages were dashed by the recommendations of the Morgan Commission, which proposed substantial wage increases, in both public and private sectors, to be retroactive to October 1, 1963. The government rejected the recommendations and made counterproposals for smaller increases to be retroactive to April 1, 1964. The second general strike followed, lasting thirteen days. A settlement was reached on June 29, 1964, which was a compromise between the Morgan Commission's recommendations and the government's counterproposals, and wage increases were made retroactive to January 1, 1964.

In sum, the June 29 agreement provided for the following:

1. Minimum-wage levels were established:

		Minimum Monthly Rate
Area I	Lagos	£10
Area II	Eastern, Western, and Midwestern Nigeria	£8/2/6
Area III	Kaduna and Kano (Northern Region)	£6/18/8
Areas IV-VI	Other parts of Northern Region	£6/7/10 to £5/4/0

These levels increased applicable wages in Lagos and Eastern Nigeria by 30 to 35 per cent; by 7 per cent in Western and Midwestern Nigeria, where prevailing wage rates were already higher; and by 26 per cent in Kano and Kaduna.

2. The daily-wage system is to be gradually abolished for workers with more than five years of service.

3. Salaries of junior employees were to be increased: salaries up to £318 per year, £24 per year increase; salaries between £319 and £442 per year, £16 per year increase; and salaries between £433 and £588 per year, £8 per year increase.

4. No junior employee should receive a salary less than the minimum agreed for wage earners in Area I (Lagos), *i.e.*, £120 per year.

5. Legislation and appropriate machinery is to be established to deal with the application of the new minimum-wage and salary increases, in both public and private sectors, and to provide for wage reviews on a continuing basis, through national joint industrial councils to be set up in each major industry.

6. Wage increases were made retroactive to January 1, 1964.

7. The government agreed to give urgent attention to introducing reduced fares and improved transportation facilities in urban areas, to accelerating low-cost housing development, and to controlling rents and prices.

The impact of this program on the 1962-68 Plan remains to be seen, but it is likely to increase the capital costs of the economic development program by some £8 to £10 million and to raise the recurrent expenditures of government by some £2.5 to £3.5 million per year. After this successful encounter by unions and workers, it can be assumed that Nigerian wage levels will never again be as static as in the past. It behooves the government to temper this wage increase and the future demands of the unions, which are to be expected, by insisting on the absolute necessity of increasing productivity. The alternatives are equally dangerous for the future of Nigeria: inflation, which will wipe out the wage increases; cutting back on capital expenditures that are vital to economic growth; or a further decline in Nigerian foreign reserves. This is a message that must be spelled out in forthright and intelligible terms to the Nigerian wage earner.

VI

Taxation, Incentives, and Handicaps

The effective administration of income tax on individuals or corporations requires a carefully-thought-out legal code and a corps of capable and honest administrators. It is often argued that these taxes are really too difficult for the less-developed countries to cope with, and it would be better if they concentrated on simpler forms of taxation. But the fact is that there is no suitable alternative. A graduated system of commodity taxation can never succeed in mitigating growing economic inequalities (and the political and social tensions which are associated with this process), or in reducing the resources devoted to socially unnecessary luxury consumption, in the same manner as progressive taxes on income and wealth.

Nicholas Kaldor in Foreign Affairs, *1963.*

TAXATION OF BUSINESS

"We are concerned to use the fiscal weapon of taxation not simply to raise additional revenues but also actively to further our declared aim of social justice and to facilitate the execution of the Development Plan," the Nigerian Minister of Finance declared in 1962. "It is our deliberate intention to place the major burden of taxation not on the very poorest classes of the community, but on those better able to meet it, the salary earners and the wealthier sections of the community."[1] The corporation is viewed, of course, as a member of "the wealthier section" in every economy, but, despite a complete revision of Nigerian income-tax statutes, in 1961, the rate of tax on corporate income remained unchanged.[2]

The basic corporate tax rate in Nigeria is "eight shillings in the pound,"[3] or 40 per cent of taxable income, which compares favorably with corporate tax rates in industrialized nations but is relatively high, in view of Nigeria's great need for foreign capital and its competitive position for such capital among the ranks of the developing nations.[4] There appears to be no inclination to raise this rate; rather, prospective legislation will probably attempt to close loopholes and prevent evasion. At present, profits of the following types of organization and activities are exempt from corporate income tax: statutory or registered friendly societies; religious, educational, and charitable societies and trade unions (except profits from trade or business); registered co-operatives; corporations formed for the purpose of, and which spend all their profits in, promoting sports; interest on deposits in the Nigerian Post Office Savings Bank; non-Nigerian companies operating aircraft in Nigeria and operating certain ships in external waters (on the basis of reciprocity); regional marketing boards; regional statutory development corporations (except profits from trade or business); profits of non-Nigerian companies merely brought into, or received in, Nigeria.[5]

Corporate taxes are assessed and collected only by the federal government, under the provisions of the Companies Income Tax Act of 1961. The regions are precluded by the constitution from doing so,[6] although they may lay taxes on income and profits other than the income and profits of companies.[7] The tax on companies is administered by the federal Board of Inland Revenue, whose assessment may be contested before the appeal commissioners;[8] their decision may be appealed to the high court if the commissioners permit. In cases involving over £200, appeal to the high court is provided for by law,[9] and where £500 is at stake, beyond the high court to the federal Supreme Court.[10] The board can, in all cases, appeal from the commissioners' decisions to the courts. The normal fiscal year runs from April 1, and taxes are charged on the income of the preceding year.[11] Taxes are usually payable in two equal installments; the first within two months of the date that notice of assessment is served, and the second on, or before, March 21 of the year in which assessment is made.[12] A penalty of 10 per cent may be assessed for late payment.

The profits of a Nigerian corporation are treated as arising in Nigeria, no matter where they are, in fact, earned and whether or not they have been remitted to Nigeria.[13] Income of non-Nigerian corporations, doing business both abroad and in Nigeria, might create a problem in allocation on which no experience is as yet available.[14] Non-Nigerian companies not engaged in trade or business in Nigeria are not subjected to taxes on dividends received from Nigerian companies,[15] nor is any tax withheld by the Nigerian company remitting the dividend.

TAX INCENTIVES FOR BUSINESS

While retaining a relatively high tax rate on corporate profits, the Nigerian government has, by special legislation, recognized the need for incentives to attract foreign capital to Nigeria and to stimulate the formation of local capital and entrepreneurial activity. Income tax relief is available under the Industrial Development (Income Tax Relief) Act, 1958.[16] This gives benefits to public corporations organized under Nigerian law, which qualify for "pioneer industry" status as distinguished from private corporations. Although application is made to the Ministry of Commerce and Industry, whether pioneer status is to be granted is determined at the Cabinet level, on a showing that the proposed industry will be beneficial to the Nigerian economy and that either it does not now exist in Nigeria or, if it exists, functions on an inadequate scale. At present, over fifty categories of industries have been declared as eligible for pioneer status.[17] Twenty-one companies were granted pioneer status in 1963, as opposed to eleven in 1962. Specific approval of individual proposals within established categories is, nevertheless, required, since a new category is created by the granting of pioneer status to the first comer, and a decision as to the desirability of competition must be made when a second applies. Where initiation of the enterprise is dependent on the granting of pioneer status, application may be made before incorporation in Nigeria, and a three-month period after granting of pioneer status is permitted to complete the formalities of incorporation.[18] The application must give an estimated date on which production is to begin and a year's leeway is permitted. The pioneer industry must concentrate its efforts on the production for which it was certified, and, during the time that it enjoys the benefits of pioneer status, it cannot engage in any other business, except that it may petition for the right to engage in the production of an additional pioneer product or products.[19] The application for pioneer status or the certificate granted may not be published without the permission of the company concerned.[20]

It is possible for a pioneer industry corporation to enjoy a complete tax holiday for a period of five years. An initial two-year period of relief is granted, provided the company has fixed assets in excess of £5,000 when production begins. Additional years of relief depend on increases in assets; thus, a third year of freedom from tax is given if fixed assets have increased during the initial two-year period to £15,000; a fourth year, if they have increased to £50,000; and a fifth year, if they have increased to £100,000. This schedule is, obviously, designed to encourage reinvestment of profits, rather than remittance to parent companies abroad.

For any year in which the enterprise was originally entitled to tax relief under the scheme but incurred a loss, another year of complete tax relief may be added. On this basis, a pioneer industry establishment may be in business over a period of ten years before it begins paying Nigerian income taxes. It is, thus, possible to incur initial losses while the business is being built up, rather than taking narrow profit margins, and postpone profits to years when returns from the established business may be expected to be high. Needless to say, the structuring of operations for such an objective must be within reasonable limits lest excessive costs of doing business be disallowed.

The tax-holiday benefits extend to the shareholders of the pioneer industry, as well as to the corporation itself. This applies to profits earned during the tax-relief period, whether distributed during, or after, the expiration of the period. Profits for this purpose are computed without making any deduction for capital expenditures, as are the profits of the company itself. Depreciation is separately charged off.

Additionally, it may be possible to secure agreement from the Ministry of Finance to exempt from tax the receipt of interest paid by a pioneer company on debenture stock held, or loans made, by non-Nigerian companies and individuals not resident in Nigeria. Such an exemption was granted in the application of the Nigerian Sugar Company.[21]

The amount of discretion that may be administratively employed by the Minister of Finance is wide.[22] One report, issued in connection with a company stock prospectus, went so far as to say that it was expected that tax treatment would ultimately be settled by negotiation rather than by the strict application of particular rules.

After the expiration of the tax holiday period, tax liabilities may still be kept low for the pioneer industry. Additional tax benefits that are applicable to all companies operating in Nigeria, whether incorporated there or not, inhere in the accelerated depreciation provisions contained in the Income Tax (Amendment) Act of 1958.[23] These enable companies to amortize capital assets in the formative years and rapidly build up liquid reserves. The special initial write-off is 40 per cent for machinery, on top of a normal permissible annual depreciation of 5 to 15 per cent. As a result, a company can write off approximately 50 per cent of its machinery capital value during its first taxable year in calculating taxable income. The initial write-off for industrial buildings is 20 per cent; for developmental costs on mines and plantations, 25 per cent. Regular annual rates, which may be claimed in addition, vary. No special treatment is permitted for other than industrial buildings, but a maximum of 10 per cent annual regular depreciation is permitted. For the pioneer company, depreciation allowances may be deferred until the end of the tax holiday, when they may be claimed in full. If taxable income is then less than the capital allowances claimed, the unabsorbed balance may be carried forward indefinitely to offset taxable profits.[24]

Similarly, unabsorbed losses may be carried forward for as long as ten years and set off against future profits resulting from the particular trade or business in which the loss was incurred.[25]

Limited tax relief is available, also, for private companies over a maximum period of six years, where profits do not exceed £3,000 per year.[26] To qualify, the private company must be incorporated and controlled in Nigeria and cannot claim pioneer status. Such private companies are allowed a remission of the full company tax for the first two years of operation, two-thirds of the rate is remitted during the third and fourth years, and one-third of the rate is remitted during the fifth and sixth years. When total profits exceed £1,000, the tax relief is reduced by one-half of the amount exceeding £1,000, until a profit level of £3,000 is reached, when tax relief ceases.

Nigeria is a party to a number of double-taxation agreements with other nations, including the United States,[27] whose provisions supersede the Companies Income Act in case of conflict.[28] The U.S.–Nigeria treaty covers income from commerce, copyrights, dividends, interest, mining royalties, and real property rentals.[29]

In the case of profits derived by a Nigerian company from a source country with which Nigeria has no treaty for relief of double taxation, the foreign tax paid on such profits is allowable as a deduction.[30]

TAXATION OF INDIVIDUALS

Individual incomes are taxed by the regional governments and, in Lagos, by the federal government. However, personal income-tax administration and procedures are uniform throughout Nigeria, by virtue of the Income Tax Management Act, 1961,[31] "An Act to regulate the taxation of incomes of persons other than companies. . . ." Uniform rates are not set under this act, as to either type (flat or progressive) or amount. Previous to independence, income-tax rates were uniform throughout Nigeria, under the Income Tax Ordinance of 1943.[32] The rate was progressive, beginning at 4.5 pence in the pound, for the first £200 of taxable income (after deductions and exemptions), and moving to 15 shillings on every pound in income over £10,000. Since April 1, 1961, the rates have varied: in Lagos, there is a flat tax of 10 shillings on all taxable income up to £100 and then a graduated tax takes over. The old maximum rate remains: 15 shillings in the pound on income exceeding £10,000. Exemptions are £200 for a wife, £72 for each unmarried child up to the age of sixteen, and £100 for each adult dependent relative. Additionally, up to £210 is allowed for expenses incurred in the education of a child abroad. The 1961 Act ended tax discrimination that previously had favored women. The income of both men and women is now subjected to the same taxes.

Evasion of personal income taxes is widespread in Nigeria,[33] owing, in part, to lack of education but principally to the lack of adequate administrative machinery and the general prevalence of cash transactions. In 1963, an Investigative Branch of the Board of Inland Revenue was constituted to combat tax evasion. Smuggling is also a serious problem for Nigerian fiscal authorities, increasingly so now that customs duties have been raised over the past few years, and stronger measures for detection, including the use of aircraft, are being employed.

The "pay-as-you-earn" withholding tax was introduced in the Federal Territory of Lagos, in 1961, and applies to all residents of Lagos, irrespective of where the income is earned in Nigeria and whether the employee is temporarily outside of Nigeria or receives his pay outside Nigeria. It covers all employment income and pensions exceeding £25 per month. Employees earning more than £300 per year, but whose "free pay allowance" (i.e., exemptions and deductions) results in no taxable income, must file a "nilcard," which, if approved by the tax office, relieves the employer of the duty of withholding tax. Employers are required to deduct tax from wages and salaries of employees earning less than £25 if they receive a "tax deduction card" for such employee; this would result if an employee held two jobs, each of which paid less than £25, but the total wages earned on the two jobs amounted to more. This system reveals "moonlighting" to the employer, which may have its merits, but it is really outside the scope of the taxing authority's role. The taxes withheld by the employer (less refunds authorized) must be paid by the employer to the Inland Revenue Department within ten days of the close of the month for which they were deducted.[84]

IMPORT CONTROLS

Income-tax relief may provide an incentive to the entrepreneur to invest in a business in Nigeria, but the incentive must be predicated on the realistic possibility of making a profit. An agrarian, near-subsistence economy, setting out on the path of industrialization, can produce few manufactured goods in its initial stages which are competitive with those of industrialized nations. Semifinished materials must be imported, initial capital costs are high, labor is unskilled, and consumer preferences in favor of imported goods are well-established—there is, in fact, a marked lack of consumer acceptance of locally manufactured goods. Thus, for example, a high-quality transistor radio, assembled in Nigeria from foreign-made components, went begging on the market and was finally offered for sale below cost.

The problem of making a profit on the local manufacture of goods previously supplied from abroad is encountered, also, in industrialized countries, although less frequently and on a narrow basis. It characterizes almost the entire industrialization process of the less-developed countries. It is universally, although reluctantly, recognized as a situation justifying national protection of an "infant industry."[35] A "tariff wall" is erected behind which the infant industry can pursue its uneconomic manufacture or service, with the pressure of lower-cost, foreign-source competition considerably reduced, equalized, or, in fact, eliminated. By equalizing costs to the seller, price is eliminated as a factor in the buyer's choice between the imported and the local product; if the tariff makes the cost of the imported product higher than that of the local product, the price of the latter gradually becomes a more important factor in choice. When the tariff is "prohibitive," in fact, the price of the local product becomes the sole determinant, regardless of quality or other factors. At this point, or even earlier, the foreign manufacturer who has been exporting finished goods to the high-tariff country may decide that, to preserve his market there, he must engage in manufacturing "behind the tariff wall." If he is permitted to do so, further local manufacture is stimulated and internal competition, important to quality, is restored. Eventually, the local industry is established, costs are reduced, and the former infant, hopefully now a lusty youngster, loses his tariff protection and faces foreign competition on his own.

Nigeria has this process as its purpose in affording two forms of business relief that are controlled at the point of import by the assessment of duties. It may take the form of reduced customs duties on semifinished materials that are required in a manufacturing, processing, or service industry within Nigeria (raw materials not available in Nigeria enter duty-free),[36] and that normally attract a duty of 10 per cent. This is "affirmative" relief that does not discriminate against the foreign manufacturer, since he may import his unassembled product at the same rate. The government merely denies itself the revenues that it would otherwise receive from duties on such imports.

The import-duty rebate on semifinished materials is authorized by the Industrial Development (Import Duties Relief) Act of 1957.[37] The applicant must satisfy the federal Minister of Commerce and

Industry: (1) that, without the rebate, the finished goods could not be produced at prices competitive with comparable imported goods, or at prices leading to the establishment of an adequate Nigerian market; or (2), that the imported finished goods bear a lesser proportion of import duty than the materials imported to produce the same goods in Nigeria; or (3), that the imports consist of fixed plant or materials therefor. Additional criteria are the cost in revenue of the relief sought and the importance of the industry to the Nigerian economy.[38]

The second form of relief is plainly intended to discriminate against the foreign manufacturer, for it imposes a protective tariff, for a period of up to ten years, on imported finished goods that are also made in Nigeria. Here, too, the government expects to sacrifice income, since the intent is to discourage the purchase of imports and, consequently, revenues from customs imports are expected to fall. However, preference for imported goods may overcome the disadvantage of their higher prices, and the result may be an increase in revenues to the government.

The rates of import duty are set forth in the Customs Tariff Ordinance, 1958, as amended. The authority to establish tariff rates has not been delegated by the legislation, and established rates may be varied downward by administrative action only within prescribed limits, such as those governing duty rebates on materials or parts used in manufacture, as described above. There is no executive discretion with respect to the setting of higher tariffs on imported goods in order to protect the Nigerian producer, except in cases of the dumping or foreign subsidy of goods.[39] Such protection must be obtained through legislation. The producer makes representations to the federal Ministry of Commerce and Industry, which examines the request in the light of whether protection is necessary to the development of an industry important to the economy. If it approves, the ministry proposes to Parliament the necessary amendment to the Customs Tariff Ordinance. Normally, finished imported goods attract a duty of 20 per cent, but the level goes as high as 75 to 100 per cent in cases where protection has been granted to infant industries.[40]

The government's policy on protectionism has been stated by the Minister of Finance in these words:

... [T]his weapon will be used with caution. The purpose of protection is not to provide undue profits for an indefinite period to the manufacturer at the expense of the consumer, nor will Government allow a high cost industrial economy to be built up under the umbrella of excessive protection. Nigerian products must be reasonably competitive with imported goods, not merely so as to provide Nigerians with quality goods at fair prices, but also so that Nigerian manufacturers may compete effectively in the markets of the world. We do not visualize Nigerian industry as catering only for the domestic market, it will increasingly become the supplier of manufactured goods throughout Africa. This it can only achieve if it remains efficient and fully competitive.[41]

When Nigeria is used as a base for warehousing goods that are for sale in a third country, or as an assembly or manufacturing base for subsequent distribution of the finished product to other countries, reimbursement of the import duties paid on such goods or materials may be claimed. Re-exported goods must be in the same state as when imported into Nigeria, in the sense that they have not been used in Nigeria; further assembly, modification, or refinements are, of course, not precluded, and the rebate would be based on the classification of the imported goods as materials used in the manufacture of goods subsequently exported.[42]

The "central" geographical location of Nigeria, the small populations and limited economies of neighboring nations, and the plans for the eventual establishment of a common market, including, at least, West Africa and, perhaps, all of "black Africa," suggest the consideration of Nigeria as a manufacturing or distribution center. Additionally, the large Nigerian market provides a basis for initiating activities there, while markets are tested and facilities established in other African countries by the Nigerian-based entrepreneur.

IMPORT PROCEDURES[43]

Open general licenses have been established that permit the importation of most goods and commodities without prior permission, and current payments for such imports may be made to most countries through banks authorized to deal in foreign exchange. A few items may not be imported for "health, safety and moral" reasons; a further list of goods, and goods imported from certain countries, require the specific approval of the Ministry of Commerce and Industry.

Principal imports for which individual licenses must be sought are petroleum products, cement, tin ore, coal and coke, cotton blankets, enamelware, meat and certain meat products, butter, produce handled by local produce-marketing boards, lemons, grapefruit, and ginger. All of these, except petroleum products, are locally produced, and, sometime in 1965, production of those will begin at the refinery now under construction. Gold articles, secondhand clothing, and household rummage from the dollar area also require specific approval.

Nigeria's continuing, disproportionate, unfavorable trade balance with Japan led, in September, 1963, to discrimination against imports of textiles and cordage from Japan (including such goods originating in Japan but shipped from Hong Kong), and such imports, since then, have required individual licenses. Nigeria has bilateral trade agreements with a number of Eastern bloc nations, and imports from those countries may be brought in under general license. However, imports from Albania, Red China, East Germany, North Korea, North Vietnam, and Rumania must be specially licensed, as must also imports from Yugoslavia, South Africa, and South West Africa. Imports of wheat and sugar from countries not participating in the International Wheat Agreement and the International Sugar Agreement are similarly treated.

If import-licensing requirements have been complied with, exchange for payment is automatically granted, including payment to non-sterling countries. No advance approval is required to open normal letter-of-credit facilities or to arrange for deferred payment of imports, but advance payment for imports on consignment requires the approval of the Ministry of Commerce and Industry.

REGIONAL INCENTIVES

Regional competition for new industry has both advantages and disadvantages for the foreign investor who is surveying the scene for the best place in Nigeria to establish his enterprise. It can bring about inducements, such as facilitating the acquisition of land or providing participating capital,[44] although the latter is severely limited and is conserved for projects in which the governments have the "felt necessity" (most pervasive in the Eastern Region) to invest for the sake of participating in management, exerting control, or for financing of Nigerian private enterprise. On the other hand, because of the political power structure of Nigeria at the federal level, it can cause certain difficulties. Northerners hold the reins of power in Nigeria, but their region, while large and populous, is the most backward, the most remote, and the least desirable area in which to establish new industry from a purely business point of view. Distances are great, many of its people are nomadic, large population centers are rare, and markets are relatively undeveloped. The southern, coastal areas are generally preferred for plant sites because of the proximity of raw materials and large markets, the availability of good transportation, and the relatively high levels of worker skills and consumer tastes. As a result, the south has attracted a much larger share of new investment. In 1963, total domestic and foreign investment in Lagos and the southern regions was estimated at £53.3 million; the total for Northern Nigeria, in 1963, was estimated at £23.6 million. (Both figures are probably overstated.)

It is widely suspected that much of the delay in processing applications for pioneer status, or simply for permission for a foreigner to do business in Nigeria, is attributable to contention among federal officials (backed by regional politicians) expressing regional points of view, particularly those of the north. Given the urgency that is expressed on every side for rapid industrialization, the need for foreign capital and know-how, and the wide variety of enterprises that could find room in Nigeria, this appears to be the only plausible explanation for delay.[45]

Because the overwhelming majority of factors that affect the choice of plant location are under the control of the federal government, such as the companies act, corporate taxation, and immigration, little regional initiative remains to take the form of legislative or administrative incentives for new investment. As a result, where to locate one's business is a management and marketing decision, except to the extent that political factors or pressures may intervene. Such differences in the law as exist between the regions, as for example with respect to the law of property, are not sufficiently consequential to the investor to affect this decision.

FOREIGN-EXCHANGE CONTROL

The American businessman, who has never encountered foreign-exchange controls in his own country, reacts negatively to such controls when he finds them abroad and weighs them along with other "disincentives" when he is considering where to invest. "Disincentives" they are, and the country without them is to be preferred (other things being equal, which they rarely are). But they are, also, facts of life, with which everyone doing business abroad must reckon at some time, in some form, even in highly developed countries. The postwar European recovery program demonstrated that exchange controls are necessary concomitants of economic growth when scarce resources must be carefully allocated and when large capital formation is required. Since it is generally recognized that such controls exact a heavy price for their benefits, by diverting trade and discouraging foreign investment, they are tools that monetary authorities use reluctantly. Of greater interest to the investor than the power to impose controls, which exists almost everywhere as "reserve" legislation, or than the presence of controls are the factors that may lead or have led to activation of stand-by statutes. Are exchange controls looked upon and used as monetary tools that help to allocate resources? Have they been used as "last-ditch" maneuvers to rectify irresponsible fiscal action somewhere further up the line? Is careful consideration given, in the statements of government leaders and central banks, to the nation's foreign-exchange position? Are development plans centered on wealth-producing capital investment, on prestige items that do not produce wealth, or on social programs (however desirable) that require increasing recurrent expenditure?

Happily, Nigeria can be counted among the developing nations that have demonstrated a high degree of fiscal responsibility. Its leaders, in their statements and in the 1962-68 Plan, reflect a maturity in this respect that might well be emulated by others. The power is there to impose controls, and one cannot argue with the wisdom and necessity of that. The willingness to impose them, if necessary, is also there. But it has been made clear again and again that control legislation will be brought out of reserve only if other monetary measures and self-policing, on the part of Nigerians and aliens doing business there, fail.

Under the Exchange Control Act, 1962,[46] the Minister of Finance has the authority to institute controls over all foreign-exchange transactions, both sterling and non-sterling.[47] Before 1962, he had this authority only with respect to non-sterling transactions.[48] The present act insures Nigerian independence, if it is deemed necessary, from fluctuations in sterling and permits closure of an escape route for the flight of Nigerian capital; the main effect of the new act has been to bring certain sterling transactions under the same requirements as previously applied only to non-sterling transactions. Thus, at present, prior permission of the Ministry of Finance is required for the following transactions, whether with sterling or non-sterling countries: transfer of profits, repatriation of capital, new foreign borrowing, transactions in securities, and compensation deals. As a rule, permission is granted freely. All other payments (principally, payment for imports, fees for services, and licensing fees) to sterling-area countries may be made without formality, and, while such other payments to non-sterling countries nominally require prior approval, authorized dealers in foreign exchange have, in fact, been delegated power to approve such payments in most cases. As of mid-1964, no application for remittance of current payments had been rejected.

The act is administered by the Central Bank, but applications are passed on by the Ministry of Finance. It applies equally to government and private transactions, and it also empowers the Minister of Finance to control internal borrowing by Nigerian companies that are controlled directly or indirectly by foreign interests. Such borrowing currently requires prior approval.

The requirement that a company have "approved status" before exchange conversions and transfers can be made no longer applies, but foreign capital that has been granted such status is assured of "sympathetic consideration" when requests are made for repatriation of profits and capital. Since these remittances are freely approved at present, the intent apparently is to give preferential treatment to companies having "approved status," in the event that the foreign-exchange situation becomes tight in Nigeria. Because of the continued drain on Nigerian foreign reserves, it is highly advisable that the foreign entrepreneur negotiate for and secure "approved status" before committing his capital to Nigeria. Whether it will be granted depends on the nature of the investment and the "reasonableness" of the probable foreign-exchange costs. Thus, the industry that fits into national or regional economic development needs and presents a program of expansion through the reinvestment of part of its profits should have no difficulty in securing approval. Approved status is, of course, subject to withdrawal in the discretion of the Minister of Finance. Companies without approved status must seek approval for individual non-sterling remissions; while licenses for remittances of profits and royalties, and payments for rentals and technical assistance, appear to be readily granted, permission to repatriate capital, at this stage, is reported to be subject to some delay.

In his 1962 budget speech, the Minister of Finance clearly set forth his reluctance to reimpose controls such as those that existed during the 1950's:

There can be no doubt that the progressive dismantling of our physical controls during the past few years, and the liberal policies adopted towards the few controls which remain, have played a major role in confidence in our monetary stability. They have contributed to the creation of a climate conducive to the channelling of domestic savings into productive investment and to the inflow of foreign capital into the public and private sections of the economy.... It would be folly to throw away these hard won advantages. Should balance of payments pressures arise, it will therefore be the policy of the Federal Government to seek to contain them by the more flexible fiscal and monetary means; by selective tariff increases, by stepping up the tempo of domestic savings, overall budget policies and by use of the monetary weapons increasingly available to the Central Bank.[49]

Nevertheless, the minister went on to say, a situation might arise which such measures could not control. To prepare for such a contingency, he proposed a new exchange-control bill, the one subsequently enacted. This legislation he likened "to the fire extinguisher which the prudent man keeps in his factory ... for use only in an emergency" and stated "quite categorically [that] physical controls will be introduced only in the last resort, when all other measures have proved ineffective." He stated that he had "no intention of introducing restrictions where they do not exist today. Overseas investors, in particular, will continue to be free to repatriate profits where they satisfy the authorities that they have paid their proper tax on them. My aim will rather be to continue to liberalize such few controls as are still in force."[50]

In his 1963 budget speech, the Minister of Finance reiterated this unequivocal position. He noted that the 1962 act had resulted in a "minimum of inconvenience" to trade and commerce. Repatriation of profits had remained uninhibited. In fact, "further liberalization has been introduced and commercial banks given greater discretion to approve certain remittances abroad."[51]

At the same time, the minister censured "compensation deals," in which companies privately exchange funds between Nigeria and another country, or which might involve a triangular switching of funds. But they were condemned not as evasions of exchange controls but as possible covers for fraudulent invoicing of goods and the evasion of taxes.[52]

Obviously, every interest of Nigeria, in this period of development, requires the maximum degree of monetary freedom consistent with planned objectives. Since the private foreign investor is an integral part of this plan—16 per cent of the capital required for the 1962-68 Development Plan is to come from this source—he can be assured of liberal treatment as long as the economy continues to expand. Just as obviously, the Nigerian government will see its interest in prohibiting the remittance of profits and repatriation of capital if foreign-exchange earnings and reserves drop. Although almost entirely dependent on commodity sales for foreign-exchange income, the Nigerian economy is more buoyant than that of most African states because of the variety of commodities exported and the generally consistent world demand for some of them at all times.

"DISINCENTIVES"

Delay—the inability to get decisions made by Nigerian authorities who are charged with the responsibility for doing so—probably accounts for the disillusionment of more would-be foreign investors, particularly Americans, than any other cause.[53] Some of this can be attributed, as noted above, to political reasons. But it must be frankly stated that, while there are many able Nigerians in posts connected with "processing" would-be investors, the number of knowledgeable, responsible, hard-working, and clear-thinking officials is all too few. There is still too much preoccupation with status and perquisites in the Nigerian Civil Service, although it is receding at the higher levels, and the officers concerned with economic development are no exception. Found lacking are the keen sense of dedication; the profound awareness of needs and deficiencies; the urgency to accumulate expertise, by reading, by inquiry, and by discussion; and the determination to work long and hard hours. One has the impression in visiting office after office, in both federal and regional governments, of officials who have "arrived" and are quite content with being, rather than doing. The atmosphere one encounters is almost always friendly, but it is much too relaxed in terms of the objectives that the Nigerians have set for themselves.[54] All too often the impression is one of a haphazard operation, where the compass of competence and knowledge of individual officials is very narrow, self-criticism is rare, co-ordination is sparse, records are unevenly maintained (complaints of lost files are numerous), and the presumption is against initiative and action. Frequently, one can find greater concern and enthusiasm for moving ahead with

Nigerian industrial development among expatriates than among Nigerians.

To some extent this reserve derives from an ambivalent attitude among Nigerians toward foreign capital and expatriate business. There is a real sense of uneasiness that the drive to industrialize is committing Nigeria to economic servitude. This combines with a sense of frustration that the opportunities of Nigerian development must be proffered to foreigners because Nigerians have not the capital and skills required. The result is indecisive or reluctant action. Self-assertiveness vis-à-vis the foreigner is another factor contributing to bureaucratic delay and inefficiency. The lack of opportunity to develop and use initiative under a colonial administration must take its share of the blame also.

Nowhere is the combined effect of these factors more evident than in the "over-administration" of simple but critical controls, such as the issuance of visitors' visas, the whole process of clearing customs and immigration upon arrival in Nigeria, and the securing of "expatriate quotas" for the essential staffing of new enterprise. Since these strict controls are enforced at a relatively low level, seeking to comply with them, or seeking permission to take action within their limits, often becomes a tiresome, frustrating, and wholly negative experience.

Corruption and bribery are no longer the problems they once were, one is assured, and yet there is no doubt that they persist and that the foreign investor will encounter them. The press has done much to illuminate this problem—and its sensationalism has been effective—as have some government officials by their conspicuous consumption. Permanent secretaries in the ministries and other higher civil servants are said to exert an increasing influence as "watchdogs" of the tendency of political appointees to use the opportunity of public office for self-aggrandizement. This view of the use of power has some validity in the traditional perquisites to which the chief or traditional ruler was and still is entitled.

Thus, "dash," as bribery is termed, is not entirely "corrupt"; the word also includes a tip or gratuity. However, as a non-rational and subjective determinant, it has no place in government, especially where resources are scarce and disparities of income between the elite and the masses are great. It has been said that bribery or graft is the lubricant of economic development. This is not only cynical, it is untrue, for it presumes that the decision predicated on bribery is the right decision. If it is, it is fortuitous. The best counsel for the foreigner in Nigeria to follow is obvious: refusal to become a party to bribery. Where the problem is simply one of delay, the threat of an appeal to the ministerial level is reported as generally successful at lower echelons if inaction follows a refusal to pay "dash." Such a threat will not avail in one circumstance: "kickbacks" have not, in all cases, accrued personally to officials but have gone into the coffers of political parties; that is, the money has, for example, been extracted at the regional level, where the party controls, for use against the minority in the region or for use by the party at the federal level. This is a political factor worth exploring before one selects the region in which to locate one's business. Hopefully, inquiry will disclose that this form of corruption has disappeared.

Other "disincentives" are discussed more fully or adverted to in other parts of this study. However, they may again be mentioned briefly here, in an effort to give in one place a more complete picture of the difficulties that face the foreign investor in Nigeria and to attempt an evaluation of their total effect.

For all practical purposes, it is, at this time, extremely difficult to attract large amounts of Nigerian private capital to any undertaking unless it promises phenomenal returns. Such capital exists, but it can earn 20 to 30 per cent, or even higher, without difficulty, either as short-term loans or in speculative enterprises in land or construction. Federal or regional governmental participation, if it is desired, can be secured, generally, only for "high priority" enterprises, and, in such cases, it may, in fact, be difficult to avoid government participation, particularly in the Eastern Region, where the predilection for state participation in industry runs highest. Such investments are made by the various regional development corporations that are financed largely by the profits of the regional marketing boards.

The lack of local management skills, compounded by the reluctance of immigration authorities to grant adequate expatriate quotas, is a severe "disincentive" to the prospective investor. To ask him to assume (as he sees it, at least) not only the non-market political risks of investment in a new African nation but also to take chances on how efficiently ordinary market risks will be met by his Nigerian management is likely to discourage him even from attempting to enter the field. The explicit recognition by the new investor of the goal of Nigerianization and the presentation of plans for training and upgrading Nigerian employees are the investor's best approach to this problem. While skilled technical labor is still lacking, the educational programs of the six-year development plan should go a long way toward remedying this shortage over the next few years, more readily than the shortage of skilled management people will be overcome. If the investor's program warrants a training program, he can overcome the shortage himself, since the Nigerian is a quick learner if he is well-motivated. Work performance is higher than generally supposed, and absenteeism and turnover are lower. The problem in staffing an enterprise, then, centers chiefly about securing adequate management and technical staff people.

Markets must be developed for products unknown or little used in Nigeria. This may take considerable time and effort, particularly since it is said that Nigerian "brand-loyalty" to established imports is high, and low incomes preclude experimentation with new and untried products that may be looked upon as luxuries.

Racism and xenophobia are not widespread, although they exist. One of the pleasures of visiting Nigeria is the sense one has (with some exceptions in places where price serves to segregate the expatriate from all but the wealthiest Nigerians) of experiencing a fully integrated society. Generally, the matter of color does not raise itself. One of the consequences is that the American Negro does not find the special acceptance he expects in West Africa. Resentment against whites is more likely to derive from their affluence or their rudeness, and the Nigerian elite is not immune to this reaction. Xenophobia is often likely to be mistaken for racism because to the non-discerning white all foreigners in Africa are white or Asian. But the two should not be confused. Ethnic Nigerians "spill over" into neighboring countries, either by reason of the old, artificial colonial borders that split tribes or by reason of Nigerian venturesomeness, particularly on the part of Ibos from the east, who have migrated into neighboring countries in search of work or economic opportunity.[55] There is a flow the other way, but of much smaller proportions. Within Nigeria, numbers of southerners have moved into the Northern Region, and many Ibos have made their way into the Western Region. All of these "foreign" groups garner their share of resentment and difficulties, from time to time, probably as much as or more than the white man (or more properly, the European man) in the Nigerian urban center, since the white man retains a status that protects him. Levantines and Asians, on the other hand, tend to be less tolerated than Europeans. These peoples are generally clannish, they have a reputation for driving hard bargains and charging high rates of interest, and, very often, for being hard employers.

All of these are concerns of management, rather than directly of the lawyer. Yet, the lawyer should be aware of them since they reflect Nigerian conditions and attitudes that, in one form or another, may find expression in, or have relevance to, legislation or administrative action. The largest problems for the lawyer and his investor-client remain those of security of investment against expropriation and the repatriation of profits and capital. These are assured in Nigeria to a much higher degree than in most of the developing countries. There are, additionally, attractive inducements. Once the initial, discouraging "disincentives" are overcome, obstacles remain, to be sure, but they should not deter the investor bent on a reasonable and deserved profit who believes that profit is the reward of risk-taking.

VII

Land Tenure

I am very much inclined to declare all married men who have been allocated separate pieces of land to be the owners of the same. My reasons are: In the traditional tribal society the right of use is by far the most important. Second comes the right of inheritance. Where land has not yet become a commodity, the right of disposal is immaterial; nobody has it anyway. But I admit that, due to the considerable amount of group coherence, it is also safe to consider the group itself to be the true owner of the land; at least the smaller groups, family or clan, especially if one regards the spiritual relationship of the Africans to their land. In this respect a Nigerian chief is reported to have made the following notable statement to the West African Lands Committee in 1912: "I conceive that land belongs to a vast family of which many are dead, few are living and countless numbers are unborn."

> H. Fliedner in "Some Legal Aspects
> of Land Reform in Kenya,"
> Proceedings of the East African
> Institute of Social Research
> Conference, 1963.

NATIVE LAW AND CUSTOM

Under native law and custom, which still obtain in most of Nigeria with respect to land tenure, land belongs to the tribe or extended family.[1] An individual member of the group can neither sell nor mortgage the portion of the tribal lands allocated to him by the chief or head of the family, unless he has the consent of all members of the family entitled to a voice or a court has ordered partition. He has what might best be described as "an inalienable right of occupancy during good behavior."[2] He cannot devise the land allocated to him, although his heirs receive his right of occupancy in undivided shares. A court order effecting partition, where a family dispute regarding division or alienation cannot be resolved, may accomplish the same end as family consent: "each breaks down the family structure with all its incidents of customary tenure."[3] The result is an absolute property right in the portion, whether alienated or partitioned by family consent or partitioned by court order. Thus, a fee simple may result, except in Northern Nigeria.[4]

The traditional sale of land between Nigerians, under native law, is highly informal; no formal document of conveyance is required. The purchase money is handed over and possession given in the presence of witnesses. Receipts or other documentation are not employed in such transactions.

ENGLISH LAW

European influences and the need for greater formality imposed by the rise of trade and commerce, particularly in population centers where demand for land arose and a market price developed, have made inroads into this communal system. For example, although native law knows no principle of prescription, English equity has been interposed in a chain of cases, beginning in 1913, that precludes the application of strict rules of native law and custom in support of a stale claim.[5] Similarly, the rigid rules inhibiting the alienation of land were modified. Thus, in the present federal city of Lagos, which was part of the original colony (the rest of Nigeria was penetrated from Lagos by private traders and came under British dominion much later as a protectorate),[6] individual ownership of land became quite common, until today very little land in Lagos is family held.[7] English property law was applied, by the colonial administration, where land could be held in fee simple by an individual. English statutes of general application, including property statutes, were made applicable by ordinances, first to the Colony (Lagos);[8] subsequently, to Southern Nigeria;[9] and, then, to Nigeria as a whole, including Northern Nigeria.[10] Thus, for many years, and even today, except where they have been superseded by Nigerian statutes, the Statute of Frauds of 1677,[11] the Real Property Act of 1845,[12] the Vendor and Purchaser Act of 1874,[13] the English Conveyancing Acts of 1881,[14] 1882,[15] and 1892,[16] and the Land Transfer Act of 1897[17] have been and are the law where customary law does not apply.

REGIONAL PROPERTY LAW

The result has been described as an attempt to fit tenures, under native customary law, into deeds designed for English feudal conveyancing, for the adopted English law remains subject to native law and custom. Western Nigeria has, at least, modernized and consolidated its inherited English property law, as, indeed, it has done with all English statutes of "general application." In that region, the Property and Conveyancing Law of 1959[18] incorporates the basic features of the English Law of Property Act of 1925[19] and, thus, supersedes the pre-1900 English acts. Nevertheless, the 1959 statute operates on land subject to native law only if the parties agree thereto,[20] and, consequently, the statute affects only a minor portion of land in the Western Region, principally that in the Colony Province.

In the largest region of Nigeria, the Northern, the adaptation of English concepts, family consent, and court partition cannot create a fee simple. In fact, in Northern Nigeria the fee simple does not exist, except with respect to lands of the Niger Company and its successors in title, or in cases in which title was established by a "nonnative" earlier than 1927 in Sardauna Province and earlier than 1916 in the rest of the region.[21] All any Northern Nigerian can claim is a right of occupancy. The vast majority of people live under a customary right of occupancy and without any tangible evidence of such right. The customary right may give rise to the statutory right of occupancy that, if the former is established, is evidenced by a certificate.[22] The holder of such a statutory right has exclusive possession against all persons other than the Minister of Lands and

Survey,[23] for "all native lands and all rights over the same are... under the control and subject to the disposition of the Minister,"[24] who may revoke the certificate for cause. The holder of the certificate is bound to whatever conditions and provisions are stated or implied in the certificate of occupancy "under this Law or under any written Law replaced by this Law."[25] If the holder fails to comply, his right of occupancy may be revoked.[26] A customary right of occupancy may also be withdrawn, but only on narrower grounds.[27]

The idea of family consent, then, not in the meaning of consensus but of the specific agreement of all individual members having a right to participate in the decision,[28] is of the essence in most Nigerian land transactions. Its lack may destroy the symmetry of an English-style conveyance whose cold formalism has appeared impregnable for decades.[29] The same effect may obtain where customary non-possessory rights are disregarded.[30]

The second fundamental concept that shapes Nigerian land law is one originally fostered by Lord Lugard in the formative colonial days,[31] which prevented the widespread acquisition of land by Europeans and, thus, happily precluded the development of a "white settler" problem in Nigeria, such as has plagued East Africa.[32] Except for the minor exceptions noted with respect to the north, aliens can own land outright only in the federal Territory of Lagos, which covers an area of only some twenty-seven square miles, and in the Colony Province of Western Nigeria. Freeholds exist in the three southern regions[33] and may be freely transferred between Nigerians, but they may not be transferred or mortgaged to aliens without the permission of the government. In practice, however, approval is never given for a sale to an alien. Leases of ninety-nine years to aliens are generally consented to, and, of course, it follows that a mortgage to an alien can only be a demise for a term not exceeding ninety-nine years. Once a non-Nigerian acquired a legal right in land from a Nigerian, the right could formerly be transferred to another non-Nigerian without reference to these statutory inhibitions,[34] but consent of the responsible minister is now required.[35]

While, in the southern regions, an alien is taken to be a non-Nigerian,[36] and there is no attempt to discriminate among Nigerians, the definition of "native" in the north includes only a person whose father is a member of any tribe indigenous to Northern Nigeria.[37] Any other person is a non-native, and thus aliens and southerners are under the same disabilities. Since the customary right of occupancy is that of a native community that is lawfully occupying native lands under native law, a non-northerner or a non-indigenous family cannot qualify for this "inchoate" right but must seek a certificate granting a statutory right of occupancy on the same footing as the non-Nigerian. In a sense, the Southern Nigerian's position may be less favorable, for he is generally discriminated against in the north.[38] The principal restriction placed on the occupancy of land by non-northerners, beyond that which may inhere in the discretion of the minister, is that no single right of occupancy granted to a non-native may be issued with respect to more than 1,200 acres to be used for agricultural purposes or 12,500 acres for grazing purposes.[39] A native holding a customary or statutory right of occupancy may transfer his rights, under native law and custom, to another native, but he may not alienate his right, or any part of it, to a non-native by sale, assignment, mortgage, sublease, or bequest without first obtaining the consent of the Minister of Lands and Survey. Without such consent, the transaction is void.[40] The same applies with respect to a non-native's statutory right of occupancy: the fact that a non-native holds a certificate does not permit him to transfer or encumber the land he occupies without first obtaining permission. To do so is to provide the minister good cause to revoke the certificate under §34 of the Land Tenure Law.

Aliens have long been able to purchase freeholds by agreement with the owner in the old colony, since the Native Lands Acquisition Ordinance of 1917, which governed what was the Southern Regions at that time and prohibited the alienation of land to non-Nigerians, did not apply to the Colony, which then included both the present city of Lagos and what is now the Colony Province of Western Nigeria. Registration of titles is possible in some parts of Lagos,[41] and in the remainder deeds are registered and previous transactions may be traced. In some of the public estates managed by the Lagos Executive Development Board, freeholds may be obtained, and, in others, leases are granted.[42] State (formerly Crown) lands are available for leasing in the Colony Province of Western Nigeria for industrial and housing estates or developments.

LAND AND ECONOMIC DEVELOPMENT

The combined effect of the inability of the alien to own a freehold and the need for family consent has proved to be a serious obstacle in the path of the foreign investor who responds to the

Nigerian drive for industrial development.[43] Happily, although space in the federal territory is severely limited, the adjacent Colony Province of the Western Region offers freeholds for alien investors. Otherwise, special measures have been adopted in the regions to ease the problem of securing suitable land for factories, offices, and homes for expatriate technicians and managers. One measure provides for the regional government to supply public lands (formerly Crown lands) on lease,[44] or for the regional government to exercise its right of eminent domain to clear all claims and to lease the land to the alien investor. Several industrial estates (or parks) have, thus, been created by regional authorities, where substantial economies have been effected in taking over large tracts, putting in utilities, and concentrating industry convenient to transportation, labor sources, and markets.

Under the Public Lands Acquisition Act,[45] the government is empowered to take private land when required for public purposes. These purposes are for "exclusive Government use or ... general public use": sanitary improvements (including reclamation); laying out of new towns or developing planned rural settlements; creating housing estates; promoting economic, industrial, or agricultural development; establishing or extending government stations; port expansion; building roads or public works; mining, and "obtaining control over land the value of which will be enhanced by the construction of any railway, road or other public work or convenience about to be undertaken or provided by the Government."[46] In the exercise of this right of eminent domain, customary law, regarding family consent, is rudely brushed aside by the sovereign prerogative. Section 7 provides: "Where lands required for public purposes are the property of a native community, the recognized head chief of such community may sell and convey the same for an estate in fee simple, notwithstanding any native law and custom to the contrary." Compensation is provided for by the act[47] and by the regional statutes that have supplemented it.[48] The right to compensation is guaranteed by the Nigerian Constitution for property acquired compulsorily by government anywhere in Nigeria, as is the right of access to the courts to determine an interest in such property and the amount of compensation to be paid.[49] This section of the constitution is not restricted in its application, as are some others, to Nigerian citizens.[50] There is no provision for compensation for damages to land not taken (injurious affection).

It had been held under the act that the acquisition of land for the purpose of leasing it to a commercial company is not a public purpose.[51] This disability was overcome by amendment of the definition of "public purpose" in order to permit the creation of industrial estates that may be leased or sold to private business.[52]

Aliens in Northern Nigeria must apply to the permanent secretary of the Ministry of Lands and Survey, at Kaduna, or through the provincial secretary where the land is located, for either a Certificate of Occupancy or for governmental consent to the acquisition of an interest in land under a native's Certificate of Occupancy,[53] such as a lease or sublease.[54] The length of time for which the Certificate of Occupancy will be granted depends on the scheme for investment and development presented by the applicant, chiefly the value involved, and may go as high as ninety-nine years. Rents payable annually under the leases vary from £6 to £500 per acre.

Under the 1958 regulations, made under the Western Region's Native Lands Acquisition Law, 1952, the alien applies on a specified form to the permanent secretary, Ministry of Lands and Housing, Ibadan, for approval of the Minister of Lands, together with the stipulated fee. When consent is given, the alien has, for the first time, the right to enter the land about which he has come to agreement with the Nigerian owner. Before governmental consent, however, occupation of the land by the alien is unlawful and subject to penalties. If a lease has not already been made, it must be completed within one year of the minister's letter of consent. The lease cannot be for longer than ninety-nine years, with a provision for rent revision every twenty years (rent cannot be paid in advance for a longer period), by arbitration if the parties fail to agree on new terms.[55]

In the Eastern Region, the provisions of law regulating aliens' land tenure are similar to those in the west. The Acquisition of Land by Aliens Law, 1957, is the governing statute, and applications are submitted to the permanent secretary, Ministry of Town Planning, at Enugu.

Public lands may be made available to aliens under lease by public authorities.[56] In the north, of course, all land, except that subject to a private customary or statutory occupancy, is in effect public land. Applications for public lands in the Federal Territory must be made to the chief federal land officer at Lagos and, in the regions, to the appropriate ministries or to their sub-offices in such commercial centers as Ibadan, Warri, Sapele, Port Harcourt, and Onitsha. Once a lease is granted, any further dealings with the land by the lessee again require the consent of the authorities. In effect, any person claiming a right under a lease of public lands must have governmental approval, by virtue of law, not merely by reason of the terms of the original agreement. The lease, however, will also spell out particular conditions, such as those pertaining to the use and development of the land. Consent to changes, in these respects, should be obtained, and it is advisable, also, to secure approval of specific building plans.

Under the pertinent acts, all buildings and improvements pass to the government at the end of the lease term, without compensation, unless the term is for less than thirty years. In the latter case, buildings erected by the lessee may be removed, unless the lease provides to the contrary and no damage is done to the land by the removal.

VIII

Credit Transactions

... Thus it suffices that a person believe or could believe that a right would be acquired, for the right to be set up. The shadow of a prey to be grasped is transformed, by a happy metamorphosis, into a genuine right.

Such is certainly the spirit of many of the solutions adopted by modern legal systems. The object of all these dispositions is the same, to make transactions easier. A man will evidently be induced to perform a juridical act to acquire a right, if he knows that, if certain things appear to be true, the result to him will be the same as if they were true.... I will the more readily lend on a mortgage if I know that only such mortgages as preceded mine on the records have a prior right to mine in the realty. The security thus assured is a leaven of activity, a bounty given to active individuals, which may be as important as a bounty on exported goods or on manufacture.... These solutions favorable to security are entirely in the spirit of Western European law, dominated as it is by an ideal of business, by the idea that the object to be sought is to produce more, to manufacture more, to sell more, to multiply enjoyment, to satisfy more, and more varied, needs.

René Demogue *in* Analysis of Fundamental Notions, *1916.*

PROTECTING THE CREDITOR

No modern industrial or agricultural economy can exist without a sophisticated system of credit to expand the uses of a limited supply of money. A smoothly functioning system of credit, in turn, depends on the confidence that participants in the system have that obligations will be serviced and paid when due. Confidence is assured when credit is secured on property that will be sacrificed if payment is not made, and by laws that assure the creditor he will not be frustrated in proceeding against the property pledged as security. Confidence is further heightened, and a system of credit permitted to operate even more expansively, if unsecured credit is made possible by the fact that (while the integrity of the debtor is paramount) the law and the courts provide swift and certain remedies for proceeding against the debtor's assets or, as a last resort, a bankruptcy statute assures an equitable division of those assets among the creditors.

Thus, it is important to know, in estimating the level of Nigerian commercial development, to what extent Nigerian law provides for the creation of secured indebtedness, how the creditor may have recourse to the security, what provision is made for the enforcement of unsecured debts, and what is available, as a last resort, by way of bankruptcy legislation.

We may dispose of the last-mentioned at once. There is no bankruptcy statute in Nigeria, and, as early as 1881, in the very first reported Nigerian case,[1] it was stated that the English Bankruptcy Act[2] was not in force in the Colony of Lagos. It has been suggested that this derives from the fact that the English Act is one of general application but that "local circumstances do not permit it."[3] Thus, it was never applied as a pre-1900 English statute, and the deficiency has not been made up by Nigerian legislation. Consequently, the sole remedy available to the vendor, under a hire-purchase agreement or agreement to purchase, is to rush to the scene and repossess the goods before they disappear. With respect to corporations, the Companies Act[4] provided for their liquidation and winding-up, and, in so doing, applies English bankruptcy rules. Generally speaking, when everything has been done that needs to be done, under corporation or companies acts that provide for liquidation and winding-up, a bankruptcy act adds nothing in the case of an insolvent corporation.

Ghana recently acquired a bankruptcy statute drafted by Professor L. C. B. Gower, who also wrote Ghana's new companies legislation. Ghana acted on the assumption that "adequate legal machinery for the determination and settlement of debts" is important to "a modern agricultural, commercial and industrial system" and that "the need for this machinery is urgent."[5] If one underlines the word "adequate," one may agree. There may be a sound reason for not having a bankruptcy act. Bankruptcy legislation is only as effective as its administration. In Nigeria, company liquidations conducted by statutory authorities, rather than by "commercial liquidators," have shown that there is no effective administration and that there is unlikely to be any for some time to come. The effect of bankruptcy legislation, in these circumstances, might well be to substitute "no shares for anyone" for the present rule of "first come, first served."

MORTGAGES ON REAL PROPERTY

The pre-1925 English law applies to transactions in land throughout Nigeria, except where entered into by Nigerians under customary law and except in Western Nigeria, where the equivalent of the English Law of Property Act of 1925 was enacted in 1959.[6] Thus, in Western Nigeria, a mortgage is effected by making a charge by way of a legal mortgage or lien upon the land, or it may be achieved by a demise for a term of years, subject to cesser upon redemption. Under native or customary law, both sale and mortgage (known as a pledge or pawn)[7] may be accomplished orally in the presence of witnesses. With these two exceptions, the pre-1925 English mortgage predominates. In the transaction, which must be under seal, legal title of a freehold is transferred from mortgagor to mortgagee, subject to the mortgagor's right of redemption. The equity of redemption precludes the mortgagee from becoming the absolute owner until the entry of a decree of foreclosure, following default or the exercise of a power of sale after default and notice, where notice has not been waived.[8] When the mortgagor pays the money due under the agreement, in accordance with its terms, the mortgagor is entitled to have the property reconveyed to him. Possession, during the mortgage, is normally retained by the mortgagor, and he is entitled to rents and profits,[9] in contrast to the indigenous pledge, under which the mortgagee takes possession and enjoys the usufruct.

A mortgage may also be accomplished by a demise or by assignment of a leasehold estate. Assignment of a lease to effect a mortgage is not practical if the lease is burdened with covenants, and it is not possible in Western Nigeria. In both of these cases, the mortgage of a leasehold estate is accomplished rather by sub-demise or, in Western Nigeria, also by a legal mortgage. Where native lands are concerned, a mortgage can only be by a demise not exceeding a term of ninety-nine years,[10] and foreclosure by an alien of a mortgage on native lands requires governmental consent for the mortgagee to realize anything.

An equitable mortgage is a simpler, less costly, and less rigorous security arrangement than a legal mortgage. It is not sealed, stamp duty amounts to 3 shillings per £100, rather than 7.5 shillings per £100, as on a legal mortgage,[11] and it may be created orally. The deed to the mortgaged property is deposited with the mortgagee, and when, as is usual, a document is drawn up to record the transaction, it is termed a memorandum of deposit of deeds. Under it, the mortgagee has the power of foreclosure but not the power of sale, and it usually gives him the right to have a legal mortgage, in place of the equitable, if he so desires.

In Western Nigeria, an equitable mortgage may be created in three ways: (1) by an agreement to create a legal mortgage, which can be specifically enforced if there is a sufficient memorandum or if there has been partial performance; (2) by a deposit of title deeds, either with an oral agreement or, more usually, by a memorandum under hand, with a power of attorney that enables the mortgagee to exercise the power of sale and to convey a legal estate to the purchaser; and (3) by equitable charge or lien with a memorandum under hand.

A second mortgage is, essentially, a mortgage only of the equity of redemption, since the legal title is already with the mortgagee in the case of a legal mortgage and, until the first mortgage has been redeemed, is no more than an equitable mortgage.

With respect to specific regional requirements, over and apart from those arising from English law that are applicable to the transaction and its consequences, governmental consent is required for all mortgages, legal and equitable, with some few exceptions. In the north, an equitable mortgage, for which consent has been given, may be converted into a legal mortgage without further consent, and the reconveyance, following exercise of the equity of redemption, does not again require governmental consent. In the west, governmental consent is not required to effect a mortgage in the Colony Province (adjacent to Lagos) except on public lands. In the remainder of the west, blanket consent has been given by the Minister of Lands for all equitable mortgages on land, subject to the Native Lands Acquisition Law of 1952, but not for legal mortgages, where consent must be specifically sought. It has been suggested that, under the 1952 act, the Minister, in fact, has no power to give such blanket consent; if so, a serious cloud could at some time be cast on all equitable mortgages in the west.[12] The rationale of "practical necessity," which has been given as the reason for using the device of blanket consent, is hardly an adequate substitute for the simple legislation that could remedy this defect. Blanket consent to the creation of equitable mortgages, it should be added, does not comprehend conversion of an equitable into a legal mortgage.[13]

Leaseholds of the former Crown Lands may be freely subjected to equitable mortgages, but legal mortgages require governmental consent. This is true in the southern regions as well as in the Federal Territory, including also land leased from the Lagos Executive Development Board. No Crown Lands existed in Northern Nigeria, and, as has been noted, all land in the north is "public land," subject to customary or statutory rights of occupancy, revocable for cause.

Because stamp duties on mortgages are regional revenues, mortgages must be stamped in the region where the land is located. This causes obvious problems when one master mortgage is sought to cover land in various regions. Since it is impossible to stamp a mortgage in all regions, even if one were able to allocate the revenue properly, time limitations and transportation difficulties have resulted in the practice of drawing up separate mortgages or using a master mortgage plus collateral mortgages. The latter course recommends itself when the mortgage is to secure facilities, and the amount of the mortgage is limited only by the amount of the stamp duty.[14]

A corporation should provide, in its objects' clause, for the power to mortgage its property and to secure the obligations of third parties if that is desired. The doctrine of *ultra vires* retains some viability in Nigerian corporate law, since the Nigerian Companies Act is the English Act of 1908. Mortgages on corporate property must be registered with the registrar of companies within twenty-one days.[15]

CHATTEL SECURITY DEVICES

The indigenous pledge of land has its counterpart in the use of chattels as security. Again, when made under native law or custom, it is an oral transaction that others are called upon to witness. Upon repayment of what was lent, the pledged goods are returned; if the borrower fails to repay, the pledgee becomes full owner of the goods pledged. Elias appears to distinguish this transaction, which can have sizable commercial dimensions, from that of the pawn,[16] which he characterizes as a "socio-economic" loan contract for petty cash, where the amount of the loan runs between 5 shillings and £5 and interest may run as high as 50 per cent and, in some cases, even higher. In substance, there does not appear to be any difference in the law applicable: both pledge and pawn are treated as bailments up to the point of default, upon which the bailee becomes absolute owner.[17]

In modern transactions, actual possession of the goods pledged necessarily gives way to constructive possession. Without possession the lender can have an enforceable security only by having documentary evidence of his interest. This he has in the bill of sale, by which the borrower, while retaining possession, grants the legal ownership to the lender, subject to the borrower's right to redeem on, or before, a certain date. If the borrower defaults, the lender's (or mortgagee's) title becomes absolute, the right of redemption is extinguished, and the mortgagee is entitled to possession. A bill of sale is also used to convey absolute title in a sale between vendor and purchaser, where possession and legal title usually pass together to the latter. No security problem is there involved. But, if the vendor retains possession, in such a case, the bill of sale is evidence of both the purchaser's legal title and his right to possession.

Whenever title and possession are thus separated—as when borrower or vendor retains the chattels involved—the danger arises that creditors may be defrauded by appearances. It was to meet this practice that the first English Bill of Sales Act was passed in 1854.[18] The Nigerian Bills of Sale Ordinance of 1923[19] incorporated the English Acts of 1878 and 1882, as amended in 1890 and 1891. All of them have the same purpose: to create a public record of secured interests by compelling the registration of bills of sale and, thus, to prevent "frauds ... frequently committed upon creditors by secret bills of sale of personal chattels, whereby persons are enabled to keep up the appearance of being in good circumstances and possessed of property, and the grantees or holders of such bills of sale have the power of taking possession of the property of such persons, to the exclusion of the rest of their creditors."[20]

Originally, registration of bills of sale in Nigeria was provided for only in Lagos, and the registrar of the High Court of Lagos was designated as registrar under the 1923 ordinance. Subsequently, a registrar of bills of sale was appointed, and appointment of regional registrars was provided for.[21]

The bill of sale, as a security device, was developed to facilitate loans and was not readily adaptable to sales transactions where payment of the purchase money was deferred. Instead, two other devices came into use: the agreement to purchase (or, the credit-sale agreement, which is to be distinguished from the sale on credit) and the hire-purchase agreement. Under the first, title remains in the vendor while possession of the chattel passes to the buyer, who agrees to buy and to pay installments on the price; when he has paid in full, or in part, depending on the terms, the sale is consummated, and he becomes the owner.[22] Under the hire-purchase agreement, title also remains in the one who lets (the vendor), and the hirer takes possession; the hirer also agrees to pay installments but becomes the owner only when he has paid in full. The principal distinction, however, lies in whether the putative buyer has the option of returning the chattel and terminating the contract before he has paid in full.[23] If he has no such option, the contract is one to purchase; if he has the option, it is one of hire-purchase.

Thus, the agreement to purchase and the hire-purchase agreement transfer possession, but not ownership, while the bill of sale, as a security device, transfers ownership, but not possession. The Bills of Sale Act applies only to the latter transaction.[24] Thus, since neither the agreement to purchase nor the hire-purchase agreement is a bill of sale,[25] neither is subject to compulsory registration under the Bills of Sale Act. There is no separate statute requiring registration of such agreements, either in England or in Nigeria.

Early in May, 1965, the Federal Parliament passed the Hire-Purchase Act of 1965. It did so in the course of one day and without amendment. The Explanatory Memorandum that accompanied the bill stated:

The object of this Bill is to make provision for the regulation of hire-purchase and credit-sale transactions. It is based primarily on the U.K. Hire Purchase Acts of 1938 and 1954 with modifications to suit conditions prevailing in Nigeria.

The main purpose of the Bill is to afford protection to the buyer of goods on hire-purchase or similar terms against certain abuses which have become apparent in the practise of hire-purchase trading. However the Bill is also designed to secure that the owner is not put at an undue advantage, and thus to maintain a reasonable balance between the owner and the hirer or buyer. Thus, for example, Clause 9 restricts the right of the owner to recover the goods otherwise than by action where the "relevant proportion" of the hire-purchase price has been paid; but Clause 10 enables the court to order specific delivery of all or part of the goods to the owner or to postpone the operation of such an order subject to the fulfilment of such conditions by the hirer as the court thinks just.

Clause 5 of the Bill enables the Minister of Trade to regulate the terms of hire-purchase and credit-sale transactions by restricting the rates of interest and other sums which may be charged and providing penalties for breaches of the regulations. Clauses 18 and 19 enable the Minister to obtain information from hire-purchase and credit-sale traders and finance-houses and to exempt any class or description of goods and any statutory corporation from the operation of the Bill.

The Bill applies to Lagos only, but it is envisaged that legislation in similar terms will be enacted by the legislature of each Region.[26]

The "relevant proportion" has been established at 60 per cent in respect to automobiles and 50 per cent in respect to other goods. After the hirer has paid that amount on the contract, the owner must have a court order to repossess the goods, or must fall back upon his remedy to sue on the debt. Neither is satisfactory from the view of the owner: courts have historically favored the hirer, and Nigerian lower courts are notoriously lenient with Nigerian debtors where the creditor is an expatriate firm. Bankers have cited cases of court-decreed installment payments on debts extending over years, rather than permitting the creditor to proceed against the debtor's assets. If additionally, the interest rate on hire-purchase contracts is set too low (whereas costs, including those connected with court actions, will increase), hire-purchase will be sharply restricted, to only the best credit risks, or perhaps entirely eliminated.

The majority of hire-purchase agreements in Nigeria, heretofore made entirely as a matter of private contract under a form generally in use, have involved motor vehicles. Since depreciation is very rapid owing to poor roads, difficult traffic situations, and lack of adequate maintenance by hirers, the terms and conditions of hire-purchase contracts must be rigidly enforced to protect the owner. This situation has been greatly resented by Nigerians, as it has been by consumers everywhere.

Under the hire-purchase agreement, it is clear that the hirer cannot pass good title of goods he has hired to an innocent third party. The reasoning is highly legalistic: the hirer's right to return the chattel before all payments are made is implied in every such agreement. As a rule, the right is expressly stated in the contract. Thus, it is not a binding agreement to buy, and the hirer is not a person who has bought or agreed to buy the chattel. He has, therefore, not gotten possession of it within the meaning of §25(2) of the English Sale of Goods Act, 1893,[27] also applicable in Nigeria.[28]

But a credit-sale agreement, where transfer of title is deferred, is an agreement to buy goods. The buyer does not have the option of returning the goods and terminating the contract. Thus, under §25(2) of the Sale of Goods Act, 1893, a bona fide purchaser takes good title to the same effect "as if the person making the delivery or transfer were a mercantile agent in possession of the goods or documents of title with the consent of the owner."[29]

At common law, landlords are permitted to distrain for rent in arrears any goods and chattels found on the tenant's premises, including goods there under a hire-purchase agreement or agreement to purchase. Since neither the English Law of Distress Amendment Act, 1908,[30] nor the English Hire-Purchase Act of 1938[31] are law in Nigeria, whatever protection may be afforded to the owner/seller by these two acts is not available in Nigeria.[32]

Goods may not be seized in execution that do not belong to the person against whom execution is levied in satisfaction of a judgment. The owner of goods, under a hire-purchase agreement, can, therefore, protect himself, if he knows of an impending levy, by notifying the proper officials of his title. If the goods are, nevertheless, sold, the purchaser at a judicial sale gets good title, but the owner has an action against the official who wrongfully sold the goods.

DEBENTURES, FLOATING AND FIXED CHARGES, TRUST RECEIPTS

A debenture, it is said, has never been reduced to a precise and absolute definition. So stated Justice Chitty in *Levy v. Abercorris*,[33] in 1887: "[I]t is not, either in law or commerce, a strictly legal technical term or what is called a term of art."[34] In the same year, in another case,[35] Chitty attempted a definition: "The term itself imports a debt... an obligation or covenant to pay... in most cases... accompanied by some charge or security."[36] Goodeve states:

It generally signifies a document under the seal of a company given to secure the repayment of money (or money's worth) to a creditor of the company. The debenture may only be a certificate of indebtedness, but it generally contains or imports a covenant to pay, which is usually accompanied by some charge or security on the property of the company, so that some debentures are secured and some are not secured.

Although as a general rule debentures are issued in series to different persons whose debentures rank *pari passu*, there is nothing to prevent all the debentures, or one debenture for the total amount ... being issued to one person.[37]

A Nigerian lawyer describes a modern debenture more precisely in this manner: "It is an instrument under seal of a company providing for the payment of a principal sum at a specified date, and for the payment in the meanwhile of interest half-yearly and being either a single debenture or one of a series of like debentures ranking *pari passu*, and carrying a charge or secured on the company's undertaking and its property present and future."[38] The debenture is employed only by corporate bodies—limited companies and government and statutory corporations. They are made payable either to the registered holder or to the bearer.

Needless to say, a company's debentures must be issued within the scope and powers of the corporation, as defined in its articles. If they are *ultra vires*, they are invalid as debentures, even as to bona fide purchasers (except to the extent of subrogation of such purchasers to creditors paid out of debenture funds), and are afforded no priority.[39]

The debenture is issued subject to certain conditions endorsed on the instrument, the principal one reading as follows: "This debenture is a first debenture issued by the Company for securing the sum of ...... [the face amount]. The debenture is to rank as a first charge on the property hereby charged, and such charge is to be a floating security, but so that the Company is not at liberty to create any mortgage or charge on any of its property and assets in priority to the said debenture."

The floating security is an equitable charge which, it has been said, "floats or hovers like a hawk over all the assets of the company as they change in the ordinary course of business." Lord MacNaughton described it as "dormant until the undertaking charged ceases to be a going concern, or until the person in whose favor the charge is created intervenes."[40]

While it hovers, the floating charge is an immediate and continuing charge on the property of the company, but the company is free to deal with it in the ordinary course of business, without seeking the permission of, or accounting to, the debenture holder, unless it is so specified in the agreement. The agreement always specifically prohibits the creation of mortgages ranking in priority to the floating charge; but the charge, while floating, is not effective against judgment creditors.

When a company that has an interest in land issues a debenture as security, a mortgage (or fixed charge) is necessary if the land is to be part of the security, since it is not possible under Nigerian law to create a floating charge over land.

Where the transaction is highly formalized, as in the case of the issue of debenture stock, the instrument employed is termed a trust deed. An example is the "Trust Deed securing £425,000 7½ Percent First Mortgage Convertible Debenture Stock" made between Alcan Aluminium of Nigeria, Ltd., and the Royal Exchange Assurance, dated May 8, 1962, and forty-eight legal-sized pages in length. The pertinent sections of the deed, for our purposes, are marginally labelled as "Fixed charge," "Floating charge," "Carrying on business," and "Restrictions on creation of mortgages." They read as follows:

6. THE Company as Beneficial Owner with the consent of the Minister of Town Planning, Eastern Nigeria and subject to the provisions of the Crown Lands Ordinance hereby demises UNTO the Trustees ALL THAT leasehold property of which particulars are given in the Second Schedule hereto together with the buildings erected or to be erected thereon and the fixed plant, fixed machinery and fixtures now installed or to be installed thereon or therein TO HOLD to the Trustees for all the unexpired residue (except the last day thereof) of the term of years granted therein by the lease of which particulars are given in the said Second Schedule subject to the proviso for redemption following namely that if all moneys herein covenanted to be paid shall be paid accordingly then the hereditaments and premises hereby mortgaged shall at the request and cost of the Company or the persons deriving title under it be duly reconveyed to it or them or as it or they shall direct.

7. THE Company hereby charges in favor of the Trustees its undertaking and all its property and assets for the time being both present and future including its uncalled capital (except the specifically mortgaged premises for the time being) with the payment of all moneys intended to be hereby secured.

8. THE charge created by the preceding clause shall be a floating charge and accordingly unless and until the security hereby created has become enforceable and the Trustees shall have determined or become bound to enforce the same shall in no way hinder or prevent the Company from selling alienating leasing paying dividends out of profits or otherwise disposing of or dealing with its properties and assets in the ordinary course of its business and for the purposes of carrying on the same but so that the Company shall not except as expressly authorized as hereinafter provided create or permit to subsist any charge upon and so that no lien shall in any case or in any manner be permitted to arise or affect any part of such assets ranking in any such case *pari passu* with or in priority to the floating charge hereby created. The Trustees shall permit the Company to hold and enjoy the mortgaged premises and subject as hereinafter provided to carry on therein and therewith the business or any of the businesses authorized by its Memorandum of Association until the security hereby constituted becomes enforceable as hereinafter provided.

9. EXCEPT with the previous sanction of the Stockholders by an Extraordinary Resolution the Company shall not create or permit to subsist any mortgage or charge whether fixed or floating upon its undertaking property or assets present or future (including any uncalled capital) or any part thereof ranking in priority to or *pari passu* with the charges securing the Stock

PROVIDED THAT the Company may:

(i) create a floating charge ranking in priority to or *pari passu* with the charge created by Clause 7 hereof for the benefit of the Company's bankers for securing amounts borrowed from or obligations incurred towards them not exceeding an aggregate amount of £750,000 at any one time outstanding; and

(ii) permit to subsist specific mortgages or charges ranking in priority to the charge created by Clause 7 hereof on freehold or leasehold property hereafter acquired by the Company being mortgages or charges existing at the time of acquisition and the Company may with the consent of the Trustees create specific charges on specific assets by way of substituted security for any such mortgage or charge.

The right of the debenture holder to intervene for the protection of his interest is spelled out in the conditions endorsed on the debenture: default, distress or execution levied against the company, or winding-up or appointment of a receiver by a court. These can cause the hawk to descend or the dormant charge to awaken. But the charge does not crystallize automatically unless the company goes into liquidation. Otherwise, the debenture holder must act, and this requires more than a written demand for repayment, which is insufficient to fix the charge. Until the charge is fixed, and while it is still floating, it is a breach of contract for the holder to interfere in the conduct of the borrower's business.

What must he do to fix the charge? He may sue for payment.[41] He may enforce his debenture by sale, usually by the appointment of a receiver and, if necessary, a manager, for which the endorsed conditions provide. As a creditor, he may also petition for an order to wind-up the company. What generally happens, as a matter of practice, is for the holder to demand payment and immediately appoint a receiver, or have one appointed.

While the debenture must be registered within twenty-one days of issuance and, thus, becomes a matter of public record,[42] it does not of itself operate to defeat subsequent specific mortgages, unless the debenture contains language prohibiting them. This is usually included, and the holder is protected against third-party claims outranking his. His principal risk is the conduct of the borrower and the power the borrower has to dispose of assets in the ordinary course of business. Thus, as a rule, a lender on a debenture will create a fixed charge over fixed assets (including a legal mortgage on realty), together with a floating charge over the floating assets—inventory and accounts receivable, as demonstrated in the Alcan Aluminium trust deed—that is, over the whole undertaking and assets, except land and buildings. If the borrower wastes the floating assets before the lender can fix or crystallize the floating charge, other collateral is then available. Otherwise, the lender will have to watch the borrower's business activity carefully, in order to fix his floating charge at the first sign of danger.

While this type of debenture may appear to the American reader to resemble the trust receipt facility, the floating charge does not hover specifically over the proceeds of sale of goods by the borrower; they are not held in trust for the creditor, as under the trust receipt. A trust receipt is a document by which the borrower acknowledges the lender's lien on goods, and, for all intents and purposes, it hypothecates the proceeds of sale in discharge of the lien. It is still necessary for the vendor (or financier), before the creating of the trust receipt, to have actual or constructive possession of the goods, *i.e.*, he must have his interest by retention and not by conveyance. If the borrower attempts to convey an interest to the vendor/financier, that interest would be ownership, while the borrower retains possession. This would bring the transaction within the concept of a bill of sale. But, since this does not occur, and since the trust receipt is not a bill of sale, it need not be recorded.

Again, this device depends largely on the honesty of the borrower in observing the pledge. If greater security is desired, the next step is to warehouse the goods and to release them to the borrower or purchaser, only on the specific authority of the lender. The transaction is, nevertheless, carried out under a trust receipt. The trustee undertakes the insurance of the goods, and, where imports are involved, a bonded warehouseman is employed to obviate the expense to the lender of customs duties.

IX

Nationalization, Socialism, and Nigerianization

It must be obvious that no Nigerian can be content so long as any major sector of the economy is controlled by foreigners. But we are realists and we say so long as there is a dearth of Nigerian capital, so long must there be an opportunity for foreign capital in Nigeria. We do not seek the withdrawal of foreign capital from any area of the economy before Nigerian enterprise is able to replace it. When the time for withdrawal has come, due notice will be given.
Sir Abubakar Tafawa Balewa before the Nigerian House of Representatives, 1964.

NATIONALIZATION

No one, today, seriously questions the right of the state to take private property within its territory, whether it is termed the right of eminent domain or the right to nationalize or expropriate. The right is an attribute of sovereignty, but it is generally held to be subject to certain qualifications: there cannot be a bare taking of alien-owned property under international law.

These qualifications were given expression by the United Nations, General Assembly, in 1962, in adopting its resolution on "Permanent Sovereignty Over Natural Resources,"[1] a statement ten years in the making. Discussions first began in 1952, and what evolved was a statement expounding what the representatives of the industrialized, capital-exporting nations have long argued: a state not only has rights in its natural resources but it has obligations, as well, toward foreign interests, both public and private, which help the state to develop those resources.

As amended through the efforts of the western industrialized states, the key clause reads:

Nationalization, expropriation or requisitioning shall be based on grounds or reasons of public utility, security or national interest which are recognized as overriding purely individual or private interests, both domestic and foreign. In such cases the owner shall be paid appropriate compensation, in accordance with the rules in force in the state taking such measures in the exercise of its sovereignty and in accordance with international law.[2]

The statement begs the question in that international law in this area is yet ill-defined, and what constitutes "appropriate compensation" remains unsettled. The United States' delegation sought to include the adjectives "prompt, adequate, and effective" but was unsuccessful.[3]

Nigeria was one of eighty-eight nations that approved the resolution. Although the resolution is not legally binding on U.N. member states, including those which voted for it, it may, indeed, be creative of a new norm of international law.[4] It must also be noted that nothing in the above-quoted Article 4 "prejudices the position of any member state on any aspect of the question of the rights and obligations of successor states and governments in respect of property acquired before the accession to complete sovereignty of countries formerly under colonial rule."[5] Nevertheless, it is a significant step forward, when such a large number of nations, including the overwhelming majority of less-developed nations, agree as they did on "appropriate compensation" for property taken, to honor government-to-government investment agreements,[6] to observe agreements to arbitrate,[7] and to adhere to the principles of international law.[8]

Nigeria's adherence to the U.N. resolution merely reflected what was already Nigerian law and policy. The Independence Constitution had already provided for "adequate compensation" in cases of compulsory acquisition,[9] and "adequate," while capable of wide definition, is a stronger word than "appropriate." But the assurance of "adequate compensation" in a constitution or statute is, of itself, not enough to put the foreign investor entirely at ease. Whether the right to nationalize is exercised and, if so, how it is exercised are questions of critical interest to the investor. Can the constitution be amended, circumvented, or callously disregarded? What are the stated policies and objectives of the national leaders and political parties? How profound is the commitment to principles expressed in formal context?

The assurance of "adequate compensation" is more than a remedy of last resort. If such an assurance is honored, and if compensation is also prompt and effective, the assurance itself operates as an inhibitor of nationalization, for the reasons set out below. The Nigerian government, since independence, has accomplished three nationalizations, all in areas of economic activity that, in many non-socialist countries, although not in the United States, are typically or often government-owned: airlines, shipping, and external communications. In all three cases, evaluation of assets was made by third parties, the compensation figure was reached by agreement between the parties, and the price was paid in convertible funds.[10] Additionally, Nigeria and the United States have signed an investment guarantee agreement, under which Nigeria recognizes the subrogation of the United States to claims of its nationals, if payment is made by the United States for "assets expropriated or assets made useless by reason of expropriation."[11]

While the sovereign right to nationalize may be firmly established, the wisdom of exercising the right remains open to question. The urge to nationalize is strongest when it can least be afforded, when a nation, having achieved political independence, seeks economic independence and growth. Nationalization is not the route to either.

When compensation must be paid under the law of the nationalizing state, money must be diverted from the funding of needed new capital projects to the purchase of existing plants, merely to acquire ownership and oust the alien.[12] If compensation is not paid, the flow of private foreign capital will dry up, and the nationalizing country will find itself operating entirely on its own, with the limited aid of international institutions (providing they remain convinced of the nation's credit-worthiness), or pursuing its economic objectives at the sufferance of, and with the uneven assistance of, sympathetic Soviet- or Chinese-bloc nations.

In either event, other serious consequences follow. The nationalizing authorities may find they now have ownership but that, since they must retain the former owner or his employees to operate the plant, they do not have true control. If the expatriates are ousted, skilled management and technicians must be diverted from other purposes, if they are, indeed, available,[13] or they must be imported again at great expense, either in money or in terms of political integrity. Foreign markets, and even domestic markets where there are competitors, may disappear because they were "tied" to the former alien owner. The flow of technical information and advice from the former owner's home plant is cut off. The state-owned enterprise must now purchase such information or generate it through research, if possible; more likely, the product will stagnate and cease to be competitive. Finally, in developing countries, government ownership and management very often open the operation to the rankest kind of nepotism and favoritism, which can greatly reduce efficiency and stifle initiative.

Those who hold power in Nigeria and are responsible for its political and economic development are aware of these facts, although they are not widely appreciated below the elite level. Upon independence, Nigerian leaders stated the policy of the new government on the use of its right to nationalize. Assurances have emanated from the very highest levels, including the prime minister, on numerous occasions, that stress the primary role of private capital and entrepreneurship in Nigerian economic development and restrict nationalization to public utilities.[14] Under this ostensible criterion, Nigerian Airways, the Nigerian National Line (shipping), and Nigerian External Communications were created, after independence, out of nationalized properties.

Undoubtedly the most definitive statement of policy, with respect to nationalization on behalf of the government of Nigeria, is that made by the Minister of Finance, Chief Festus Okotie-Eboh, in 1961, when the leader of the opposition, Chief Obafemi Awolowo, moved in the House of Representatives: "That this House approves in principle the nationalization of basic industries and commercial undertakings of vital importance to the economy of Nigeria."[15]

Chief Okotie-Eboh moved to substitute the following, which was adopted: [That this House]

(i) resolves that the nationalization of industries and commercial undertakings beyond the extent to which public utilities: Shipping, Airways, Railways, Power, Communications and Marketing Boards are already nationalized is not in the best overall interests of Nigeria;

(ii) welcomes the review of company and other legislation now being carried out by the Federal Government and other measures to ensure such undertakings are conducted in the best interests of Nigeria;

(iii) welcomes the increasing participation by Nigerians in the ownership and direction of such undertakings; and

(iv) deplores irresponsible statements on nationalization which have recently been made in Nigeria and overseas.[16]

Chief Okotie-Eboh explained his motion at length and with considerable force:

We all know that Nigeria's most urgent need to-day is for the rapid and orderly development of our economy to raise the standard of living of all our peoples. But this cannot, and will not, be achieved at the expense of other values. The Federal Government, which reflects the views of the great majority of this country, does not believe in indiscriminate nationalisation, whether it be termed expropriation, confiscation, or what you will. Fundamentally, we believe in a future under a system of democratic socialism which respects the rights and liberties of individuals and in which both public and private capital have their proper parts to play. We see in this that system in which a truly Nigerian society can best flourish and prosper. Within this broad concept, however, we accept the necessity for measures to ensure that all economic activity in Nigeria is carried on in accordance with our own best interests and that, where those interests conflict with those of any other person or country, Nigeria's interests must prevail.

At the same time, we do not believe that in order to achieve these aims it is either necessary, or desirable, for the State itself to own and operate every important organ of economic activity. On this we are at one with the Premier of the Western Region, who is reported as having stated during his recent tour of the United States of America:—"Private enterprise takes precedence in Government planning. We believe in private enterprise. In Western Nigeria we have offered every guarantee against any form of appropriation, sequestration or confiscation of foreign capital."[17]

This does not mean that government's place in commerce and industry is restricted entirely to "public utilities" as Americans think of them. Government is viewed as having a right—and even a duty—to participate in those enterprises that are highlighted by the public interest and those deemed to be of sufficient importance, for economic, prestige, or security reasons, to require their initiation. Government may become involved in the latter for any one or more of several reasons not derived from any hostility to private enterprise. The enterprise may fall within an area of economic activity in which foreign control or participation is not desired (this results from the policy of "Nigerianization," or economic nationalism), and, while it is open to Nigerian private capitalists, local capital is simply inadequate or not forthcoming. There may be no preconception regarding the desirability of foreign or local private ownership, but capital is not forthcoming from either, perhaps because of the large amounts required, perhaps because of the nature of the risk. The "public interest" may be found in felt prestige or security needs that seem to dictate government ownership or control.

Two aspects of this require further elaboration.

First, the definition of "public utility" becomes very broad and flexible. Nationalization of the airline and shipping properties, which became Nigerian Airways and the Nigerian National Line, had to be subsumed under this rubric because of earlier government statements restricting nationalization to public utilities. But, in truth, since transport is not generally a public utility (in Nigeria road transport is one of the strongest elements in the private sector), both nationalizations can better be explained in terms of public interest, prestige, and, perhaps, security. The nationalization of the majority of interest in Cable and Wireless, while clearly within the "public utility" criterion, was further justified on security grounds.

Second, by giving its assurance that only public utilities will be subject to nationalization, the Nigerian government by no means forecloses itself from entering into or initiating enterprises that are not public utilities. The context of statements regarding nationalization makes it quite clear that the Nigerian authorities are only referring to the take-over of existing institutions or enterprises and are not delineating any preserve for private enterprise that government cannot enter, unless it demonstrates that a public utility is involved, however defined. This was made very clear, for example, in the parliamentary debate during consideration of the Insurance (Miscellaneous Provisions) Act in March, 1964. After a number of speakers had expressed strong hopes that the insurance business should someday be nationalized, the Minister of Finance said: "I must say ... that we do not contemplate in this country, the nationalisation of insurance business.... Nationalisation is not our policy.... It is not the policy of this Government to nationalise any private industry. When the time comes for us to set up our own insurance business, we will do so...."[18] The colonial government, of which Nigerians are the heirs, took a similar view. Thus, wherever Nigerian authorities perceive a public interest, in the initiation of a new enterprise where national prestige or security appear to demand government control, or where ultimate Nigerian private control is deemed desirable, government may enter the picture as an owner of equity.

A number of concerns that were established in the colonial era by government framed the broad concept of public interest, which is still applied: the railways, domestic telephone and telegraph services, radio broadcasting, electricity plants, the coal mines (but not the tin mines located in the north), and the marketing boards.[19] Concerns established since 1960 which reflect that policy are the federal and regional television broadcasting services, the oil refinery, and, possibly, the projected steel mill. The government's part in the steel mill, however, may additionally be explained in "non-ideological" terms; even if foreign private capital were available for what may well be an uneconomic "prestige" investment, regional competition as to the mill's location requires a political decision and, therefore, government control. Other equity investments of the federal and regional governments, made principally to protect the future Nigerian shareholder or at least to insure some Nigerian participation, are in a wide variety of industries, including cement, textiles, sugar, tires, and metal fabrication. Whether governments will continue to view their role in new industry as catalytic and be willing to open their portfolios to Nigerian share-purchasers as they appear remains to be seen. The need for increased capital formation demands that government turn over its capital as quickly as possible. Its most useful role is to supply venture capital to create new sources of wealth in Nigeria for Nigerians and to move its venture capital to meet new needs, as soon as the initial risks have been overcome and private resources are willing and able to replace it. To immoblize government capital in enterprises where private capital is willing to replace it and to deny private capital formation the resulting incentive is to serve a doctrinaire ideal but not economic growth.

SOCIALISM

"Democratic socialism," a phrase used by the Minister of Finance in his statement on nationalization, is one of various similar terms employed to describe the idea of a unique African or Nigerian social order that maintains its roots in the tradition of the "classless" society of the extended family or tribe, while it seeks economic modernity. This is, essentially, what is meant or attempted to be conveyed by "African socialism," "Nigerian socialism," and "pragmatic socialism." In a sense, it is the social counterpart of the concept of *négritude*, which Ezekiel Mphahlele defines as "a word coined to embrace all Negro art, or the negroness of artistic activity,"[20] but which, in fact, now has wider connotations than art. It reflects a search for identity by the former colonial African.[21] In developing his new ego, he proclaims his uniqueness, discovers his own history, and asserts values derived from his own culture. Thus, Dr. Alioune Diop of Senegal has suggested that Graeco-Roman culture derived from Africa through Egypt. One commentator has suggested: "The starting point—rather a negative one—is the need to react against the colonial myth which pretended that African history and culture presented a mere blank sheet for European influence."[22] This may require the repudiation of received or impressed ideas and values, or, more often, the placing of them in a new context, so that they can be "legitimately" acknowledged by independent Africans.[23]

What is the real content of socialism for Nigerians? First, we must appreciate that "socialism ... has been the pristine condition in Africa in the form of communalism."[24] Taken in the modern, political sense, however, socialism to the African means economic modernity without its "dehumanizing" effects:[25] rootless urban masses, slums, unemployment, excessive preoccupation with materialism and self, a society in which individuals are linked principally by a cash nexus, and a society in which the African joy of life gives way to the hard and competitive attitude of "life is earnest, life is real." In sum, it might be described as the idea of the welfare state that seeks a total and equitable participation in the wealth of the nation by a people who are devoid of sharp social and economic distinctions and disparities, a people who have not lost what Abraham described as "the egalitarian and humane mentality of traditional African society."[26]

Hunter has this to say:

Socialism in West Africa has certain definite meanings at the leadership level—Dr Nkrumah, M. Senghor, M. Sékou Touré are men well read in political philosophy. It also has a vague popular appeal, particularly since leaders under Marxist influence equated the battle against imperialism with one against capitalism, and much oratory in press, radio and public meetings has published the equation abroad. The serious content includes above all the devotion to central planning of the use of resources, both human and material, for the common good.... Planning, in African circumstances, does in fact mean not only State control but a great deal of State enterprise, particularly in the field of industry, finance and marketing."[27]

As economic philosophy, these generalizations apply more to Ghana and Guinea than to Nigeria. "Planning" is hardly, any longer, the mark of a socialist economy, and, if "central planning" remains such, Nigeria can point to its true federal system, where a wide range of powers inheres in the regions, which devise their own development plans and display considerable variation in their respective approaches to economic problems. The "African circumstances," the almost sole ability of the state to muster the required capital, to train the manpower, and to allocate resources, in short, to provide the "take-off" basis for economic development, are a set of operative facts in Nigeria as elsewhere, but, in Nigeria, are not widely viewed as the predicate of a doctrinaire socialist ideology. They are rather viewed as requiring government financing and participation at this early stage, with the expectation that, as private capital formation takes place and as knowledge and confidence in the share market develop, governmental initiative will be replaced by private. It is not generally a commitment to economic centralism or statism.

Even where the "circumstances" are viewed as necessarily dictating a particular political ideological approach, as they are by President Senghor of Senegal, the resulting "socialism" is highly qualified. At the conference on socialism held in Dakar, in late 1962, which was attended by representatives of 18 African states, including Nigeria, Senghor stated:

We maintain, that given our geographical and historical situation, as well as the teething troubles of our societies, only socialism can resolve our development problems. It is not a question of a particular brand of socialism nor even of Marxist socialism. For us, socialism is merely the rational organization of human society, considered as a whole, according to the most scientific, modern, and effective means. That is to say that, from the start, socialism demands equality of opportunity and liberty for peoples and individuals.[28]

Nigeria's delegate, Pro Vice-Chancellor of the University of Ife Dr. Biobaku, defined socialism as "a sense of the community," as Senghor also has. He went on to describe it as "the essence of African-ness.... [I]n a society which has never really been stratified into classes, a redistribution of wealth is a perfectly normal process.... [I]n the family circle, for example, we have always taken care, and still do, of the aged and infirm and the disinherited, without the need for pensions and unemployment benefits."[29] But, when Dr. Biobaku then said that he was quite satisfied if this militated against the formation of local capital, since Nigeria's goal was socialism, not capitalism, he was posing a choice between two philosophies that do not exist in such categorical fashion in Nigeria.

There is little emphasis in Africa on the "economic and political imperatives" of socialism, which the Westerner—Communist or anti-Communist—perceives. The class struggle, for example, is regarded by African socialists as irrelevant to Africa. Hunter, also, claims that "except for a few younger intellectuals in Lagos and Accra, mainly in salaried and professional jobs," there is little or no emphasis on "the moral aspects of socialism, the gap between the rich and the poor ... between the Chevrolet society and the bicycle society."[30] One suspects that many claim the label of "socialist" because that of "capitalist" is identified with colonialism and is, therefore, anathema. One observer has stated his opinion: "So far as Communism is concerned ... the borrowings which African nationalism has made from Marxism/Leninism are opportunist accretions to a political philosophy which is essentially libertarian and essentially democratic."[31]

Whether the trend in the new African nations toward the single-party system[32] should be viewed as a "main element in the African idea of socialism," as Hunter sees it, is, perhaps, questionable. It seems more accurate to characterize it as a technique for the consolidation of power, devoid of political ideology, but often "opportunistically" clothed with the socialist mantle. The most successful practitioners of socialism, after all, the Scandinavian nations, are hosts to vigorous opposition parties. In Nigeria, the principal proponents of the unitary system have been conservatives from the north, and the principal opponents have been trade unionists, the main source of ideological socialist strength in Nigeria. It is necessary to recall, also, that periods of stress have brought about coalition governments in a number of non-socialist democracies and have served to still the opposition temporarily in others.

The idea of a unitary party derives from circumstances—the felt requirements of forced-draft national political and economic development, rather than doctrinaire notions. As one writer puts it,

To a country fighting for its freedom, multiple parties are a luxury since they divide and dissipate nationalist strength. Apologists for the one-party, one-leader state carry the argument further by contending that this system is necessary for a decade or so after independence if a united nation is to be welded out of freedom. Africans often argue that a multiplicity of parties intensifies and consolidates tribal divisions. Similarly, many Asians affirm that a single party makes for national cohesiveness. The argument is plausible and would be justifiable if within a single-party state the values of democracy, quite apart from its institutional forms, were able to thrive.[33]

Where those in power enjoy security for themselves within a constitutional framework that assures the security and continuity of the state, and where they possess a level of sophistication that not only tolerates dialogue but values it, organized opposition will be permitted. But this sophistication swiftly evaporates if the opposition is unwilling or incapable of engaging in meaningful dialogue and is merely searching for routes to power, or if its criticism exceeds "permissible" limits, by threatening national stability or, perhaps, even impeding progress toward goals ordained by those in power.

Unhappily, many of Africa's new leaders are insecure. Their power does not rest on a broad base of popular support but on their control of the apparatus of government—"the means of violence"—or on a slim or regional majority. Denying legitimacy to those in opposition enhances control and, thus, security, stability, and progress. Happily, this phenomenon is less marked in Nigeria, as the handling of the Western Region crisis of 1962-63 by the federal government amply demonstrated. The leadership is both secure and sophisticated. Panic and demagoguery do not characterize the reaction of Nigerian leaders to security threats, although there are, as one might expect, some high officials, at both national and regional levels, who do not contribute to this reputation. But, as the events of 1962-63 showed, the Nigerian remedy is applied with deliberation and with due regard for constitutional requirements and legal process. Security was assured throughout the crisis by the government's control of the army and the federal police force (there are no regional police), and the incipient threat was dispelled, not by ruthless or even harsh repression, but by the legislative declaration of an emergency as provided by the constitution, the displacement of the Western Region government, and eventually the holding of treason trials, all under law and "due process."[34]

NIGERIANIZATION

"Socialism" should not be equated with "Nigerianization," which is economic nationalism, compounded by latent racial, or at least "anti-neo-colonial," feelings. At the same time, one must not limit Nigerianization merely to a demand that Nigerians should displace, as rapidly as possible, expatriate employees and managers in Nigerian business and industry. It is that, too, but more. Nigerianization is directed, more broadly, at the dilution and, at the extreme, the removal of foreign interests from the commanding position that they now occupy in Nigerian economic life. It is increasingly being felt among Nigerians that, while they have thrown off foreign political dominion and have almost entirely Nigerianized the government positions held by expatriates even after independence, Nigeria has yet to win its "economic independence." Without any precise analysis of what role foreign capital and business interests play in Nigerian life, to determine whether it is beneficial, harmful, or mixed, many Nigerians tend to think that "political independence," without "economic independence," is meaningless. It is widely assumed by Nigerians, including highly-placed officials, that the particular business interests of foreigners who are operating in Nigeria do not entirely coincide with Nigeria's interests and, in fact, that they are often necessarily antithetical. The fact or legend of "colonial exploitation" clings to the expatriate concerns whose fortunes paradoxically were not diminished by independence but were, rather, enhanced by reason of the necessary demands made on ready access to capital, qualified management, technological resources, and skilled labor, as economic development became the first business of the newly independent nation. Ironically, and inevitably, the economic development program and its heavy dependence on new foreign investment are enlarging and fortifying the position and scope of foreign business interests in Nigeria. Unavoidably, the source of new investment is the white nation and, most often, the former colonial power. Quite understandably, the Nigerian wants greater participation in what he sees as the fruits of foreign enterprise: the good life, as lived by expatriates—the fine car, the large house in Ikoye or Apapa; and the income to shop in Kingsway and patronize the luxury hotel. He feels locked out; success breeds success, but the Nigerian cannot enter the charmed circle. He has no capital, and the banks are reluctant to lend. Foreign exporters to Nigeria seek established channels of distribution, and they turn to the expatriate firms. Foreign manufacturers require skilled technical partners, as well as capital, in joint manufacturing ventures. The resulting attitude is aggravated by a lack of sense of process.[35] The assumption is that the present position of foreign business in the developing country was primarily the conscious creature of the colonial administration, rather than resulting, in larger part, from the advanced stage of the parent nation's economy, which had earlier gone through its own developing and maturing process.

The continued domination by expatriate firms of the distributive and retail trades and of the banking business is a constant fact before the average urbanized Nigerian. The alien could hardly be more conspicuous than he is in these roles. Generally, when the Nigerian buys anything beyond the simplest necessities of life, he buys from an expatriate—British, Levantine, or European. There are exceptions, of course, but expatriate firms sell almost all durable goods, such as radios, tools, machinery, and automobiles. Nigerians abound as petty traders, and a few have established themselves as producers of finished products in baking, printing, tire retreading, etc., of some scale, but, in the private sector, volume, quality, efficiency, and "style" are almost entirely expatriate monopolies. In the foreign firms, the number of expatriates grows smaller in relation to the number of Nigerians employed, but, again, the Nigerians are employed mainly as clerks, mechanics, and supervising personnel. Few are in positions in which they exert direction and control. In numerous foreign-owned and foreign-controlled companies, Nigerians sit as directors, and there may, indeed, be a Nigerian minority stock interest, but the image presented is, nevertheless, alien.[36]

A recent exposition of the xenophobic view was made at a surprisingly high level. The federal Minister for Economic Development, in March, 1964, is reported to have told a "cheering" House of Representatives that "most of Nigeria's economic difficulties could only be solved when foreign business concerns operating in Nigeria were in the hands of Nigerians."[37] The minister "regretted that the bulk of Nigerian business was in the hands of expatriate concerns" and said that, as long as the present trend continued, "all talk about economic progress will be useless."[38] Finally, having pointed to foreign banking as one instance of what he had in mind, the minister said, "If we protect our people, if possible by legislation, and give them credit facilities which have been denied them by foreign banks, nothing will stop them from growing in the same way as foreign firms have grown."[39] One is reminded of the remark, reported by Hunter, of a Nigerian who watched a Boeing 707 jet take off from Kano Airport and commented "We could have made those if you had given us our independence ten years ago."[40]

As the Minister for Economic Development well knows, one might reply to him that capital is only the means whereby knowledge and skills are translated into the production of goods and services. Where a nation possesses that knowledge and those skills, as Nigeria some day surely will in full measure, it need no longer pay for their provision by expatriates in the form of salaries for employees and profits for entrepreneurs.[41] And when it has adequate capital of its own, it need no longer pay rent, in the form of profits, on the overseas capital that it now seeks to entice into Nigeria.[42]

But this "logical" reply does not take into account the understandable emotional content of the attitude reflected in the minister's statement, nor does it acknowledge the political capital that can be made of this issue.[43] This problem cannot be easily resolved, but restraint on both sides is certainly the key. Nigerians in positions of responsible leadership must present Nigerianization as the eventual end-product of economic development and not as a means to it, for in no sense is it the latter. The Nigerian content in capital and skills of the developmental process is simply not large enough at this time.[44] These leaders must appreciate, as many already do, the non-essentiality of ownership and the use of legislative devices to assure the legitimate control of Nigeria's economic life. They must present to the Nigerian people the idea of the foreign investor's Nigerian venture as a participation in the creation of wealth in Nigeria, which otherwise would not be created, at least for a long time; profits and dividends must be shown as the legitimate fruit of the endeavor, not as exploitation.[45] There are, probably, only two ways in which an independent less-developed nation may be exploited today: if its rulers are willing for it to be exploited (a process in which they then share), or (it may be claimed) by the vicissitudes of demand in the industrialized countries for the primary products of the less-developed nations.[46] While it is true that the foreign investor very often takes the country's leaders as he finds them and may, thus, be a party to corruption, it should be understood that one of the purposes of economic modernization, in which the foreign investor plays an essential part, is to permit the less-developed country to escape the tyranny of the commodity markets through diversification and industrialization.[47] This could not happen, either in a controlled and directed world economy or in one in which classic free trade obtained. Both would perpetuate as economic and rational the present division of labor between the industrialized nations, on the one hand, and the primary-commodity-producing nations, on the other. However, where relatively free competitive forces are permitted to seek their particular interests, within agreed larger national interests, the theory of comparative advantage can be set aside long enough to permit new industry to be established in new countries with capital provided by their would-be industrial competitors, to the ultimate advantage of both.

X

The Western Region Crisis of 1962-1963

The second development concerns the great debate as to whether the newly independent African states and those about to follow them must pass through a period of political absolutism now as a condition of achieving liberal democracy at some future date when all the fissiparous tendencies of tribalism shall have disappeared. The protagonists of this view point for examples to Bismarck in Germany and Garibaldi in Italy in the last quarter of the 19th Century. There is something to be said for the case against the all too frequent phenomenon of sectional self-assertiveness among the polyethnic communities in the countries of Africa and Asia today. Where some of us are in doubt is the extent to which highly restrictive measures may legitimately be taken to repress incipient revolt or resentment that is animated by sentiments of separate group identities. The need for Government security might, if pursued in too single-minded a manner, lead to a situation where personal liberty could be overlooked or even jettisoned.

T. O. Elias before the African Conference on the Rule of Law, Lagos, 1961.

THE ACTION GROUP FACTIONS

Until the national election crisis of January, 1965, the most severe test to which the new Nigerian nation had been put since independence came in May, 1962, when the federal Parliament declared a state of emergency in the Western Region and replaced the region's elected government with a federal administrator who ruled until the end of the year. The crisis is discussed here at some length because of the insights it provides into personalities, attitudes, approaches to problems, and the machinery of government. Even if one may find fault with how the crisis was met in certain particulars, its history demonstrates the resilience and "sense of orderly processes" that is to be found in Nigeria and that again served Nigeria well in the subsequent election crisis. The latter is too recent an event to evaluate here: furthermore, the Western Region crisis extended well over a year—a period of prolonged agony that, it is submitted, few of the new states could have weathered successfully.[1]

The crisis was precipitated by a split in the ruling party in the west, the Action Group, and the struggle for control between the two factions. The rival leaders were Chief Awolowo, leader of the Action Group and leader of the opposition at the federal level, and Chief Akintola, deputy leader of the party and premier of the Western Region. At Awolowo's behest, the national executive of the Action Group deposed Akintola as deputy leader of the party and requested that he resign as premier. Akintola refused and, in turn, asked the governor that the legislature of the Western Region be dissolved.[2] The governor denied this request, apparently aware that Chief Akintola had simultaneously asked the speaker to convene the House of Assembly three days later, in order to try to muster a vote of confidence, or simply because he favored Awolowo. The next day, the governor was presented with a letter that bore the signatures of 66 of the 124 members of the House of Assembly and stated that Premier Akintola no longer enjoyed their confidence.[3] Akintola again requested a dissolution. The governor refused Akintola's request and, instead, dismissed him, relying on the power he believed resided in §33(10)(a) of the regional constitution: "the Governor shall not remove the Premier from office unless *it appears to him* that the Premier no longer commands the support of a majority of the members of the House of Assembly...." The governor read the italicized words literally, and the letter bearing the sixty-six signatures was his evidence. He appointed Alhaji Adegbenro as premier in Chief Akintola's place, effective May 21.[4]

Chief Akintola at once sought to challenge his dismissal in the high court, which subsequently removed it to the federal Supreme Court.[5] Meanwhile, the Western House of Assembly was summoned for May 25, and two attempts that day to convene the house ended in riots on the floor, requiring the use of tear gas by police to disperse the fighting members. Several persons were injured, and the mace and furniture of the house were damaged. After a second attempt to meet, attended by even greater violence, the chamber was cleared by the police and locked.

The same day, Prime Minister Sir Abubakar Tafawa Balewa presided over a meeting of the federal Council of Ministers and that evening made a nationwide broadcast in which he said: "No responsible Government of the Federation could allow an explosive situation such as that which now exists in Western Nigeria to continue without taking adequate measures to ensure that there is an early return to the Region of peace, order and good government."[6]

By May 29, the plan of action was completed and the necessary documents drawn up. The prime minister moved a resolution in the House of Representatives for the declaration of a state of emergency in the Western Region, under the authority contained in §65(1) of the Independence Constitution of Nigeria: "Parliament may at any time make such laws for Nigeria or any part thereof with respect to matters not included in the Legislative Lists as may appear to Parliament to be necessary or expedient for the purpose of maintaining or securing peace, order and good government during any period of emergency."

A "period of emergency" exists, §65 went on to explain, when the Federation of Nigeria is at war,[7] when there is in force a resolution passed by each house of Parliament declaring that a state of public emergency exists,[8] or when two-thirds of both houses resolve that "democratic institutions in Nigeria are threatened by subversion."[9] Acting under the second provision, both the House of Representatives and the Senate passed the resolution moved by the prime minister declaring an emergency to exist in the Western Region.

The resolution brought into force the Emergency Powers Act of

1961,[10] which, in turn, authorized the numerous regulations promulgated by the federal government. These included the Emergency Powers (General) Regulations, which suspended the offices of the various Western Region officials—that of the governor, the premier and his ministers,[11] and members of the legislature; the Emergency Powers (Essential Services) Regulation; and the following other emergency powers regulations: Retention of Services; Requisition; Billeting; Misleading Reports; Protected Places; Processions and Meetings; Control of Arms and Explosives; Curfew; Detention of Persons; Restriction Orders; and Reporting of Persons Advisory Tribunal; Statutory Corporations Inquiries; and Prerogative of Mercy.[12] Most engendered controversy, and several brought forth important constitutional law cases.

Additionally, the Emergency Powers (Jurisdiction) Act[13] gave the federal Supreme Court, "to the exclusion of any other court in Nigeria . . . during any period of emergency within the meaning of section 65 of the Constitution . . . original jurisdiction with respect to any question as to the validity of the Emergency Powers Act, 1961" or any regulations or acts thereunder.[14]

The prime minister, on June 9, appointed Dr. Moses Majekodunmi, a senator and the federal Minister of Health, as administrator of the Western Region, effective May 29. The two contending premiers, several Western Region ministers, and Chief Awolowo were restricted in their movements, as were Chief Rotimi Williams, legal adviser of the Action Group and the leading constitutional lawyer of Nigeria, several other lawyers, and several journalists.[15]

Sweeping powers were conferred upon Dr. Majekodunmi by the emergency regulations. The general regulations authorized him to exercise "executive authority of the Region on behalf of Her Majesty,"[16] subject only to the chapter on fundamental rights of the Nigerian Constitution,[17] "to do such things as appear to him to be necessary or expedient. . . ."[18]

Under §5, the administrator was given power to:

(a) detain persons within the emergency area or elsewhere, and to remove or exclude persons from the emergency area;

(b) take possession or control of any property or undertaking in the emergency area;

(c) authorize the entry and search of any premises;

(d) amend, modify, or suspend any law in force in the area;

(e) provide for compensation to persons affected by the order;

(f) provide for the apprehension, trial, and punishment of persons offending against the order; and

(g) provide for maintaining essential supplies and services in the emergency area.

A copy of each order made by the administrator was to be transmitted to the prime minister, who could, from time to time, give directions to the administrator in the exercise of his functions.[19]

While the political executive of the region was suspended from office, the civil service, regional and local, was ordered to remain on duty. Commissioners were appointed to replace ministers, and, very shortly, Dr. Majekodunmi, demonstrating unusual administrative skill, had the processes of government functioning smoothly. Except for the restriction on movements of persons, Dr. Majekodunmi's administration was almost entirely free of any repressive measures, although his powers were ample. Nor was there any significant physical resistance by the people of Western Nigeria to the action taken by the federal authorities. In what will surely go down in the annals of African history as one of the most remarkable episodes of constitutional and judicial process, the issues, instead, were joined in court.

Three important cases came out of the crisis, which helped give shape to Nigerian constitutional law and to its political order: Chief Akintola successfully challenged the governor's power to dismiss him,[20] Chief A. O. Adegbenro (Akintola's purported successor) unsuccessfully challenged the constitutionality of the Emergency Powers Act,[21] and Chief Rotimi Williams succeeded in his challenge of the restriction order served upon him.[22] By good fortune, the writer was present in court when, on July 7, 1962, judgment was handed down in all three cases.[23] A judgment of less importance, and handed down at a lower level, was that given in the case of *Awolowo v. Minister of Internal Affairs*,[24] in which Chief Awolowo failed in his effort to secure an order permitting entry into Nigeria of a British lawyer chosen by Awolowo to defend him against charges of felonious treason.[25] These cases are discussed subsequently. On the heels of the declaration of the emergency and the suspension of elected government came the Coker Commission, appointed on June 16, 1962, to inquire into the alleged financial mismanagement of the Western Region. Charges had been made, more than a year before the emergency, that widespread misuse of public funds was taking place, particularly those of the Western Region Marketing Board, for the benefit of Action Group politicians and the party itself. In the Western Region 1961-62 Appropriations Bill debate, the leader of the NCNC opposition, Mr. Fani-Kayode, had demanded a "comprehensive White Paper" on the operations of the Marketing Board since 1954, alleging that almost £1 million had been "stolen" from the board.[26] The Coker Commission inquiry showed that even larger sums had been involved, including £4 million that was "handed over" to the Action Group.[27]

The debacle of the spring and summer threatened the very existence of the Action Group and its leaders apparently decided to take desperate measures. They allegedly plotted to seize power in September. Awolowo and other Action Group leaders were arrested and shortly went on trial, in late 1962, charged with felonious treason. One of the accused, Chief Anthony Enaharo, the "shadow cabinet" foreign minister, had fled to England and became the center of a dispute between Nigeria and the United Kingdom when the Nigerian Government sought his return under the Fugitive Offenders Act.[28] British officials, under the pressure of certain members of the House of Commons, who viewed Enaharo as a victim of political oppression, hesitated to comply and cast serious aspersions on the integrity of the Nigerian courts. "Assurances" were sought that Enaharo would be given a fair trial and that the death penalty would not be imposed. Enaharo was, finally, returned and tried. All of the defendants in the treason trials, except four against whom charges were dismissed, were found guilty and sentenced to prison for terms of up to ten years each, in September, 1963.

Chief Akintola resumed the premiership of the Western Region on January 1, 1963, while Awolowo and other Action Group leaders were in prison. By this time, numerous prominent members of the Action Group had left the party. A number had made a display of their defection in the May 29 debates. Chief Akintola and others formed a new political party in the west, known as the United People's Party (UPP). In May, 1963, the Judicial Committee of the Privy Council reversed the federal Supreme Court's decision in the premiership dispute and held that the governor could, indeed, dismiss the premier if "it appears to him," apart from a vote of no confidence in the House of Assembly, that the premier no longer has the support of a majority. The Western Region legislature promptly met and retroactively amended the Constitution of Western Nigeria to frustrate the decision of the Privy Council.[29]

In July, 1963, Nigerian leaders of all parties, including the Action Group, met to consider constitutional revisions in anticipation of

Nigeria's becoming a republic in October, 1963. There had been dissatisfaction with the status assumed upon gaining independence on October 1, 1960, which perpetuated the sovereignty of Elizabeth II as Queen of Nigeria. The move to a republican form of government within the Commonwealth was inevitable, and, if it was not hastened, it was confirmed by the events of 1962-63: specifically, the posture of the British government in the matter of the return of Chief Enaharo; the reversal by the Privy Council in the case of *Akintola v. Adegbenro*;[30] and, more generally, the unsympathetic treatment in the British press of the Western Region crisis, which was widely pictured in Britain as signaling the degeneration of Nigeria into a police state.

In summary, the events that came out of the Western Region crisis, that were speeded to their climax by it, or that were suddenly and dramatically brought into focus as the result of it, were these: (1) a number of important constitutional law decisions and ensuing developments, (2) the Coker Commission inquiry into corruption in Western Region finances, (3) the trials for felonious treason of Action Group leaders, (4) the crippling of the Action Group as an effective political force and the dispersal of its leaders to prison, to the UPP, or to the NCNC, and, perhaps (5) the firm resolve of the Nigerian leadership to effect an early changeover to a republican form of government.

THE JUDICIAL DECISIONS

The resort to legal process to resolve issues raised by the political upheaval in the Western Region is, perhaps, the most telling evidence of the basic adherence to the rule and processes of law that characterizes the Nigerian political order. There have, of course, been episodes of violence in recent Nigerian history—the Egba Uprising of 1918 and the Aba Riots of 1929, both revolts against colonial policy and, therefore, properly characterized as "early resistance movements";[31] recurrently, since independence, there have been disorders among the Tiv people of Northern Nigeria, but this is a very primitive tribe and the causes and events appear to have been entirely localized.[32] The violence that attended the two attempts to convene the Western House of Assembly, although not resulting in loss of life, was one of the most serious and, certainly, the most spectacular lapse from the orderly resolution of issues that Nigeria has witnessed in modern times. It severely marred the Nigerian image. To recover and stabilize the situation strong measures were required, as the federal government saw it, and these followed. But the legal basis of the government's compulsive measures was tested in court. It is believed that it was honestly tested and done so by the Supreme Court, in the face of considerable impatience and even hostility on the part of government leaders and certain newspapers. Dr. Odumoso includes in his study several statements reflecting this attitude. True, these were made with reference to the expulsion of Mr. Dingle Foot,[33] the British barrister, and must, therefore, be discounted somewhat, but they were revealing.

Dr. M. I. Okpara, a medical doctor, premier of Eastern Nigeria, and head of the NCNC, is reported to have said: "There is an emergency in a part of the country and you don't need to fumble in court in such a situation. If there were an emergency in Britain, would any Nigerian lawyer be allowed into Britain to challenge the authority of the British Parliament in declaring an emergency? . . . I think this democracy of ours is being misinterpreted."[34] The premier of the Northern Region, the Sardauna of Sokota, let it be known that he agreed with Dr. Okpara.[35] The leading NCNC newspaper, the *West African Pilot,* stated editorially (again, with reference to the Foot incident): ". . . Nigeria is most certainly committed to the principle of the rule of law . . . [but] Each time the Government tries to uphold the sovereignty and integrity of this country, doctrinaire constitutionalists will plead liberal democracy. . . ."[36]

Early in May, the prime minister, himself, had expressed impatience with legal process: "We were dragged to court on the bank inquiry and now we are being dragged to court on the Mid-West. Well, if our courts will allow themselves to be used in the way they are being used on any minor thing, I am afraid people will make a mockery of our courts. . . . Personally, I think it is wrong for every small constitutional matter to go to court, people will soon come to laugh at our courts. . . ."[37]

Neither the arrogation of power by the executive, which the constitution does not grant, nor the creation of a new Mid-West state out of territory of the Western Region, whose legality the latter sought to test in court, are by any stretch of the imagination "small constitutional matters." Almost as startling is the fact that the prime minister would so express himself when the Mid-West matter was *sub judice.*

As Dr. Odumoso says, "There seems to be a dangerous misconception among these leaders of governments in the Federation about the role of the Supreme Court under a federal system."[38] But the prime minister apparently saw things quite differently by May 29, for, in the debates on that day, he criticized the governor of Western Nigeria and the Action Group for lacking regard for the court. His reason apparently was that the Western Region House of Assembly had been convened, on May 25, to seek a vote of confidence for Adegbenro, when Akintola's suit contesting his dismissal was *sub judice*. He adverted, again, to the federal government's being stymied in the bank inquiry:

But the Court ... stopped us, they said we could not go ahead. We had to listen to the Court and obey the Court. We did not go ahead. We could easily go ahead but we did not.

We called a meeting of Parliament; Parliament gave us approval to go ahead and we did. When we appointed the inquiry again, the inquiry sat for only fifty minutes and the court stopped us. We did not disobey, we had to wait. . . .

We have to respect our Courts and we have to respect our Constitution. One side cannot say that they do not wish to respect the Court or the Constitution and because the Federal Government is taking certain action they regard the Federal Government as trying to kill democracy. . . .[39]

Fortunately, the more recent pronouncement of the prime minister was heard more clearly in the land than his earlier words or those of the two regional premiers. The justices of the federal Supreme Court were not intimidated. Early in July, 1962, there was an air of expectancy in Nigeria as to how the court would rule on the three important questions before it. One gained the clear impression that the Supreme Court and not the political leaders, the objective process of adjudication and not political expediency, were expected to provide the answers.

The machinery of justice was, as noted, put into action by the principals concerned, Chief Akintola contesting his dismissal as premier, Chief Adegbenro challenging the constitutionality of the Emergency Powers Act of 1961, and Chief Williams denying the validity of the restrictions placed on his movements.

The *Akintola* case turned on the interpretation to be placed on §33(10) of the Constitution of Western Nigeria and the words "it appears to him," mentioned earlier, as to whether they authorized the governor to dismiss the premier on evidence other than a vote of no confidence in the House of Assembly. Chief Akintola argued, of course, that such a vote was a necessary condition precedent to his removal and that the governor could not act on evidence extrinsic to proceedings of the legislature. The defendant argued the plain language of the section: if it "appeared" to the governor that the premier had lost the support of a majority, no matter what evidence he relied upon, he was empowered to dismiss him. The majority of the court agreed with Chief Akintola, relying on constitutional conventions, as they believed them to have developed and to exist in the United Kingdom, as qualifying the plain language of the Constitution, notwithstanding the fact that the British conventions did not develop out of a written document.

Federal Chief Justice Sir A. A. Ademola said, in giving judgment:

To my mind the conclusion is inescapable that the framers of the Constitution wanted the House to be responsible at every level for the ultimate fate of Government and the Premier. The horizon must be larger than leaving it to one man. The Governor might eventually be the instrument used to effect this, but his position as final arbiter must be dictated by events in the House or events emanating from the House, and not by a letter, however well meaning, signed by a body of members of the House. Law and convention cannot be replaced by party political moves outside the House.

I believe that the Constitution contemplated proceedings in the House as being the touchstone of whether the Premier (and his Government) commands the support of a majority of members or no longer commands such support.[40]

Mr. Justice Brett dissented, insisting that what was before the court was a written document whose meaning was clear and into which United Kingdom conventions could not be properly imported. Furthermore, he pointed out that no parallel question had ever arisen in United Kingdom constitutional practice and, therefore, no convention specifically existed as precedent. As Davies points out,[41] "It is possible that, if attention had been given to Commonwealth experience, particularly up to and including the Imperial Conference of 1926, there might have been more support for the view of Brett F. J."

The Judicial Committee of the Privy Council ultimately agreed with Justice Brett:

The difficulty in limiting the statutory power of the Governor in this way is that the limitation is not to be found in the words in which the makers of the Constitution have decided to record their description of his powers. By the words they have employed in their formula, "it appears to him," the judgment as to the support enjoyed by a Premier is left to the Governor's own assessment and there is no limitation as to the material on which he is to base his judgment or the contacts he may resort to for the purpose.[42]

This judgment was undone by the retroactive amendment of the Constitution of Western Nigeria,[43] and the provision for appeal to the Privy Council contained in the Independence Constitution of 1960 was subsequently omitted from the Republican Constitution.

British commentators on the case prefer the dissent of Justice Brett and the decision of the Privy Council.[44] Dr. Allott, for example, sees the retroactive amendment of the constitution as recognition of "the fundamental principle ... that it is the actual words of the constitution which are to be consulted, and conventions are not to be deemed to have been impliedly attached to the constitution."[45] Dr. Odumosu, in his book on the Nigerian Constitution, agrees with Justice Brett's dissent[46] and emphasizes the lack of parallels and precedent in English constitutional practice.

Another Nigerian, Dr. C. Ogwurike, lecturer in law at the University of Nigeria, suggests that the more liberal approach of the federal Supreme Court comported more with the realities of the political situation in Nigeria, and he raises (but does not answer) the problem of "political expediency and the rule of Law":[47]

The second important factor which has emerged from the divergent views of the Supreme Court and the Judicial Committee ... is the problem of maintaining and applying strictly legal principles in constitutional interpretation while at the same time recognizing the fact that the constitution is designed for prompt action and effective administration.

The members of the Judicial Committee, unlike the judges of the Supreme Court, possessed no firsthand knowledge of the political and administration problems confronting Western Nigeria. Their decision was given in isolation from the real social and political problems in the Region....

The decision came in less than two months short of a year after the Supreme Court decision, and at a time when it could be said that things were returning to normal in Western Nigeria. A reversion therefore to the *status quo ante* was bound to be regarded as a retrograde step—even though by strict law [*i.e.*, obedience to the Judicial Committee's decision] the right step to take.[48]

The British critic would ask, but do all of these considerations matter, in the face of "a clear and unambiguous provision" of the constitution? On the other hand, is the rule of law necessarily sacrificed to political expediency, if they are, indeed, held to matter? These are serious questions, for much depends on whether one views the court as performing a valid function in interpreting, even where the language appears plain, to arrive at the precise meaning in which "plain" words are understood, by placing them in context. The alternative is to suggest that a court that is engaged in interpretation is really "embellishing" plain words, "reaching for a decision," in order to sanctify an accomplished political act, or anticipating a political act with which it sees a necessity to conform. If such is the case, the rule of law is a hollow thing indeed. That was quite plainly not the case here.

A constitution is not a contract,[49] nor is it subject to the parol evidence rule. It is a living document, in a very real sense; it must be read and applied in context. It regulates a dynamic and changing society, not a static condition or relationship. This is not to deny Parliament or the people the last word; they may have it, by way of amendment. But there will always be unanticipated gaps that present themselves and must be bridged until the legislature or the people act. If the court is informed of what the true meaning of language in the constitution is, it should not strip language of the custom or understanding in which it rests, most certainly not if the insistence upon the naked juxtaposition of words is to become the handmaiden of confusion or chaos. Its function is to supply the totality of meaning, at any given time, regardless of the outcome, to language that, because of the fundamental and pervasive nature of a constitution, must always suffer from lack of precision[50] and, to be truly viable, is always in need of explication.

The decision, while a defeat of strict construction, is not to be taken as a victory of liberal construction. As the fundamental rights cases demonstrate,[51] the federal Supreme Court is not so inclined. But it does show that the court reserves the right to construe the language of the constitution and not to rely on bare words when orderly processes are at stake. While it did establish the sole initiative of the legislature, in providing the basis for the removal of the premier, the case is not to be taken as suggesting the supremacy of the legislature over the existing constitution. The court found the role of Parliament within what was then the language of §33(10), and the judgment of the court and the subsequent amendment of §33(10) are two wholly distinct acts. The supremacy of the existing constitution was definitively settled the year before, in *Doherty v. Balewa*.[52]

In the *Adegbenro* case, the plaintiff, appointed by the governor of Western Nigeria to succeed Akintola as premier, sought, by an original action before the federal Supreme Court, to legitimize his position by having the Emergency Powers Act, 1961, declared unconstitutional and the regulations made thereunder declared void.[53] He also sought an interlocutory injunction to prevent the administrator of the Western Region, appointed by the governor general in council, from exercising the powers conferred upon him; and he requested a declaration that he, Adegbenro, had been lawfully appointed premier and that his government was duly constituted. Chief Adegbenro also challenged the restriction order served upon him.

The judgment of the court, in this case, was unanimous but inconclusive. It held that plaintiff's proof went only to the validity of certain portions of the Emergency Powers (General) Regulations and to the validity of the restriction order and that "the plaintiff has put forward no grounds on which we could hold the whole of the Act or the regulations invalid...."[54] But the question of whether Adegbenro was, in fact, premier was *sub judice* in the pending *Akintola* case, and "unless those proceedings are decided in his favour he has not shown that the declaration to which his arguments have been directed would be of any value to him."[55] Adegbenro, thus, lacked standing to challenge the regulations. With respect to the restriction order, Federal Justice Taylor found it reasonably justifiable. As to the allegation that the plaintiff was the lawful premier and that a duly constituted government existed in Western Nigeria, the court held that these matters were not only *sub judice* but involved the interpretation of the Constitution of Western Nigeria (*i.e.*, going back to the lawfulness of Akintola's dismissal) and did not arise under the Emergency Powers Act, 1961. Hence, as to these claims, the federal Supreme Court lacked original jurisdiction, which the Emergency Powers (Jurisdiction) Act, 1962, had provided only with respect to matters arising under the Emergency Powers Act, 1961.

Owing to the bases of decision, the court did not consider the profound question of the constitutionality of the Emergency Powers Act. Davies reviews the arguments, made on the motion for the injunction, that §65 (empowering Parliament to declare and provide for an emergency) "must be read and circumscribed by the purpose of the Constitution as a whole and by the provisions of section 64 in particular,"[56] particularly since the Emergency Powers Act did not specifically state it was enacted under the authority of §65. Section 64 provides the general legislative authority of the federal Parliament with the power to make laws "for the peace, order and good government of Nigeria" and the individual regions, in accordance with the distribution of powers contained in the legislative lists. Since the purpose of §65 was to authorize legislation "with respect to matters not included in legislative lists," any power that inheres in §64 cannot be subsumed under §65, since an emergency need not exist to implement §64. But §64 is clearly subject to the entrenched safeguards that protect fundamental rights and that may be overcome only by following the complex amending processes of §4.[57] Short of amendment, such a law, if it encroaches on a fundamental right, must be "reasonably justifiable in a democratic society"[58] and is, thus, subject to judicial review.

This argument was actually made earlier in the case of *Williams v. Majekodunmi*[59] and, perhaps, tacitly accepted.[60] In *Adegbenro*, it was further argued that, although §65 may obliterate the distinction made by legislative lists with respect to the division of powers between federal and regional government, a declaration of emergency could not be taken to obliterate regional authority, for this would be tantamount to this section's permitting the overthrow of the constitution itself. Thus, §65 would displace §4, the amending section; but entrenched sections of the constitution, such as §5, which states that a regional constitution may be altered only by an act of the regional legislature, may, in turn, be altered only under the provisions of §4. If such a radical power had been intended, it should have been expressly granted. Since it was not, §65 remained subject to the limitations of §64, since only thus could a constitutional balance between the branches of government be maintained. While certain steps to meet an emergency may be taken under §65, it is doubtful if it contains the authority for the federal government to suspend the government of a region. Ekineh argues:

> The suspension of the executive of a Region entails important departure from the Constitution itself; and power to do so ought clearly to be given. Since a State of War automatically means an emergency under Section 65, it seems to mean that by the precedent of 1962 the Federal Executive can suspend the executives of all Regions whenever this country is engaged in war.
>
> It is submitted that the section only empowers the Federal legislature and executive to make laws for the maintenance of law and

order, such as by imposing curfews, banning processions and imposing restrictions on persons during an emergency.[61]

The federal Supreme Court may yet have to meet this question directly.

The *Williams*[62] case has been previously discussed. Its importance, however, should be reiterated. The court held, with respect to the principle of delegation, that Parliament could properly delegate to the governor general in council its powers to legislate, since Parliament retained ultimate control and the power to revoke under the delegating act,[63] and that these powers could be redelegated by the governor to the administrator. However, the court also held that there was no evidence from which it could be fairly inferred that the restriction placed upon Chief Williams' freedom of residence and movement was "reasonably justifiable in a democratic society," as §26 of the constitution requires that a restriction on the movement or residence of a Nigerian citizen must be. The net result, although the court did not spell it out with precision, may be that legislation under §65, like §64, is subject to the safeguards of the chapter on fundamental rights. However, it will be recalled that §4(2) of the Emergency Powers (General) Regulations specified that the administrator was to exercise the executive authority of the region, subject to the chapter on fundamental rights.[64] The court may have relied on this, and we do not, in fact, know whether implementation of §65 is subject to the chapter on fundamental rights if no proviso similar to §4(2) is interposed. Obviously, "[I]t may well make a difference, when one comes to consider the reasonableness of legislation which restricts free movement, whether there is a state of emergency on, and what it is."[65]

It is to be noted, however, that the court's role does not extend to examining the judgment of parliament that an emergency exists, if it so declares under §65. During oral argument in the *Williams* case, the chief justice, by way of dictum, stated that this question was "within the bounds of Parliament, and not one for this Court to decide."[66] If this is, indeed, the case, the need to restrict the powers of the federal government under §65 should not await an eventual test in court. Amendment of the constitution would seem to be in order. For if Parliament by a simple majority vote of both houses can declare an emergency to exist under §65(3)(b), and legislation that follows is not subject to any pre-existing constitutional restraints, the constitutional "guarantees" exist at the whim of the majority in the federal legislature.[67]

In Chief Awolowo's suit in the High Court of Lagos,[68] to secure the admission into Nigeria of counsel of his choice—in this case, the British barrister, Mr. E. F. N. Gratiaen—it was held that §13 of the Immigration Act, permitting the governor general, in his absolute discretion, to bar the entry into Nigeria of any non-Nigerian, did not conflict with §21(5)(c) of the constitution, which provides: "Every person who is charged with a criminal offence shall be entitled to defend himself in person or by legal representatives of his own choice."

To the plaintiff's argument that §13 should give way, Mr. Justice Udo-Udoma said:

The Constitution is a Nigerian Constitution, meant for Nigerians in Nigeria. It runs only in Nigeria. The natural consequence of this is that the legal representative contemplated in §21(5)(c) ought to be someone in Nigeria, and not outside it.
Nothing which has been urged before me has suggested that the framers of this Constitution ever had any special reason to contemplate, at the time of framing the Constitution; that in the ordinary course of events, Nigerians involved in criminal charges would normally engage legal representatives outside Nigeria.[69]

This also set at rest the matter of the expulsion of Mr. Dingle Foot,[70] but since both Gratiaen and Foot were members of the Nigerian bar, it brought to a head the matter of the practice of law by expatriates. After the Gratiaen episode, the Bar Association stated that it was unable to support the government's action in barring Gratiaen, although it believed "the time is more than ripe to stop expatriate lawyers from coming to practise in Nigeria."[71] The result was the enactment of the Legal Practitioners Act, 1962, requiring Nigerian citizenship for entering the practice of law but permitting resident expatriates already enrolled to continue their practices.[72]

As was stated earlier, one cannot yet generalize with respect to the constitutional decisions of the federal Supreme Court. The cases that arose out of the emergency have been set forth in some detail to demonstrate the vitality of the court's role in the crisis, whether one agrees with its conclusions or not. Its approach is variable and, perhaps, not entirely consistent in theory. But there is a consistency in its seeking to establish orderly processes in a political order that is still finding its way. The emphasis on order necessarily exacts its price in the liberality with which the rights of individuals and political minorities are protected against encroachment by government. In the Western Region crisis cases, the caution that the court

The Western Region Crisis of 1962-1963   191

had previously exhibited in the few earlier constitutional cases may be said to have served it well; no retreat was necessary. The methodical search for orderly processes went on. Yet, where it could strike a blow for individual rights and against arbitrary action by government, the court did so.

THE COKER COMMISSION OF INQUIRY

In November, 1962, after ninety-two days of hearings, the Coker Commission, appointed[73] in June to investigate the financial affairs of the six statutory corporations of Western Nigeria, adjourned to write its report. The commission was composed of Mr. Justice G. B. A. Coker, at that time Judge of the High Court of Lagos and since appointed to the federal Supreme Court; Mr. J. O. Kassim, chief magistrate, Eastern Nigeria; and Mr. Akintola Williams, chartered accountant. It had sifted through a mass of evidence, it had heard fifty-nine witnesses attended by numerous counsel, and, in the process (as the commissioners said in their report), it had unfolded "the great tragic story... of a people who had trusted their leaders and had identified their interests with the interests of their Government in the hope and settled conviction that all was well... only to be told when their leaders fell apart, that the security into which they were lured was not real."[74]

That is somewhat overdramatized, and the statement catches reflections of other, more serious events of the Western Region crisis. The question that the Coker Commission sought to answer was on everyone's lips: "Where did the money go?" The balance of the Western Region Marketing Board, on September 30, 1959, had stood at £64 million. Its assets, in the summer of 1962, were £8.7 million.[75] It had no liquid reserves and was living on an overdraft from an expatriate bank.[76] Where, indeed, had the money gone?

The answer, detailed in the commission's report of four volumes,[77] is a story of corruption and venality, of political manipulation, and of financial mismanagement and ineptitude. A few individuals profited directly on their own account, but the amounts involved were not large. Of course, the greater portion of £64 million was not misappropriated—it went into the development program of the Western Region, even, as one commentator put it, if it was not used for the purposes for which it was originally intended.[78] But there was a good deal of slippage, if not leakage, and, in instance after instance, the inquiry revealed the fruits of favoritism, nepotism, poor planning, bad management, and the Action Group's struggle to assert itself on the national political scene. For the chief beneficiary was the Action Group, into which some £4 million is supposed to have been funneled through various devices. This explained, among other things, the expensive election campaign conducted by the party in 1959 when it "invaded" the north to challenge the Sardauna of Sokoto on his own ground, and the nationwide network of offices maintained by the Action Group. The instances of wrongdoing uncovered by the commission are many and varied. An island in Lagos, sold in 1958 for £11,000, was sold by the National Investment and Properties Company (NIPC), which was owned by prominent members of the Action Group, to the Western Region government for £850,000 in 1960. A total of £6.2 million was also loaned to the NIPC by the Western Region corporations which was never repaid and on which £700,000 accrued interest was due. By various means, much of the money was routed to the Action Group, with the insolvency of the NIPC as the ultimate result. Almost £1 million, for example, supposed to have been paid to a firm of engineers, was diverted to the party, with the engineers co-operating by endorsing the checks. Funds of the Western Region Marketing Board were invested in banks without investigation. A number of projects of the Western Nigeria Development Corporation were found to have been launched without proper studies. Two soft drink bottling plants, operating at a loss at the time of inquiry, were erected at a cost of £672,000 as part of the development scheme, without the participation of the foreign licensor in the equity. After the purchase of Arab Bros. (Motors), Ltd. by the Western Region Finance Corporation for £1.1 million (described by the commission as exorbitant), Chief Awolowo insisted that the father-in-law of Chief Shonibare, managing director of the NIPC, be appointed managing director of Arab Bros., Ltd. Board members of the Western Region Housing Corporation passed a resolution permitting themselves to have loans at 5 per cent interest, rather than the 6 per cent interest charged staff members. These are some examples of the commission's findings. The initial reaction was one of shock, and foreign investment dropped off, not only in the Western Region, but in Nigeria as a whole, and the 1962-68 Development Plan has suffered as a result.

But the over-all effect was salutary. The commission helped substantiate, in the eyes of the public, the claim of the federal government to the right and the necessity to intervene in the affairs of the Western Region. The revelations of the commission were easier to understand than the sophisticated legal proceedings in the courts, and they revealed something more profoundly wrong than was manifested by the parliamentary contest between Awolowo and Akintola, or even by the one day of rioting in the House of Assembly in May. The accusations of treason against Awolowo and others were yet to be made when the inquiry opened—it is not clear when the evidence of the plot was uncovered (the day of seizing power was alleged to have been set as September 23, 1962). When the charges were made, of course, the Coker Commission had revealed enough, together with everything else that had gone on before, to show up the Action Group leaders as desperate men whose only salvation lay in resort to violence. This is not a role the Coker Commission was, perhaps, intended to play; however, it was the role it did play, owing to the train of events. Its quasi-judicial procedure, its careful attention to the formulation of rules of procedure, its rulings on appearances of counsel (particularly with respect to conflict of interest), its meticulous handling of items of evidence, and its detailed final report gave a deserved high credibility to the hearings and findings of the commission. All of this affirmed, once again, the importance of duly constituted bodies and processes to examine and pronounce on allegations of wrongdoing.

Political revenge may well have been an ingredient of the Western Region crisis and its aftermath, perhaps indeed of the appointment of the Coker Commission, for certainly the Western Region leaders were not the only offenders against financial rectitude. Nevertheless, the inquiry had an important cathartic effect and has probably done more to drive home the idea of responsible management of government offices and funds than any other measure might have done. The commission in its report stated: "This Inquiry . . . has come and gone, but no doubt exists about [its] historical significance. The fires lit by the proceedings glowed over every nook and corner of the Federation and . . . the embers of these fires shall remain alive for many years to come."[79] It is believed that Nigeria is a better place to invest than it was before the crisis.

Although the Action Group was badly hurt by the events of 1962-63 and its leadership was lost, it retains a great vitality in the west, especially at the local level, which must continue to be reckoned with. Only a few months after the crisis erupted, for example, the Lagos Town Council elections, in the fall of 1962, returned a majority of Action Group candidates to office.

Political diversity and differences have many roots in Nigeria. No sooner had the Action Group been eliminated as a political force at the national level, for the time being at least, and the prime minister had made some exploratory remarks about a unitary party system, than the preliminary figures on the 1963 census were released. These revealed that Northern Nigeria had a population exceeding that of the three southern regions combined, by a margin sufficient to insure the north's perpetual control of the federal Parliament and government. This gave rise to strong feeling in the south and, particularly, in Eastern Nigeria, since the allegedly inflated figures of the east, in the 1962 census, were the ostensible reason for taking a new census in 1963. At one point, early in 1964, there was a separatist call from the Ibo Union (the Ibo tribe predominates in the east). This brief clamor subsided, but the tensions remain and, during 1964 found expression in a realignment of political parties and forces in anticipation of the 1964 elections. The tensions now pull most strongly between north and south, whereas, during the Western Region crisis, they pulled between government and opposition. One might say that as to whether Nigeria can survive as one nation, the issue has now been joined, since authoritarian and consolidative forces derive from the north, while liberal and fragmentive forces derive from the south. These were the forces that came into conflict following the national elections of December 30, 1964.[80]

Differences in religion, culture, language, political outlook, level of education and development, allocation of resources, all contribute to the rich variety of Nigerian life. As long as they are not permitted to spill over into conflict, these differences ultimately strengthen Nigeria as a nation, for only a resilient political order can absorb the strains that are generated. Maintaining a fine balance between the control necessary to maintain national unity and the liberty that the natural diversity of Nigerian life requires is, then, the most important task that Nigerian leadership has. A certain amount of economic waste is bound to occur in the continual process of reconciling, adjusting, and compensating regional and sectional differences. But there is more to nation-building than rapid economic development, and, if Nigerian leadership can maintain balance and flexibility, the political order that evolves by 1975 will be strong, cohesive, and purposeful.

Abbreviations

LAW REPORTS:

    All N.L.R.   All Nigeria Law Reports
    N.L.R.   Nigerian Law Reports
    W.A.C.A.   West African Court of Appeals Reports

COURTS:

    F.S.C.   Federal Supreme Court
    H.C.   High Court
    W.A.C.A.   West African Court of Appeals

STATUTES:

    C.C.L.   Customary Court Law
    C.C.(A.)L.   Customary Court (Amendment) Law
    E.R.H.C.L.   Eastern Region High Court Law
    H.C.L.O.   High Court of Lagos Ordinance
    N.C.L.   Native Courts Law
    N.R.H.C.L.   Northern Region High Court Law
    W.R.H.C.L.   Western Region High Court Law

MISCELLANEOUS:

    L.N.   Legal Notice
    N.R.   Northern Region

NOTE: The 1960 Constitution, herein referred to as the "Independence Constitution," is found in *Laws of the Federation of Nigeria and Lagos* (1960), where the regional constitutions also appear. The 1963 Constitution, herein referred to as the "Republican Constitution," is found in *Laws of the Federal Republic of Nigeria* (1963).

Notes

CHAPTER I

1. James S. Coleman, "The Foreign Policy of Nigeria," in *Foreign Policies in a World of Change,* eds., Joseph E. Black and Kenneth W. Thompson (New York, 1963), p. 381.
2. The so-called *Ashby Report.* [Nigerian] Federal Ministry of Education, Investment in Education, *The Report of the Commission on Post-School Certificate and Higher Education* (1960).
3. At the end of 1962, foreign investment in fixed assets in Nigeria was distributed as follows, with percentages shown in parentheses: United Kingdom, £113.6 million (74.9); United States, £15.0 million (9.9); Western Europe £5.9 million (3.9); others, £17.2 million (11.3). "Foreign Investment Survey," [Central Bank of Nigeria] *Economic and Financial Review,* June, 1964, p. 12.
4. Colin Legum describes Nigeria as "the only really 'open society' in the continent." Legum, "What Kind of Radicalism for Africa?" 43 *Foreign Affairs* 244 (1965).

CHAPTER II

1. 8 & 9 Geo. 6, c. 20 (1945). An act by the same name was passed in 1940, and others in 1949, 1950, and 1955.
2. Sources of external funds available to Nigeria for economic development in the public sector, up to 1954, were as follows: since 1900, £36 million had been raised by loans in London, of which £18 million went into the railway system, and £6.5 million into harbors (mostly pre-World War II). The only such postwar loan was made in 1951 and amounted to £6.8 million. By 1954, £14 million had been received as grants under the Colonial Development and Welfare Acts, of which £6.5 million had gone into welfare projects. Internal sources of financing, under the 1945 plan, were restricted almost entirely to the reserves of the commodity marketing boards, which, by 1954, had committed £34 million to economic development and research. See *Commonwealth Development and Its Financing, No. 5, Nigeria* (London: H.M.S.O., 1963).
3. Members are the federal prime minister, regional premiers, and the regional ministers concerned with economic development.
4. Arnold Rivkin, "Economic Development Planning in the Federation of Nigeria," 3 *Journal of Local Administration Overseas* 28 (1964).

5. *Ibid.*

6. This assumption of population growth rate was shaken by the 1963 census, which showed an annual increase, since the 1952-53 census, of 5.5 per cent. It is doubtful if this figure is correct, since comparable African nations show increases of 2 to 2.5 per cent.

7. It is generally accepted that adequate reserves are equal to the cost of a nation's imports for six months. Rivkin suggested, in 1961, that because of Nigeria's stable export earnings, it may require less. U.S. AID, *Special U.S. Economic Mission to Nigeria: Second Report* (Washington, Oct. 27, 1961), p. 71.

8. U.S. AID, *Special U.S. Economic Mission to Nigeria Report* (Washington, June 17, 1961), pp. 62-70, which discusses a series of papers presented to the Special Economic Mission by officials of the Nigerian government, laying out their tentative plans for the period 1962-66.

9. The plan was also influenced by the two surveys made by Rivkin and his associates, in 1961, on behalf of AID, which was considering the U.S. share of external financing of the plan (above nn. 7 and 8).

10. See *Report* (above, n. 8), p. 27.

11. *Federation of Nigeria National Development Plan 1962-68* (Lagos, 1962), p. 3.

12. *Ibid.*, pp. 22-24, and *Report* (above, n. 8), p. 29.

13. *Ibid.*

14. It is generally considered that a ratio of 3.5 or 4 to 1 obtains between savings and growth rate. Thus, 16 per cent annual savings is a precondition to a 4 per cent annual growth rate.

15. Under the 1955-61 Plan, 29.3 per cent went for administration.

16. H. M. A. Onitiri, "People and Plan in Nigeria," *West Africa*, Feb. 16, 1963, p. 182.

17. The External Loans Act, 1962, *Laws of Nigeria* A35 (1962), enables the Minister of Finance, in any manner authorized by the General Loan and Stock Act, 1960, to raise loans outside Nigeria not exceeding, in the aggregate, £300 million net of procurement costs, the proceeds to be paid into the Development Fund, where they must be employed in the federal portion of the 1962-68 Plan or may be on loan to regions where the regional authority has authorized the raising of such loans for development purposes approved by the regional legislature.

18. Additionally, the major technical assistance programs are those of the U.S., the U.K., the U.N. and its specialized agencies, Canada, the Ford Foundation, and the Rockefeller Foundation. Figures of these programs are not fully comparable to those for capital assistance or among themselves.

19. Cocoa, seed cotton, groundnuts, benniseed, soya beans, palm oil, and palm kernels.

20. About 60 per cent of Nigeria's revenues come from taxes on imports and exports. See *Report* (above, n. 8), p. 80, and note 26, below.

21. Under the Central Bank of Nigeria (Amendment) Act, 1962, *Laws of Nigeria* A77 (1962), "The value of the reserve external assets shall be not less than forty *per centum* of the total demand liabilities of the Bank." *Report* (above, n. 8), p. 34. At the close of 1963, total demand liabilities of the banking system were £133.2 million, against net foreign assets of £64.9 million. The latter declined from £75.4 million since December, 1962.

22. Public debt service on external loans is now relatively modest. In 1960-61, interest payments amounted to but £1.2 million; this is expected to peak in 1966-67, with interest and capital payments of £8.5 million due, but this amounts to only 5 per cent of expected exports for that year. A prudent public-debt service to earnings ratio, according to Rivkin, is fre-

quently suggested at 1 to 10 (or 10 per cent). The average external debt service cost over the next decade is estimated at only 2.5 per cent of exports.

23. Estimated for 1962-68 at £149.4 million.

24. See *Second Report* (above, n. 7), p. 30.

25. See the chapter on "The Western Region Crisis of 1962-63," p. 175.

26. Revenue, in 1962-63, fell £9 million short of expectations, owing to the decline in customs revenues because of increased duties and the rapid growth of import-substituting industries. Nigeria's heavy reliance on customs as a principal source of revenue is declining. In FY 1963-64, it was 61 per cent.

27. Described by the Minister of Finance in his 1964 budget speech. Federal Ministry of Information, *The National Budget* (1964), p. 5.

28. Under the Savings Bonds and Certificates Act, 1962, *Laws of Nigeria* A81 (1962), the Minister of Finance, "with a view to provide further facilities for the investment of small savings," may raise loans in Nigeria for the purposes of the development program. The Internal Loans Act, 1962, *Laws of Nigeria* A37 (1962), authorizes borrowing within Nigeria from other sources for the Development Fund, not to exceed £100 million.

29. Insurance (Miscellaneous Provisions) Act, 1964, and *Laws of the Federal Republic of Nigeria* A179 (1964).

30. *Ibid.*, §2. One-quarter of the life-insurance premiums invested in Nigeria must be invested in Nigerian government securities. With respect to general risk insurance, all policies of insurance or reinsurance, in respect of Nigerian risks, must be effected in Nigeria, to the extent that local underwriters provide the necessary coverage. General risk companies operating in Nigeria must, at all times, hold investments in Nigeria equal to 40 per cent of the previous year's gross premium income.

31. "This is partly due to the fact that the Nigerian public has not yet become accustomed to investment in stocks and shares. Moreover, the volume of personal savings is small and probably the small number of citizens who own an investible surplus are still able to find employment for their funds at yields higher than those obtainable on the Stock Exchange." Central Bank of Nigeria, *Annual Report and Statement of Accounts* (1963), p. 33. A knowledgeable observer in Lagos says that there is a great deal of capital controlled by chiefs and extended families but that it seeks 20 per cent or more return. The maximum rate of interest permitted on unsecured loans is 48 per cent per year, Moneylenders Ordinance, 1939, 4 *Laws of the Federation of Nigeria and Lagos* c. 124, §13(1)(c) (1958).

32. Douglas Gustafson, "Development of Capital Markets in Nigeria" (Unpublished paper written in the Sloan School of Management, Massachusetts Institute of Technology, Cambridge, Massachusetts, July, 1964).

33. 1 *Laws of the Federation of Nigeria and Lagos* c. 37, §242 (1958).

34. *The Nigerian Sugar Company Limited Prospectus* (Sept. 7, 1962).

35. National Provident Fund Act, 1961, *Laws of the Federation of Nigeria and Lagos*, A85 (1961).

36. The Trustee Investments Act, 1962, gives trustees the power to invest in debentures and paid-up stock of public companies subject to certain limitations that, in effect, make only blue-chip stocks quoted on the Lagos Stock Exchange available to trustees. *Laws of Nigeria* A45 (1962).

37. Federal Ministry of Information, *The Modernisation Budget* 14 (April 2, 1963), p. 14.

38. The Central Bank of Nigeria bought up 62 per cent of the Fourth Development Loan, amounting to £9.3 million, of which it had sold off £6.8 million by the end of the year. Other initial subscriptions were: banks, 0.7 per cent; marketing boards, 13 per cent; pension and provident funds, 19.5

per cent; insurance companies, 0.6 per cent; firms, schools, and individuals, 0.8 per cent.

39. The Treasury Bills Act, 1962, *Laws of Nigeria* A33 (1962), amending earlier acts, provides that the principal sums represented by outstanding treasury bills are not to exceed 40 per cent of the estimated federal revenue during the current year, rather than 20 per cent.

40. The original 1962 cost estimate of £68 million had risen to £72 million by 1964. The cost of resettling the one town and the dozen villages in the Niger Dam Basin alone will cost £3 million, according to a report in *West Africa*, Dec. 29, 1962. In the budget, £9 million is allotted for "reservoir clearance."

41. In the 1962 projections, £12.8 was allotted for transmission lines that will be the first stage of a national power grid.

42. Other power sources being exploited are natural gas deposits in the Eastern Region. A £1.5 million gas turbine power station is now under construction for the Port Harcourt power system.

43. At least 100,000 acres are expected to be brought under irrigation.

44. Navigation is to be made possible as far as Niamey, in Niger.

45. Additionally, the federal government is responsible for all levels of education in Lagos, where universal free primary education was introduced in 1955. Under the plan, 1700 primary-school classrooms, at a cost of £3.1 million, are to be built by 1968. While the number of elementary-school pupils in Lagos, in 1961, numbered 83,000, only 960 entered secondary schools in Lagos that year. The plan's objective is to create places at the secondary level for 15 per cent of those who complete primary school. Other federal expenditures for education include technical education (£1.1 million), teacher training (£0.8 million), and university scholarships (£5.4 million).

46. The University of Ife in the west; the University of Nigeria at Nsukka in the east, and Ahmadu Bello University at Zaria in the north. University education plans for the remainder of the 1962-68 period were critically re-examined, in 1963, by the National Universities Commission, *University Development in Nigeria, Report of the National Universities Commission* (1963). The government's decisions are found in *Sessional Paper*, No. 4, 1964.

47. *Plan* (above, n. 11), p. 270.

48. This is in addition to expenditures by native authorities at the local level.

49. The Northern Regional Plan states: "Much has been learnt by experience during the past years, the main lesson being that commercial enterprises to become viable and to attract private capital from outside sources must be freed from too close Governmental control." *Plan* (above, n. 11) [Northern Nigeria Development Programme], p. 142.

50. *Federal Government Development Programme, 1962-68, First Progress Report* (Lagos, 1964), also printed as *Sessional Paper*, No. 3, 1964.

51. At the 1962 cost estimates. If the additional £70 million is added to the federal government's 1962 share of £412 million, the total is £482 million, and £140 million represents less than one-third.

52. So named because it was the first loan made after Nigeria became a republic on October 1, 1963. Otherwise it would have been the Fifth Development Loan.

53. 7 *Federal Nigeria*, March-April, 1964, p. 7.

CHAPTER III

1. English statutes were brought into force in Lagos, in 1863, by Ordinance No. 3 of 1863, §§1-2. Ordinance No. 4 of 1876 applied the common

law, doctrines of equity, and statutes of general application, as of July 24, 1874, to Lagos, and Ordinance No. 17 of 1906 extended this body of law (per the 1876 Ordinance) to the Protectorate of Southern Nigeria, while a proclamation did the same with respect to the Protectorate of Northern Nigeria. The two latter regions were made into the Protectorate of Nigeria on January 1, 1914, and the Supreme Court Ordinance (§14) of that year reiterated the application of common law and equity but set the cut-off date for statutes of general application applicable to Lagos as March 4, 1863, and for the new amalgamated protectorate as January 1, 1900. See T. O. Elias, *Groundwork of Nigerian Law* (London, 1954), pp. 17-18.

2. Interpretation Act §45, 3 *Laws of the Federation of Nigeria and Lagos* c. 89 (1958). Similar provisions were inserted into the laws of the regions. In 1959, Western Nigeria codified its statutes with the result that, while English common law and equity still apply there, English statutes, as such, do not. Before the establishment of federalism in 1954, the application in Nigeria of this body of law was authorized by Supreme Court Ordinance, c. 211 §14 (1948). This has meant, according to T. O. Elias, "... the general principles of the English law of tort, contract and crime, mercantile and commercial law, land law (where applicable in whole or in part) and, of course, constitutional law, including law of public administration ... (and) the English law of evidence and procedure (civil and criminal)...." T. O. Elias, *British Colonial Law* (London, 1962), p. 4. See also "The Reception and Modification of English Law in Africa," in Anthony Allott, *Essays in African Law* (London, 1960), pp. 3-27.

3. "An Order in Council of 1887 had provided for the exercise in 'adjacent areas' of British jurisdiction in the 'Protectorate of Lagos,' but the legal basis, if any, for British jurisdiction in much of the southwest was quite vague. However, an Order in Council, July 24, 1901, declared all territory bounded by the French territories and the Northern and Southern Protectorates to constitute 'The Lagos Protectorate'.... [U]nless one simply accepts British power over all Nigeria as something that did exist, *de facto*, one is thrown back for legal sanction onto the Foreign Jurisdiction Acts.... Parliament (Westminster) has never legislated on the assumption of power in Nigeria." W. B. Hamilton, "The Evolution of British Policy toward Nigeria," in *The Nigerian Political Scene*, eds., Robert O. Tilman and Taylor Cole (Durham, N.C., 1962), p. 31.

4. Lord Lugard, *Report on the Amalgamation of Northern and Southern Nigeria and Administration*, 1912-19 (Cmd. 468, [1920]). The boundaries of Nigeria were defined by the Colony of Nigeria Boundaries Order in Council, 1913 (Nov. 22, 1913), and the Colony and Protectorate of Nigeria was established by the Letters Patent and Order in Council, 1914 (Jan. 1, 1914).

5. Incorporation of the Northern Cameroons into the Federation of Nigeria. Exchange of letters between the government of the United Kingdom and the government of Nigeria, May 29, 1961. Cmd. 1567 (1961).

6. See Allott (above, n. 2), p. 9, for a discussion of what a statute of general application is, and Elias (above, n. 1), p. 19.

7. 53 & 54 Vict., c. 37 (1890); 11 *Laws of the Federation of Nigeria and Lagos* c. 37 (1958). The Crown's power in relation to the protectorate rested on the Foreign Jurisdiction Act; with respect to the Colony of Lagos, it rested simply on the royal prerogative. A "protectorate" is defined as a territory in which jurisdiction, but not sovereignty, is exercised.

8. See, *e.g.*, Fugitive Offenders Act, 44 & 45 Vict., c. 69 (1881). Part II, §12 states, "This part of this Act shall apply to those groups of British possessions to which, by reason of their contiguity or otherwise, it may seem

expedient to Her Majesty to apply the same." The act, Part II, was extended to West Africa, including Nigeria, by the West African (Fugitive Offenders) Order in Council, 1923, 11 *Laws of the Federation of Nigeria and Lagos*, 308 (1958).

9. Allott (above, n. 2), p. 13. He states, further, that "It is a fundamental principle or practice of English constitutional law relating to the acquisition of dependent territories that existing bodies of law and rights held thereunder are, so far as possible, maintained in force after the acquisition, whether this is by settlement, conquest, cession, or the extension of protection."

10. *H.C.L.O.*, c. 80, §27(1)(1955); *W.R.H.C.L.*, c. 44, §12(1)(1955); *E.R.H.C.L.*, No. 27, 1955, §22(1); *N.R.H.C.L.*, No. 8, 1955, §34(1).

11. The Colonial Laws Validity Act, 28 & 29 Vict., c. 63 (1865); 11 *Laws of the Federation of Nigeria and Lagos* c. 63 (1958). This power of the Crown and the U.K. Parliament to legislate for Nigeria was abolished by the Constitution of 1960, First Schedule, paragraphs 1 and 2. On the meaning of "justice, equity and good conscience," see the contribution by that name written by J. Duncan M. Derrett, "Justice, Equity and Good Conscience," in *Changing Law in Developing Countries*, ed., J. N. D. Anderson (New York, 1963), pp. 114-53.

12. For a discussion of what English statutes are considered as applying in Nigeria, see the opinion of F. J. Brett, in *Larval v. Younan*, [1961] All N.L.R. 245: "With few exceptions, statutes which have been held applicable have this in common, that grave inconvenience would follow if they were held totally inapplicable...." *Ibid.*, p. 255.

13. Allott (above, n. 2), p. 24. Cf. A. E. W. Park, *Sources of Nigerian Law* (Lagos, 1963), p. 39: "It is, of course, highly desirable that the courts' decisions should always result in justice, but the duty imposed upon them is not a general one to administer justice, but rather to administer the rules of law they are directed to apply by the relevant statutory enactments; and in the absence of a statutory power to do so it is not legitimate for them to disregard that duty when they consider that the results of adhering to it would not be satisfactory."

14. Allott (above, n. 2), p. 27.

15. See above, note 9.

16. §3 of the Independence Constitution: Nigerian (Constitutional) Order in Council, 1960, *Laws of the Federation of Nigeria and Lagos*, at B221 (1960); § 156 (1) of the Independence Constitution; *Laws of the Federal Republic of Nigeria*, at A161 (1963). Hereinafter, the two constitutions are referred to as Independence Constitution and Republican Constitution.

17. See Elias (above, n. 2), pp. 32-34.

18. See Allott (above, n. 2), p. 32. For a number of years, the West African Court of Appeals, while it was in existence, could bind Nigerian courts. Since its abolition in 1954, and its replacement, in effect, by the federal Supreme Court, "its decisions constitute persuasive precedents only for the Federal Supreme Court, but bind all other courts within Nigeria." Park (above, n. 13), p. 61. Park also suggests that, since Nigerian independence, "the only English decisions binding in Nigeria are those of the House of Lords." *Ibid.*, p. 63.

19. Park (above, n. 13), p. 33.

20. *Ibid.*

21. Elias (above, n. 2), p. 35.

22. In *Solomon v. African Steamship Co.*, 9 N.L.R. 99 (1928), Petredes had said, "The Statutes of Limitations... were statutes of general application in force in England on January 1, 1900, and they, in common with other statutes of general application which were in force on that date, are, together

with the common law and the doctrines of equity which were in force in England on the same date, in force within the jurisdiction of this court. . . ."

23. Park (above, n. 13), p. 22.
24. 3 *Laws of the Federation of Nigeria and Lagos* c. 89 (1958).
25. Park (above, n. 13), p. 54.
26. *Ibid.*, p. 44.
27. On the hazards of using foreign cases, see David L. Grove, "The Sentinels of Liberty? The Nigerian Judiciary and Fundamental Rights," 7 *Journal of African Law* 152, 166 (1963).
28. The abolition in the 1963 Constitution of the appeal to the Privy Council, following widespread dissatisfaction with the council's reversal of the federal Supreme Court's decision in *Adegbenro v. Aderemi*, F.S.C. 187/1962, is in part symptomatic of this trend.
29. See e.g., the plea of the President of Nigeria "for a monistic system of *corpus juris Nigeriensis*," in Azikiwe, "Essentials for Nigerian Survival," 43 *Foreign Affairs* 447, (n. 2) (1965); also the youthful hope of a law student for "a legal system, practice and procedure made in Nigeria, for Nigerians by lawyers 'made-in-Nigeria.'" J. E. O. Kofi, "The Made-in-Nigeria Lawyer," 1 *The Lawyer* 49, 52 (1963) (Bulletin of the Students Law Society, University of Lagos).
30. Cf. the Israeli experience described by Erwin Shimron in *Proceedings: International Lawyers Convention in Israel, 1958* (Jerusalem, 1959), pp. 43-44: "[In 1948] the law of Palestine was still a conglomerate of various laws. . . . But while . . . the law was composed of sources of various national or religious origin, English law, statutory or judge-made, had become so predominant that it governed most legal branches in their entirety. . . . Three ways were open to the Israeli legislature: (a) to replace this foreign system by its national, Jewish law; (b) to adopt another foreign code; or (c) to continue the existing system. The legislature resorted to the latter course; it was obvious that a legal system could not be changed or replaced overnight. . . . The legal profession had been trained in the present system and would not have been capable of adapting itself to another law except after a lengthy period of transition. Moreover, it must have been apparent that some of the foremost characteristics of English law were its flexibility and adaptability, most desirable attributes of the law of a dynamic and expanding population."
31. See the discussion on pages 161-70.
32. Cf. *Ghana Commission of Enquiry, Final Report on the Working and Administration of the Present Company Law of Ghana* (1961).
33. The fact that the Moslem Northern Region is tied by religion to North African nations does not mean it shares their political philosophies or the liberal interpretation of Islam being fostered in some North African states. It will be some time before the north and its essentially feudal rulers will be agreeable to a dilution of their religion as they see it, or their power, which rests in a large part on the preservation of a "fundamentalist" Islam.
34. Allott (above, n. 2), p. 18.
35. (1919) A.C. 211.
36. Allott (above, n. 2), p. 13.
37. A tribe of the Philippine Islands.
38. Robert H. Lowie, *Primitive Society,* quoted in T. O. Elias, *The Nature of African Customary Law* (Manchester, Eng., 1956), p. 30. For an interesting and colorful account of a session of a Grade D court in Nigeria, see Paul Bohannon, *Justice and Judgment Among the Tiv* (New York, 1957), pp. 6 ff. Cases reported by Bohannon in Chapter III, "A Day in Court," p. 20, include a claim for the return of a wife, a demand for the return of a goat, a request

for a divorce, a claim for the return of bride-price, a matter concerning custody of a child, a debt, and an uncle's complaint against a nephew for exceeding the privileges of his status as nephew.

39. *Cole v. Cole,* 1 N.L.R. 15 (1898).
40. Elias (above, n. 38), p. 17.
41. See the chapter on "Land Tenure," p. 137.
42. Regarding the question of whether the decisions of English courts made after independence are binding on Nigerian courts, see p. 41.
43. Customary law and its application are, by virtue of the subject matter, under the control of the regional governments. Since customary law is omitted in both the exclusive and concurrent legislative lists of items within the control of the federal government, it falls within the powers of the regional governments. See The Schedule of the Republican Constitution, (above, n. 16).
44. *H.C.L.O.* §§5, 27(1)-(3) (1955). See Anthony N. Allott, ed., *Judicial and Legal Systems in Africa* (London, 1962), p. 48.
45. E.g., in the Penal Code of Northern Nigeria Criminal Code, provisions for the prosecution of Muslims who consume alcohol for other than medicinal purposes, §403. *Quaere,* whether this does not fall afoul of §28(1)(a) of the Republican Constitution, which prohibits discrimination, in the application of law, based on communal, tribal, religious, and political differences?
46. See J. N. D. Anderson, "The Future of Islamic Law in British Commonwealth Territories in Africa," 27 *Law and Contemporary Problems* 617 (1962). Islamic law may be applied in Western Nigeria as applicable customary law under *W.R.H.C.L.* c. 44, §12 (1955) or *C.C.L.* §§19, 20 (1957), and in the Eastern Region under *H.C.L.* §22 (1955) or *C.C.L.* §23(1)(a) (1956).
47. *N.R.H.C.L.* §34 (1955). The federation and the other regions once had similar provisions in their respective high-court laws.
48. "It is clear from the context...that the principles of justice, equity and good conscience were to be relevant only to the question of whether English or customary law should apply. It was not intended to give the courts an absolute discretion to impose in any case whatever solution they thought fit." Park (above, n. 13), p. 100. See *Cole v. Cole,* 1 N.L.R. 15 (1898).
49. This is the language of the *W.R.H.C.L.* c. 44, §12 (1955). The other statutes are identical except that the references are to "natives" and "non-natives." Lagos, *H.C.L.O.* §§5, 27(1), (2), (3) (1955); East, *H.C.L.* §22 (1955); North, *N.R.H.C.L.* §34 (1955).
50. *C.C.L.* §17 (1957).
51. *C.C.(A.)L.* §33 (1956).
52. *Ibid.*
53. *N.C.L.* §15(1) (1956).
54. See Allott (above, n. 44), pp. 55-74.
55. *N.C.L.* §2 (1956) defines a Moslem native court simply as one that customarily applies the principles of Moslem law. In 1961, there were 284 Alkali's courts and 448 non-Moslem native courts in the Northern Region. "Northern Region Survey," *Daily Times* (Lagos), July, 1961, p. 7. For an excellent history and description of the native court system in the first half of this century, see *Native Courts (Northern Provinces) Commission of Inquiry Report* (Lagos, 1952). As to how the system now operates, see M. J. Campbell, *Law and Practice of Local Government in Northern Nigeria* (London, 1963), pp. 84-88.
56. Thus, customary law having been incorporated as a code, there is no longer reference to custom as a source of criminal law. By statute, native

courts in the north are permitted certain latitude in criminal procedure, Penal Code, 1959 (*N.R.*, No. 18, 1959) and Native Courts (Amendment) Law, 1960 (*N.R.*, No. 10, 1960).

57. The Imam Malik, who died in 812 A.D., was one of four founders of "schools" of Islamic jurisprudence within the orthodox Sunni sect; their teachings became the basis of the four collections in which "the legal rules that go to make up the whole of Muhammadan jurisprudence are to be found ... recognized as orthodox because they are thoroughly in accord with the traditions and with the Koran...." See Khalil, ibn Ishaq, al-Jundi, *Maliki Law* (a summary from the French translation of the Muktasar of Sidi Khalil) with notes and bibliography by F. H. Ruxton (London, 1916).

58. Sharia Court of Appeal Law, 1960 (*N.R.*, No. 16, 1960).

59. Court of Resolution Law, 1960 (*N.R.*, No. 17, 1960, §2(1)).

60. In the north, at least. Provincial Courts Ordinance, 1914 (No. 7, 1914).

61. Elias (above, n.1), p. 365.

62. *Ibid.*

63. Regarding the extensive program in Northern Nigeria for the training of customary-court judges, see the letter of S. S. Richardson, Director of the Institute of Administration, Zaria, in 1 *The Lawyer* 82 (1963): "The sum total of the training effort has embraced between 3-4,000 people, of whom 1,000 have received periods of training at the Institute of three months or more."

64. In the early part of the century, lay representatives of parties were allowed to appear, but according to Dr. Elias, these "soon abused their privilege by turning 'busy lawyers' and often touting for custom. They were, however, soon put under control." Elias (above, n. 1), p. 134.

65. See Chapter VIII, at p. 145.

66. See Arthur Phillips, "The Future of Customary Law in Africa," in *The Future of Customary Law in Africa*, ed., Afrika-Instituut (Amsterdam, 1956), p. 100.

67. Alhaji Sir Ahmadu Bello, *My Life* (Cambridge, Eng., 1962).

68. *Ibid.*, p. 229. How chiefs are selected and how native authority councils under them are constituted and operate are succinctly described in four articles on "Native Administration" in *West Africa*, in successive weekly issues beginning September 29, 1962, at pp. 1073, 1099, 1137, and 1153. The author concludes, "So long as the Emir sits outside his gate every morning, so long as N.A. Councillors retain a sense of duty and keep in touch with the public interest and feeling; and so long as the village heads and their councillors are men of substance and of integrity (as they are); so long will the Native Authority system continue to serve the Northern Region as it has done for so many centuries."

69. Republican Constitution, §42(2).

70. *Ibid.*, §63.

71. *Ibid.*, §64.

72. §4 of the Republican Constitution specifies that, while Parliament may alter the constitution, with respect to certain sections including §42, it can do so only with consent of both houses of at least three regional legislatures.

73. Republican Constitution, §4(3).

74. *Ibid.*, Chap. II.

75. See "Courts Without Justice," *West Africa*, Oct. 27, 1962, p. 1177: "Although a recent statement by the Eastern Regional Government admitted that certain local government organs were used to victimise political opponents, customary courts in the Western Region, which are for most ordinary people the only courts they ever deal with, have, in recent years, become

notorious for their political discrimination." While political discrimination may be new, other forms of injustice are not; see *Native Courts (Eastern Region) Commission of Inquiry, Report* 15-16 (Lagos, 1953), pp. 15-16: "[A] large amount of evidence was tendered to us by the people of persecution, extortion, bribery, and corruption in the native courts."

76. For descriptions of the organization and functions of the Supreme Court, see Lionel Brett, ed., *Constitutional Problems of Federalism in Nigeria* (Lagos, 1961). The following also describe the Nigerian judicial system: Allott, (above n. 44), pp. 44-46; B. O. Nwabueze, *Machinery of Justice in Nigeria* (London, 1963), pp. 85-86, 178-94; W. C. E. Daniels, *The Common Law in West Africa* (London, 1963), pp. 84-97.

77. Republican Constitution, §114(1). The abolition of the appeal to the Privy Council is discussed on pp. 55ff.

78. *Ibid.*, §114(2). E.g., Emergency Powers (Jurisdiction) Act, 1962.

79. Republican Constitution, §116(a). The Supreme Court, until 1962, had statutory original jurisdiction in admiralty. This was transferred to the high courts by the Admiralty Jurisdiction Act, 1962, *Laws of Nigeria* A413 (1962).

80. Republican Constitution, §101.

81. *Ibid.*, §116(2).

82. *Ibid.*, §115. A distinction is made in §§115(1) and 115(2) between such a constitutional question's arising in a court below the high court, in which case reference to the Supreme Court is mandatory if, in the high court's opinion, a "substantial question of law" is involved, and its arising in a high court itself, where reference to the Supreme Court is discretionary, unless any party to the proceedings requests it.

83. Republican Constitution, §§117(2) and (3).

84. *Ibid.*, §117(4).

85. *Ibid.*, §§117(2)(f) and 117(4)(d).

86. *Ibid.*, §117(2)(a).

87. *Ibid.*, §117(2)(f)(i)-(iv).

88. *Ibid.*, §119.

89. *Ibid.*, §119(1)(c).

90. See Nwabueze (above, n. 76), pp. 156-77; Allott (above, n. 44), pp. 47, 50, 58 and 65.

91. Nwabueze (above, n. 76), p. 30; including Lagos as a "region," *ibid.*, p. 84. However, as Nwabueze notes elsewhere (at pp. 88ff.), the laws of the various regions are substantially similar, since the country was unitary until 1954, and variations have only recently occurred. The heritage of British law, the role of the Supreme Court, the existence of a single bar, and the fact that the police force of Nigeria is federal are factors tending to maintain unity. But there are important differences, particularly in the Western Region, owing to the law reform of the 1950's. The Supreme Court in an appeal must apply "the law applicable to the case in the Region from the High Court of which the appeal is brought." Federal Supreme Court (Appeals) Ordinance, 3 *Laws of the Federation of Nigeria and Lagos* c. 67, §3 (1958).

92. Republican Constitution, The Concurrent Legislative List, Item 22. Sheriffs and Civil Process Ordinance, 6 *Laws of the Federation of Nigeria and Lagos*, c. 189 (1958).

93. Sheriffs and Civil Process Ordinance (above, n. 92), Criminal Procedure Ordinance, 2 *Laws of the Federation of Nigeria and Lagos* c. 43 (1958).

94. Nwabueze (above, n. 76), p. 90.

95. Evidence Ordinance, 2 *Laws of the Federation of Nigeria and Lagos* c. 62 §§228-29 (1958).
96. Sheriffs and Civil Process Ordinance (above, n. 92), Part VII.
97. Nwabueze (above, n. 76), p. 157.
98. Brett (above, n. 76), pp. 14, 25; Nwabueze (above, n. 76), pp. 86-88.
99. In the Northern Region, the civil jurisdiction of magistrates was given to district courts, in 1960, by §18, Magistrates' Courts Law (Northern Region), 1960.
100. Arbitration Act, 1955, 1 *Laws of the Federation of Nigeria and Lagos* c. 13 (1958), applicable to Lagos and Northern and Eastern Nigeria; Western Nigeria has its own statute, *Laws of Western Nigeria* c. 8 (1959).
101. Nwabueze (above, n. 76), p. 145. Magistrates' courts were, in fact, created in 1933 to fill this function. Previously, commissioners of the Supreme Court, who were untrained colonial administrative officers, had been appointed to fill the gap.
102. E.g., in 1960, while the High Court of the Western Region decided 296 cases, and magistrates' courts decided 19,898; the High Court of the Eastern Region decided 565 cases, and magistrates' courts, 32,708.
103. Nwabueze (above, n. 76), p. 147. Since October 1, 1963, of course, the proclamation would be made in the name of the president.
104. *Ibid.*, p. 150.
105. See above, n. 100. This was a re-enactment of an earlier ordinance.
106. At the Supreme Court level, the case was styled *Akintola v. Governor of Western Nigeria and Adegbenro*, F.S.C. 187/1962, decided July 7, 1962; leave to appeal to the Judicial Committee of the Privy Council was granted on July 16, 1962. The decision of the Privy Council and a discussion of it by Dr. C. Ogwurike, Lecturer in Law, University of Nigeria, are contained in 7 *Journal of African Law* 95-108 (1963).
107. In December, 1962—somewhat tardily to save the situation—an African judge first became eligible to sit on the Judicial Committee of the Privy Council. This was the Chief Justice of Nigeria.
108. For a rationalization by a prominent Nigerian commentator, Ebenezer Williams, see his article in the Sunday *Post* (Lagos), June 2, 1963, p. 4. Williams' view was that the matter was political and that the Privy Council could only advise on the matter, that parliament was supreme, and "that there is no wisdom in a court or even a Privy Council passing a judgment which it is not in a position to enforce."
109. Constitution of Western Nigeria (Amendment) Law, 1963. "[J]ust an hour after the Privy Council's decision was known, a bill for an Amendment of the Constitution of Western Nigeria was hurriedly piloted through both Houses of the Western Legislature." Note, *Adegbenro v. Akintola*, 1 *The Lawyer* 75 (1963).
110. Essentially, the question was what meaning was to be given to §§33 (10) of the Western Region Constitution that reads, "... the Governor shall not remove the Premier from office unless *it appears to him* that the Premier no longer commands the support of a majority of members of the House of Assembly." The Nigerian Supreme Court held (Justice Brett dissenting) that the italicized words did not entitle the governor to refer to extraparliamentary indices of the premier's "lack of support," but that he could dismiss only on the basis of a parliamentary vote of no confidence. The Privy Council adopted Justice Brett's view that the plain language of §33(10) permitted the governor to rely on a letter or petition, signed by a majority of the members of the Assembly and submitted to the governor, as evidence of lack of support that authorized him to dismiss the premier, as, in fact, Governor General Sir Adesoji Aderemi (the Oni of Ife) had done.

111. *Daily Times* (Lagos), May 28, 1963, p. 16.
112. *Ibid.*, p. 15. See also the deputy premier's somewhat intemperate, but telling, argument against acceptance of extraparliamentary evidence of lack of support and the desirability of assuring parliamentary regularity for acts of such political consequence as removal of a premier. See also the comment of Dr. Ogwurike (above, n. 106), pp. 95, 99. "The [Privy Council] decisions came in less than two months short of a year after the Supreme Court decision, and at a time when it could be said that things were returning to normal in Western Nigeria. A reversion therefore to the *status quo ante* was bound to be regarded as a retrograde step—even though by strict law the right step—to take. Apparently, this was the motive behind the political solution.... Nevertheless as long as the Judicial Committee of the Privy Council is the final court of appeal on Nigeria's constitutional issues there is great danger in rejecting its decision or avoiding it by political actions."
113. Privy Council Appeal No. 13 of 1962. Judgment delivered July 3, 1963. Reported in 7 *Journal of African Law* 193-94 (1963).
114. The decision was announced by the prime minister in the House of Representatives on April 29, 1963.
115. §120 of the Republican Constitution provides: "Without prejudice to the provisions of section 101 [the executive prerogative of mercy] of this Constitution, no appeal shall lie to any other body or person from any determination of the Supreme Court." §114 of the 1960 Independence Constitution provided for appeals "to Her Majesty in Council." Before World War II, Ireland had abandoned all appeals to the Privy Council, and Canada had done so with respect to criminal cases. Since 1945, Burma, India, Pakistan, South Africa, Ghana, Cyprus, Tanganyika, and Nigeria have abolished all appeals. Only appeals on interstate disputes may go from the High Court of Australia to the Privy Council, "and on rare occasions an appeal can come direct from the Supreme Court of one of the Australian States. Of those retaining it at the moment the link is tenuous. Nigeria may go; Ceylon is not likely to stay indefinitely; Kenya will go the way of Tanganyika, and so in the end will Gambia and Sierra Leone." Louis Blom-Cooper, "Privy Council and Nigeria," *West Africa*, May 11, 1963, p. 511. Blom-Cooper notes Australian dissatisfaction with the 1947 Privy Council decision holding the Banking Act, 1947, unconstitutional: "Many Australians complained that English judges, adjudicating thousands of miles from the centre of political discussion, could not hope to understand the local issues and would thus fail to interpret the constitution in spirit as well as in fact."
116. B. O. Nwabueze, "Nigerian Appeals to the Privy Council," 4 *Nigerian Bar Journal* 19 (1963). The supremacy of a Privy Council decision for Nigerian courts was stated in *Thomas v. Ademola*, 18 N.L.R. 12, 23 (1945).
117. Independence Constitution, §114(1)(a), (b), (c) and (d).
118. *Ibid.*, §114(2)(a) and (b).
119. *Ibid.*, §114(3).
120. Blom-Cooper (above, n. 115), p. 115.
121. Nwabueze (above, n. 116), p. 23.
122. Independence Constitution, §106; Constitution of the Northern Region, §51; Constitution of the Western Region and the Constitution of the Eastern Region, §50. The regional constitutions may be found in the same volume where the Independence Constitution is found.
123. As witness the removal of the Chief Justice of Ghana by President Nkrumah in early 1964.
124. Independence Constitution, §120.
125. Constitution of the Northern Region, §53; Constitution of the Western Region and Constitution of the Eastern Region, §52.

126. Independence Constitution, §105(2)—Supreme Court; *ibid.*, §116(2) —High Court.
127. *Ibid.*, §105(1).
128. *Ibid.*, §116(1).
129. Constitution of India (1950), Art. 22, pars. 3(b), 4, and 5. Act IV of 1950 is the implementing statute.
130. Preventive Detention Act, 1964, replaced the original act, having the same title, of 1958, found in *Acts of Ghana* 87 (1958).
131. See *West African Pilot*, July 24, 1963, editorial, "The Rape of Democracy"; the *Daily Express* (Lagos) of July 24, 1963, in a front-page cartoon showed the Prime Minister of Nigeria joining Nkrumah, Verwoerd, and Nyerere, arms linked, in a "Preventive Detention Club." See also the account of opposition voiced by various groups, *Daily Express* (Lagos), July 25, 1963, p. 3.
132. *West Africa*, Aug. 3, 1963, p. 853.
133. See the article "Dangers of False Sense of Security" by Wole Soyinka of the University of Ibadan in the *Daily Express* (Lagos), July 30, 1963: "This independence of the Judiciary is not a thing to be traded for the temporary surrender of an obnoxious Bill—and this is what the power schemers have counted on."
134. The Premier of the Northern Region added insult to injury when, upon leaving Lagos after the conference, he said that a detention act was needed in Southern Nigeria but not in Northern Nigeria, where the people were "law-abiding citizens."
135. Grove (above, n. 27), pp. 152-71.
136. In Brett (above, n. 76), p. 21.
137. Grove (above, n. 27), p. 168. See also his article in 1 *The Lawyer* 11 (1963) regarding the Supreme Court's interpretation of the written constitution in the case of *Akintola v. Aderemi*, F.S.C. 187/1962.
138. Compare the qualification in the Rome Convention for the Protection of Human Rights and Fundamental Freedoms, e.g., Art. 9: "Freedom to manifest one's religion or beliefs shall be subject only to such limitations as are prescribed by law and are necessary in a democratic society in the interests of public safety, for the protection of public order, health or morals, or for the protection of the rights and freedoms of others."
139. §23 (private and family life), §24 (freedom of conscience), §25 (freedom of expression), §26 (peaceful assembly and association), §27 (freedom of movement). The following rights are not thus qualified: §18 (deprivation of life), §19 (inhuman treatment), §20 (slavery and forced labor), §21 (deprivation of personal liberty), §22 (due process), §28 (freedom from discrimination), §31 (compulsory acquisition of property). However, under §29, the rights under §§18, 21, 22, and 28 may be set aside during periods of emergency declared to exist under §70 of the Republican Constitution (§65 of Independence Constitution).
140. See *Director of Public Prosecutions v. Obi*, [1961] All N.L.R. 186, where a conviction under §§50-51 of the Criminal Code (sedition) was upheld as not in violation of Art. 24 of the constitution although it was not shown that the allegedly seditious expression would lead to disorder.
141. See Denys C. Holland, "Human Rights in Nigeria," *Current Legal Problems* 145 (1962).
142. Grove (above, n. 27), p. 170.
143. Republican Constitution, §1.
144. Grove (above, n. 27), p. 170.
145. See above, note 140.
146. Holland (above, n. 141), p. 153.

147. Criminal Code, §§50ff., 2 *Laws of the Federation of Nigeria and Lagos* c. 42 (1958).
148. Penal Code (Northern Region) Federal Provisions Ordinance, 1960 (No. 25 of 1960).
149. *D.P.P. v. Obi* (above, n. 140), p. 198.
150. F.S.C. 326/1961. Reported in 7 *Journal of African Law* 193 (1963). (1963).
151. *Laws of the Federation of Nigeria and Lagos,* No. 26, §251 (1961).
152. §§32 and 115 of the Republican Constitution. This holding was affirmed by the Privy Council, see p. 57.
153. F.S.C. 166/1962 (1962). Discussed in detail in Aliyi Ekineh, *Democratic Rights during a "Period of Emergency"* (Lagos, 1963), pp. 41-47.
154. *Ibid.*
155. [1961] All N.L.R. 209.
156. *Laws of the Northern Region,* No. 28, §§33-35 (1958).
157. [1961] All N.L.R. 273.
158. *Ibid.,* p. 274.
159. Cf. Gledhill's comment regarding India: "... India has taken the problem of enforcing Fundamental Rights more seriously than any other country and has provided the world with an object-lesson. . . . The enormous body of legal literature dealing with the scope of rights has been obtained at a heavy price. . . . Although the majority of cases filed in the Supreme Court are civil appeals, in the five months of 1961 pressure of other work prevented a single civil appeal from being heard... [T]he courts cannot cope with the volume of work... and the ordinary litigant... finds himself in the queue a long way behind the person claiming protection of a Fundamental Right." Alan Gledhill, "Fundamental Rights," in *Changing Law in Developing Countries,* ed., J. N. D. Anderson (New York, 1963), p. 94.
160. See the judgment of Chief Justice Mbanefo, in *Gokpa v. Inspector General of Police,* 1 All N.L.R. 424 (High Court, Eastern Region, 1961).
161. See the judgment of Justice Fatayi-Williams, in *Aoko v. Fagbemi,* [1961] All N.L.R. 400 (High Court, Western Region); cf. Chief Justice Ademola, in *Ojiegbe v. Ubani,* [1961] All N.L.R. 277 (Federal Supreme Court).
162. 7 A.C. 96 (1881).
163. [1961] All N.L.R. 203 at 217.
164. See above, note 140.
165. See below, note 169.
166. *D.P.P. v. Obi* (above, n. 140), p. 196 (emphasis added).
167. [1961] All N.L.R. 199.
168. *Ibid.,* p. 201 (emphasis added).
169. A number of prominent Nigerians, including several well-known academic figures and editors, were prosecuted for sedition during the period of the Western Region crisis of 1962-63. Among them was Dr. Olu Odumosu, the head of the Faculty of Law at the University of Ife and author of *The Nigerian Constitution: History and Development* (London, 1963). Dr. Odumosu's offense was the publication of an article critical of the report of the Coker Commission (see p. 191) entitled "What a Huge Document of Legal Inconsistencies." The editor of the newspaper in which the article appeared, the Lagos *Daily Express* (the Action Group newspaper), was also convicted. Both men were fined £100.

Sedition is defined by §50 of the Criminal Code (2 *Laws of the Federation of Nigeria and Lagos* c. 42 [1958]) as, *inter alia,* "to bring into hatred and contempt or to excite disaffection" against the government of Nigeria or that of any region, "or against the administration of justice in Nigeria." Sedition is not committed if the intent is "to point out errors or defects in the Government or constitution . . . or in legislation or in the administration of justice with a view to the remedying of such errors or defects." *Ibid.*, §50(2)(d)(ii).

170. Henry L. Bretton, *Power and Stability in Nigeria* (New York, 1962), p. 103.

171. Estimated at 800, in 1963, by the Ministry of Justice.

172. Only one Nigerian, apparently, ever took the English examination for solicitor, *Committee on the Future of the Nigerian Legal Profession Report* (1959), p. 2.

173. Legal Education Act, 1962, *Laws of Nigeria* A41 (1962). Members include the chief justice of Nigeria, the federal attorney general, and the attorneys general of the three Regions.

174. For the syllabus for the degree of law in Nigeria, see R. Y. Hedges, "Legal Education in West Africa," 7 *Journal of the Society of Public Teachers of Law* 75 (1961). Mr. Hedges, former chief justice of Western Nigeria, also wrote "The newly-fledged African lawyer who returns to Nigeria . . . is ill-equipped in many respects for the task he has to perform, and this through no fault of his own." *Ibid.*, p. 75.

175. The courses in law at Ahmadu Bello University are described in 7 *Journal of African Law* 116 (1963).

176. See *Report* (above, n. 172), pp. 5-6, paragraph 29: "The commission considers that this provision for the establishment of a Nigerian Bar Council by the members of the Association is admirable and . . . more in keeping with the independence of the profession than a body created by statute which could be amended at any time by the legislature." See also the comments of the attorney general of the Eastern Region on the role of attorneys general in the Nigerian Bar Association in the appendix on page 14 of the *Report*.

177. Legal Education Act (above, n. 173).

178. See Ekineh (above, n. 153), p. 51.

CHAPTER IV

1. J. D. Nyhart, "Notes on Entrepreneurship in Africa" (unpublished paper for Development Seminar, Center for International Affairs, Harvard University, Nov. 11, 1961), p. 4.

2. *Laws of the Federation of Nigeria and Lagos*, No. 17, A65 (1961) which was effective on October 1, 1961, and which repealed the Registration of Business Names Ordinance of 1930, 5 *Laws of the Federation of Nigeria and Lagos* c. 179 (1958).

3. See Nyhart (above, n. 1), pp. 6-7.

4. See Sayre P. Schatz and S. I. Edokpayi, "Economic Attitudes of Nigerian Business," 4 *Nigerian Journal of Economics and Social Studies* 257-68 (1962). When asked what they considered the chief obstacle to the formation of partnerships with other Nigerians, 266 respondents replied as follows: 196 (75 per cent)—"not financially trustworthy"; 48 (18 per cent)—"conflicts with partner"; 43 (16 per cent)—"insufficient capital." Comments included: "The spirit of cheating reigns supreme among us"; "The only reason is that honesty is still wanting among indigenous businessmen"; "Established businessmen prefer to stick to the assured small profit rather than to risk losing all to a dishonest partner. This conviction will not change until morals improve, both in the business and social sphere."

5. Guy Hunter, *The New Societies of Tropical Africa: A Selective Study* (London, 1962), p. 140.

6. Kilby estimated, in 1962, that a maximum of 10 per cent of industrial firms in the Eastern Region could be said to have "minimally adequate" book-

keeping systems. He found, "Such activities as carpentry, tinsmithing, blacksmithing and shoe repair are characterized by a complete absence of records. Baking firms, having a daily turnover and a multiplicity of financial transactions, usually possess the most comprehensive set of books relative to all other small industry activities." Peter Kilby, *The Development of Small Industry in Eastern Nigeria* (U.S. AID, Lagos, 1962).

7. T. O. Elias, *Groundwork of Nigerian Law* (London, 1954), p. 338.

8. *Ibid.*

9. Matrilineal succession survives in some isolated areas of Nigeria. This entitles children to inherit from their maternal uncles but not from their fathers. According to Elias, the system is "being rapidly abandoned as contrary to modern requirements and notions." *Ibid.*, p. 340.

10. Marriage Ordinance, 4 *Laws of the Federation of Nigeria and Lagos* c. 115, §36(1) (1958).

11. See the English Partnership Act, 1890 (53 and 54 Vict., c. 39, 1890), which presumably governs. In *Farhoud v. Chama*, 20 N.L.R. 166 (1953), the court found it unnecessary to decide whether the English act applied since it was merely declaratory of the common law. Western Nigeria has enacted its own Partnership Law, 1958, *Laws of Western Nigeria* c. 86 (1959), patterned on the English Act.

12. Companies (Federation) Act, 1 *Laws of the Federation of Nigeria and Lagos* c. 37 (1958).

13. *Ibid.*, §128(1).

14. *Ibid.*, §128(2).

15. A public company that operates over six months with less than seven members (in a private company, with only one) loses its limited liability with respect to those members cognizant of the deficiency. *Ibid.*, §122.

16. *Ibid.*, §115.

17. The Banking (Federation) Act, 1 *Laws of the Federation of Nigeria and Lagos* c. 19 §9(1) (1958), requires banks to publish their balance sheets and profit and loss accounts.

18. Companies Act (above, n. 12), §28(3).

19. *Ibid.*, §5.

20. *Ibid.*, §6.

21. *Ibid.*, §7.

22. L. C. B. Gower, *Commission of Enquiry on the Working and Administration of the Present Company Law of Ghana Final Report* (Accra, 1961), p. 5. Professor Gower expresses doubt as to whether reform of company law will influence foreign investors favorably and considers that taxation, foreign exchange control, and immigration are more important to the foreign investor. *Ibid.*, p. 9.

23. *Ibid.*

24. *Ibid.*

25. *Ibid.*, p. 6.

26. Ghana Company Code Bill §8 (Feb. 12, 1963).

27. *Ibid.*, §180.

28. *Ghana Report* (above, n. 22), p. 7.

29. *Ibid.*

30. *Federation of Nigeria National Development Plan 1962-68* (Lagos, 1962), p. 18.

31. This leaves only the unpopular and unsatisfactory—and perhaps illegal—management contract as a means of assuring control in a technically competent minority. *Quaere,* whether Ghana, or the developing nations, generally, are ready for "shareholder democracy," and, in fact, whether it is truly meaningful even in advanced industrial societies.

32. I.e., in the general sense of making things easier to accomplish. Ghana's specific legislation for the inducement of foreign investment is the Capital Investments Act, April 18, 1963 (Act 172).

33. *West Africa*, Dec. 8, 1962, p. 1357.

34. See Arnold Shuchman, *Codetermination: Labor's Middle Way in Germany* (Washington, 1957), pp. 207 ff.

35. "Submission to the Commission on Company Law Revision June, 1962" (unpublished report submitted August 27, 1962, by Peat, Marwick, Casselton, Elliot & Co., Chartered Accountants, Lagos & London).

36. The Companies Act, 1948, 11 & 12 Geo. 6, c. 38.

37. Board of Trade, *Report of the Company Law Committee* (London, 1962).

38. Kilby (above, n. 6).

39. *Ibid.*, p. 5.

40. Management consultation of limited scale and value has theoretically been available from federal and regional ministries of trade and commerce but, as a practical matter, has been limited to applicants for loans from the Federal Loans Board and similar regional institutions. The best source of advice is the U.S. AID mission in Lagos and the A. D. Little Co. team attached to it.

41. Of the minority who knew of government aids for business, 255, or 54 per cent, said it was too difficult to secure them. Difficulties were ascribed variously to "favoritism" (27 per cent), "don't know how to proceed" (25 per cent), "bribery required" (9 per cent), "red tape and lack of cooperation" (5 per cent). Schatz and Edokpayi (above, n. 4).

42. Kilby (above, n. 6), p. 7.

43. *Ibid.*, p. 13.

44. "The chief federal immigration officer may, if he deems it to be in the public interest, at any time revoke a residence permit or other permit under this Act...." §34(1), Immigration Act, 1963, *Laws of the Federal Republic of Nigeria* A26 (1963).

45. Federation of Nigeria, *Ministerial Statement on Nigeria's Economic Planning Policy and Its Relationship with Distributive Trades and Road Transportation* (Lagos, 1961).

46. Speech of Robert I. Fleming before the Nigerian-American Chamber of Commerce, Lagos, May 1, 1962.

47. Immigration Act (above, n. 44), §8(1)(b).

48. *Laws of Nigeria* A51 (1962).

49. Companies Act (above, n. 12), §239.

50. See the chapter on "Land Tenure," p. 137.

51. However, if the buyer establishes "a place of business," he will presumably be required to register his company, incorporated outside Nigeria, under §239 of the Companies Act.

52. Lawrence J. Eckstrom, *Licensing in Foreign & Domestic Operations* (Essex, Conn., 1964). See also Lawrence J. Eckstrom, "Industrial Foreign Licensing Arrangements," in *A Lawyer's Guide to International Business Transactions*, eds., Walter S. Surrey and Crawford Shaw (Philadelphia, 1963), p. 95.

53. Revision of trademark legislation has been under consideration for some time and may be adopted during 1965. The new act will probably adopt the "registered user" system that prevails in most Commonwealth countries and which permits licensing. This was recommended by the Federation of British Industries team that surveyed Nigeria in 1961 (Federation of British Industries, *Nigeria: An Industrial Reconnaissance*, 1961). Under the "registered user" system, only registered trademarks may legally be licensed,

and the licensee must be registered to protect the licensor's interest. Failure to comply with either requirement can result in the loss of the licensor's ownership of the trademark. See Surrey and Shaw (above, n. 52), pp. 118-19.

54. Convention of Union of Paris of March 20, 1883, as revised, for the Protection of Industrial Property, done at Lisbon, Oct. 31, 1958. 1 U.S.T. 1; T.I.A.S. No. 4931. The 1925 revision was previously applicable to Nigeria. See U.S. Department of State, *Treaties in Force* (1964), pp. 250-51.

55. Done at Geneva, Sept. 6, 1952. 6 U.S.T. 2731. Effective with respect to Nigeria, Feb. 14, 1962. U.S. Department of State, *Treaties in Force* (1964), p. 304.

56. 6 *Laws of the Federation of Nigeria and Lagos* c. 182 (1958).

57. However, no action will lie for infringement in Nigeria antedating the Nigerian registration, §7.

58. 7 Edw. 7, c. 28 (1907) to 22 & 23 Geo. 5, c. 32 (1932).

59. Designs (Protection) Ordinance, 6 *Laws of the Federation of Nigeria and Lagos* c. 204 (1958).

60. *Ibid.,* §2.
61. *Ibid.,* §3.
62. *Ibid.*
63. *Ibid.,* §4(2).
64. Unreported, but cited in *W. B. McIvor & Co., Ltd., v. Compagnie Française de L'Afrique Occidentale,* 3 N.L.R. 18 (1917).
65. Trademarks Ordinance, 6 *Laws of the Federation of Nigeria and Lagos* c. 199 (1958).
66. The purpose was frankly to protect the Manchester cotton industry.
67. Above, n. 64.
68. *Johnson v. Orr-Ewing,* 7 A.C. 291 (1903).
69. *Ibid.*
70. Now, as then, §49 of the Trade Marks Ordinance (above, n. 65).
71. This provides for a means of contesting the refusal to register of the Registrar of Trademarks, which is a necessary predicate to the infringement action.
72. *Walkden & Co. v. Oshodi and Radcliffe, Ltd.,* 4 N.L.R. 105 (1923). §52 of the Trade Marks Ordinance (above, n. 65) specifically so provides.
73. *Montgomery v. Thompson,* 1891 A.C. 217.
74. Elias (above, n. 7), p. 263.
75. Trademark law is exclusively within the province of the federal government; see Part I of the Schedule of the Republican Constitution, The Exclusive Legislative List.
76. Trade Marks Ordinance (above, n. 65), §10(1).
77. *Ibid.,* §10(2).
78. *Ibid.*
79. *Ibid.,* §13.
80. *Ibid.,* §12.
81. *Ibid.,* §44.
82. *Ibid.,* §28.
83. *Ibid* §63(1). §63A(1) makes special provision for trademarks registered under Part I of the English Trademarks Act, 1919, 9 & 10 Geo. 5, c. 79 (1923), giving priority if the Nigerian application is made within four months of the British application.
84. *Ibid.,* §15(2).
85. *Ibid.,* §18.
86. *Ibid.,* §49.

Notes 215

CHAPTER V

1. See F. A. Wells and W. A. Warmington, *Studies in Industrialization: Nigeria and the Camerouns* (Oxford, 1962). A study therein of the African Timber and Plywood Co. in Sapele dispels two of these generalizations, absenteeism and turnover. See also P. A. L. Chukwumah, "Developments in the Search for Higher Productivity in Africa," Seminar on Manpower Problems in Economic Development with Special Reference to Nigeria, Lagos, March 2-13, 1964: "The rates of absenteeism and labour turnover, particularly absenteeism, have been shown to be much less than was commonly supposed before this investigation began. With some exceptions the verified rates prove to be not dissimilar to those experienced in technologically-advanced countries..." (p. 7).

With respect to productivity, see [Nigerian] National Manpower Board, *Report on Nigerian National Seminar on Productivity*, February 12-14, 1963, pp. 6-14: "Most of the operatives [at the West African Portland Cement Co. plant] are illiterates who were trained in their native language (Yoruba) for a period of 3 weeks. It was observed that their productivity was exactly equal to, and sometimes better than, that of their U.K. counterparts, in a timed operation requiring regularity of sequence rather than particular skill" (p. 6). "The training of the African managerial staff [at Nigerian Brewery, Ltd.] is done partly in Nigeria and partly in Europe; and it is the organisation's experience that in terms of the response of subordinate staff and output, there is no significant difference in the effectiveness of the European and the African manager" (p. 7).

2. "Compulsion was, however, confined to recruiting labour for public employment. In 1919 Lugard . . . stated that the Government will not employ it in order to procure labour for private undertakings." T. M. Yesufu, *An Introduction to Industrial Relations in Nigeria* (London, 1962), p. 9, n. 13.

3. In 1933, Nigeria passed the Forced Labour Ordinance to implement "some provisions" of the 1930 Forced Labour Convention of the International Labour Organization. However, "a few forms of compulsory labour were still legal in Nigeria, if requested by Chiefs who were entitled to them by native law and custom for specified purposes, and for porterage for (and sometimes of) administrative officers." Yesufu (above, n. 2), p. 10. All forms of forced labor, except in connection with essential communal works of a restricted nature or that required of persons under criminal sentence, were abolished by 1956. *Ibid.*

4. Henry L. Bretton, *Power and Stability in Nigeria* (New York, 1962), p. 96.

5. In 1962, Yesufu (above, n. 2), p. 14, basing his estimates on a population of 40 million, estimated total wage earners at 700,000 to 800,000, or 2 per cent of the population. The 1963 survey of the National Manpower Board estimated the total at only 550,000 (see below, n. 11).

6. It is extremely doubtful if the figures of the 1963 census are any more accurate than those of the 1962 census, which were discarded; a new census was ordered when suspicion was cast on the reliability of the figures. The returns in both enumerations were probably inflated for political purposes, reflecting regional competition for the control of government, through representation in the federal Parliament based on population. The true population of Nigeria is probably between 45 and 50 million.

The 1963 census gave the population as 55.6 million, as shown below. Figures for the first census, made in 1952-53, are given for comparative purposes:

	1952-53	1963
North	17,153,000	29,777,986
East	7,229,000	12,388,646
West	6,144,000	10,278,500
Mid-West*		2,533,337
Lagos	277,000	675,352
TOTAL	30,803,000	55,653,821

* New state, created in 1963 out of part of Western Nigeria.

7. The category is deceptive. Only a very small proportion of this group was engaged in fishing.
8. Federal Ministry of Labour, *Report on Employment and Earnings Enquiry*, 1961, Table B.
9. *Ibid.*, Table D.
10. *Ibid.*, paragraph 12.
11. Figures given hereafter for 1963 employment are taken from the survey as found in the various papers presented at the Seminar on Manpower in Economic Development with Special Reference to Nigeria, Lagos, March 2-13, 1964, especially that presented by the National Manpower Board entitled "Nigeria's High Level and Skilled Manpower, 1963-68" (draft report).
12. The emphasis must be on "relative." It is common to hear in Nigeria that labor costs are high in terms of productivity, despite other evidence to the contrary (see above, n. 1). The examples given are usually of unskilled labor, which almost everywhere in Nigeria is poorly supervised.
13. Federal Ministry of Commerce and Industry, *Industrial Labour*, 1963, p. 2.
14. See pp. 104-8.
15. *Industrial Labour* (above, n. 13), p. 2.
16. See Yesufu (above, n. 2), pp. 11-12: "Thus the escape which wage earning provides from uncertain harvests, the respect which the village often gives to the travelled man, as well as the attraction of the products of modern civilization—Gramophones, bicycles, cinemas, electric lights, and pipeborne water supplies in the towns—it is these which provide the current promptings to accept wage earning employment."
17. 3 & 4 Geo. 6, c. 40 (1940).
18. The courses are based on the Intermediate Standard of the City and Guild of London Institute Examination and the Federal Ministry of Labor Trade Syllabuses. United Africa Company also uses the London examinations in its apprenticeship program.
19. The Ministry of Labor administers standardized tests throughout Nigeria for the evaluation of skill-levels, which are used in screening applicants.
20. *Industrial Labour* (above, n. 13), p. 6.
21. "The apprenticeship system is a basic feature of small industry. Of 160 firms interviewed employing 1,741 individuals, 30 per cent of the latter were apprentices. Some industries, however, do not employ apprentices. Thus, if baking, soap-making and umbrella assembly are removed from the sample, apprentices rise to 50 per cent, and if manager/owners are also dropped the figure increases to 66 per cent.

"The age of the entering apprentice ranges from 12 to 20 years. The majority have had several years of primary schooling. Relatives tend to start at an earlier age and serve a longer term. For non-relatives, apprenticeship lasts from 3 to 5 years and requires a premium or learning fee varying from £5 to £15 depending on the trade and the length of the agreed term—the shorter the term the higher the fee. Apprentice remuneration—pocket allowance, subsistence or use of facilities for after-hours jobs—occurs in most cases." Peter Kilby, *The Development of Small Industry in Eastern Nigeria* (U.S. AID, Lagos, 1962), p. 11.

22. Professor Frederick H. Harbison of Princeton University is the author of the definitive and highly useful study on "High-Level Manpower for Nigeria's Future," published as part of the so-called *Ashby Report*, Federal Ministry of Education, *Investment in Education, The Report of the Commission on Post-School Certificate and Higher Education* (1960). For a summary of the *Ashby Report* and the recommendations accepted by the government and subsequently incorporated into the 1962-68 Development Plan, see *Educational Development, 1961-70*, Sessional Paper No. 3 of 1961 (Lagos, 1961).

23. Archibald Calloway, "Human Resources and Economic Development in Nigeria," in *The Nigerian Political Scene*, eds., Robert O. Tilman and Taylor Cole (Durham, N.C., 1962). Professor Calloway relies heavily on Professor Harbison's report.

24. *Ashby Report* (above, n. 22), pp. 51-52. Harbison defines "high-level" manpower both functionally (administrators, executives, and managers; professional personnel; technical, sub-professional, and supervisory personnel; teachers; armed forces and police officers; judges, government ministers, legislators, and local government staff) and in terms of educational background—a minimum of two years of post-school certificate work. High-level manpower is further divided into senior and intermediate. With respect to senior high-level manpower, Harbison says, "Increasingly, a university degree, or advanced teachers' college degree, or its equivalent, would be required for senior posts of this kind." *Ibid.*, p. 52.

25. *Ibid.*, p. 66; Calloway (above, n. 23), p. 210.

26. However, automation does not appear to present a problem to the individual entrepreneur vis-à-vis the government or unions. In 1964, one manufacturer, for example, was planning the introduction of machine-wrapping of his product, which would displace seventy workers. He said confidently that he expected no difficulties in making the change.

27. Calloway (above, n. 23), pp. 214-15. He estimates that, by 1970, "those engaged in factories cannot be expected to exceed 7 per cent of the then gainfully employed population." *Ibid.*, p. 225.

28. *Laws of the Federal Republic of Nigeria* A11 (1963). Under the prior 1947 ordinance, quotas were established informally and were enforced through the power to establish conditions of entry, to prosecute for breach of condition, and to deport after conviction.

In introducing the 1963 bill in Parliament, the Minister of Internal Affairs assured "all foreign investors in this country that the purpose of our Immigration Bill is not, in any way, to jeopardize their business interests. It is designed, however, to ensure that only in those categories... of employment which cannot be filled adequately by Nigerian citizens, and only in respect of those enterprises not adequately served by Nigerians will permission be granted for non-Nigerians to be employed or to participate." *West Africa*, April 13, 1963.

29. *Ashby Report* (above, n. 22), p. 186.

30. *West Africa*, Aug. 18, 1962. These were figures released to Commons in the United Kingdom. The actual totals were probably larger, since these included only "pensionable" officers.

31. *Advisory Committee on Aids to African Businessmen Report* (Lagos, 1959).

32. The report also criticized Levantines for speculation in real property and complained of their ready access to bank credit. Lagos bankers confirm that Levantine and Asian merchants are considered to be excellent risks.

33. Retrenchment in the distributive trade is not without its difficulties. As UAC closed down trading installations, it was required that workers who had no transferable skills be dismissed. This occasioned sharp criticism from politicians and unionists. See *West African Pilot,* July 6, 1962, p. 8.

34. In manufacturing establishments having 40 or more employees and in non-manufacturing establishments having 100 or more. The total surveyed was 344,000.

35. For some interesting observations on the position of women in African society and their problems in an emancipating, urbanizing society, see Guy Hunter, *The New Societies of Tropical Africa: A Selective Study* (London, 1962), pp. 78-91.

36. The 1960 survey showed that 42.4 per cent of Nigerian wage earners were employed by the federal, regional and local governments.

One result of the 1964 wage agreement (discussed below) was that minimum wage legislation should be established.

37. E.g., statistics on wages for unskilled labor compiled, in 1962, for such jobs as watchman, janitor, and truckloaders varied from 4 shillings and 4 pence (about 60¢) per day to 7 shillings and 6 pence ($1.05) per day "depending upon the type of industry and the location of industry in Nigeria." *Industrial Labour* (above, n. 13), p. 10. See also the varying minimum wage rates set by the agreement of June 29, 1964, p. 115.

38. Wages Boards Ordinance, 6 *Laws of the Federation of Nigeria and Lagos* c. 211 (1958).

39. *Ibid.,* §3(1).

40. Except with respect to employees of regional local government councils, native authorities, and certain public employees of the Western Region. *Ibid.,* §3(1).

41. *Ibid.,* §5.

42. Orders in Council were made under Chapter XIII of the old Labor Code Ordinance, repealed by the Labor Code Ordinance of 1946, 3 *Laws of the Federation of Nigeria and Lagos* c. 91 (1958).

43. Such orders survived the new ordinance by virtue of §20 of the Interpretation Ordinance, 3 *Laws of the Federation of Nigeria and Lagos* c. 89 (1958).

44. See, e.g., the minimum wage rates set, in 1957, for the "retail and ancillary trades in Lagos," 10 *Laws of the Federation of Nigeria and Lagos* c. 211 (1958).

45. Commissions of Inquiry Ordinance, 1940, 1 *Laws of the Federation of Nigeria and Lagos* c. 36 (1958).

46. The Mbanefo Commission surveyed the rates in the Federal, Eastern, and Northern Regions, while the Morgan Commission surveyed the Western Region.

47. Between 1945 and 1954, rates were increased by 50 to 300 per cent.

48. A commission may be appointed by the president to look "into any matter in respect of which, in his opinion, an inquiry would be for the public welfare." Commissions of Inquiry Ordinance (above, n. 45), §2(1).

49. The Building and Civil Engineering National Joint Industrial Council, to which both major contractors and trade unions belong. The rates were effective July 1, 1960, and have long since been outdistanced.

50. Labor Code Ordinance (above, n. 42), §125.

51. *Ibid.*, §128.
52. See discussion p. 114.
53. Before 1957, this was done by Orders in Council. Standing orders setting wages and hours for certain industries have generally been superseded. They provided 1.25 pay for normal overtime, 1.5 time for Sundays and "work-free" days, and double-time on public holidays.
54. The legislative lists are contained in the Schedule (Annex) of the Independence Constitution of 1960 and the Republican Constitution of 1963.
55. 6 *Laws of the Federation of Nigeria and Lagos* c. 200 (1958).
56. *Ibid.*, c. 201 (1958). Following creating of the federation, this ordinance was given federal application by the Trades Disputes (Arbitration and Inquiry) (Federal Application) Act, 1957. *Ibid.*, c. 202 (1958).
57. *Ibid.*, c. 222 (1958).
58. Labor Code Ordinance (above, n. 42).
59. Yesufu (above, n. 2), p. 25.
60. 3 *Laws of the Federation of Nigeria and Lagos* c. 66 (1958).
61. 6 *Laws of the Federation of Nigeria and Lagos* c. 211 (1958).
62. Yesufu (above, n. 2), p. 160.
63. These acts provide for survival of the cause of action after the death of the injured. Fatal Accidents Law (Eastern Region) of 1956, 1 *Laws of Eastern Nigeria*, No. 16 (1956); Fatal Accidents Law (Northern Region) of 1956, *Laws of the Northern Region of Nigeria*, No. 16 (1956); Fatal Accidents Law (Western Region), *Laws of Western Nigeria* c. 112 (1959).
64. Labor Code Ordinance (above, n. 42), §3.
65. *Ibid.*
66. *Ibid.*, §215(1). The court has jurisdiction if the parties are before it, regardless of where the cause arose in Nigeria, §215(2).
67. *Ibid.*, §214, gives the term the same meaning as in the Trades Disputes (Arbitration and Inquiry) Ordinance, 6 *Laws of the Federation of Nigeria and Lagos* c. 201 (1958). "Trade dispute means any dispute of difference between employers and workmen, or between workmen and workmen connected with the employment or nonemployment, on the terms of the employment, or with the conditions of labour of any person...."
68. Labor Code Ordinance (above, n. 42), §215(1).
69. *Ibid.*, §§125 ff.
70. E.g., *ibid.*, §34 (hours of work and overtime prescribed in the ordinance). See also §§45(7) and 47(1) and (2).
71. E.g., *ibid.*, §91 (recruitment). Federal action pre-empts the field in case of conflict.
72. E.g., if the federal government has not acted; *ibid.*, §183(3) (clerical service) and §184(2) (domestic service). If the federal authority approves, §138 (apprenticeship) and §210 (registration of workers).
73. Yesufu (above, n. 2), p. 20.
74. Provident Fund Act, *Laws of the Federation of Nigeria and Lagos* A85 (1961).
75. *Ibid.*, Third Schedule.
76. *Ibid.*, §12.
77. 5 *Laws of the Federation of Nigeria and Lagos* c. 147 (1958).
78. Provident Fund Act (above, n. 74), Second Schedule.
79. *Ibid.*, §8.
80. *Ibid.* See also First Schedule.
81. *Ibid.*, §§29 ff.
82. *Ibid.*, §30. However, by decision of the Minister of Finance, investment for the present is restricted to government obligations.
83. *Ibid.*, §31(3).

84. *Ibid.*, §35.
85. *Ibid.*, §36. The statute runs for six years from due date.
86. *Ibid.*, §43(1) and (2).
87. *Ibid.*, §44.
88. *Ibid.*, §11(4).
89. A majority of the workers must signify the desire for coverage. §11(2) provides for such a group to abandon voluntary coverage in the same way.
90. Provident Fund Act (above, n. 74), §11(3).
91. *Laws of the Federation of Nigeria and Lagos* A349 (1960), adding §27A to the Labor Code. Effective Jan. 26, 1961.
92. 3 *Ministry of Labour Quarterly Review* 46 (Dec., 1961).
93. The Nigerian Civil Service Union, whose stated purpose was to "promote the welfare and interests of Native members of the Civil Service." It was preceded by a similar union in Sierra Leone, and, at the inaugural meeting, it was stated "that similar Institutions existed in the old Lagos Colony and in the old Southern Nigeria Protectorate." Yesufu (above, n. 2), pp. 34, 37 .
94. *Ibid.*
95. Railway workers had formed a Mechanics Union in 1921.
96. There are exceptions, of course, but leadership "in depth" has never existed. Chief Awolowo, the imprisoned Action Group leader, and the present Minister of Labor, Chief J. M. Johnson, are two prominent Nigerians who came out of trade-union ranks. But this is one of the basic problems: the movement fails to hold its best men. Yesufu cites the cases of six union officials who were sent to the U.K. on scholarship. Three returned and joined the civil service, two secured jobs with private industry, and one took up the study of law. *Yesufu* (above, n. 2), p. 96.
97. Yesufu points out, "Other factors which militate against the organization of strikes by unions evidently include the size of the country, the difficulty of communication, and the prevalence of a large proportion of illiterate workers." *Ibid.*, p. 56.
98. §1(2)(a), 3 & 4 Geo. 6, c. 40 (1940): "...that the law of the colony provides reasonable facilities for the establishment and activities of trade unions."
99. 6 *Laws of the Federation of Nigeria and Lagos* c. 200 (1958).
100. Yesufu (above, n. 2), p. 39. While a number of Nigerian trade unionists were detained for varying periods during the war, the unions themselves remained intact and, indeed, flourished.
101. Oddly enough, the Nigerian Civil Servants Union, formed in 1912, did not register until March 7, 1949. This fact was criticized by the Tudor Davies Commission as "an anomaly and a disregard of the Ordinances by the Trade Union and by the Registrar." *Ibid.*, p. 36.
102. From a joint statement issued before the meeting, quoted in *ibid.*, p. 46.
103. Hunter says, "There is...a general likelihood that the A.A.T.U.F. will be neutralist in fact as well as in name, though much divided internally and with a strong left-wing element." Hunter (above, n. 35), p. 220. J. K. Tettegah, Secretary General of AATUF, as well as of the Ghana Trades Union Congress, was denied entry into Nigeria in 1962, presumably on security grounds.

CHAPTER VI

1. Ministry of Information, *Mobilisation Budget* (1962), p. 35.
2. "I am sometimes asked why I do not raise the rates of tax, particularly

for companies. . . . (I)t would not be in the national interest to raise company taxes at a time when we are seeking to encourage massive capital investment in industry—the present tax in practice gives Government a 40 percent stake in profits without investing a penny. . . ." *Ibid.*, p. 31.

3. §32 of the Companies Income Tax Act, *Laws of the Federation of Nigeria and Lagos* A157 (1961). The 1961 act combines the former Income Tax Act and Income Tax Administration Act, and it became effective April 1, 1961. Taxes on oil companies are regulated by the Petroleum Profits Tax Act, 1959, which established the 50-50 sharing of profits on oil production.

4. To compare the rates of other developing countries, see Walter H. Diamond, *Foreign Tax and Trade Briefs* (New York, 1960). E.g., Ghana charges a flat tax of 45 per cent on 7.5 per cent of a corporation's turnover that arises in Ghana or, if originating abroad, is brought into Ghana. Taxable income cannot be less than 2 per cent of turnover, whether or not a profit has been made. A 2.5 per cent tax is levied on remissions of profits by branches to the home office abroad, and a 20 per cent withholding tax is imposed on the remission abroad by Ghanaian subsidiaries of foreign parents.

5. Companies Income Tax Act (above, n. 3), §26(1)(k).

6. Republican Constitution §76(1), included by Item 44 in the (federal) Exclusive Legislative List (The Schedule, The Legislative Lists, Part I) appended to the constitution, found in *Laws of the Federal Republic of Nigeria* A167 (1963).

7. *Ibid.*, §76 (by implication; the Independence Constitution specifically so provided in §70[1]). The taxation of individuals by the regions is, nevertheless, regulated as to legal rules and criteria but not rates of taxation, by the Income Tax Management Act, *Laws of the Federation of Nigeria and Lagos*, A105 (1961). W. R. Cotter, "Taxation in Nigeria" (mimeographed, M.I.T. Fellows in Africa Program, Oct., 1963) suggests that this act foreshadows federal regional conflict over the definition of taxable income, including individual liability for tax on corporate dividends, and the matter of governmental tax immunities.

8. Companies Income Tax Act (above, n. 3), §§55-60. The Board of Appeal consists of eight commissioners.

9. *Ibid.*, §59(1).

10. *Ibid.*, §59(11).

11. Special provisions are made for assessing the income of new businesses and businesses ceasing to do business. See *ibid.*, §30.

12. *Ibid.*, §61(1).

13. *Ibid.*, §18(1).

14. Experience in allocation of income should not be long in forthcoming. According to a survey made in 1962-63, "About 81 per cent of investment in fixed assets of companies possessing foreign interests was in subsidiaries, the remainder equally divided between branches and other forms of organization." "Foreign Investment Survey," [Central Bank of Nigeria] *Economic and Financial Review*, June, 1964, pp. 10-14. "Other forms of organization" are believed to be chiefly joint ventures.

Since the extensive tax benefits described below are available only to companies incorporated in Nigeria, the foreign investor usually does business through a subsidiary organized as a Nigerian corporation. However, those doing business through branches should note that §18(2) of the Companies Income Tax Act (above, n. 3) provides. "The profits of a company other than a Nigerian company from any trade or business shall be deemed to be derived from Nigeria to the extent to which such profits are not attributable to any part of the operations of the company carried on outside Nigeria."

15. Companies Income Tax Act (above, n. 3), §23(a).

16. Income Tax Relief Act, 3 *Laws of the Federation of Nigeria and Lagos* c. 87 (1958), which superseded the Aid to Pioneer Industries Act of 1952 and was continued in effect by the act of 1961 (above, n. 3).

17. A list of industries that were declared pioneer up to June 30, 1962, may be found in Ministry of Commerce and Industry, *Handbook of Commerce and Industry in Nigeria* (5th ed., 1962), pp. 320-24.

18. The company's Articles of Association must not prohibit, during the pioneer status, the acquisition of company stock by the federal or regional governments or by Nigerian citizens.

19. The pioneer industry certificate may be canceled if the company fails to fulfill any estimate or proposals made in its application for pioneer status.

20. Income Tax Relief Act (above, n. 16), §9.

21. The original agreement was oral and pertained to interest on loans. It was later published in the Official Gazette, Aug. 9, 1962, exempting "interest on any money lent by a company other than a Nigerian company ... (or) by an individual ... resident outside Nigeria." By a subsequent letter, the acting secretary of the Federal Board of Inland Revenue stated that these benefits were transferable and that exemptions extended to cover any of the debenture stock issued, provided the debenture stockholder is a company other than a Nigerian company or is an individual, executor, or trustee resident outside Nigeria.

22. Companies Income Tax Act (above, n. 3), §26(2) provides: "The Minister may exempt by order (a) any company or class of companies from all or any of the provisions of this Act, or (b) from tax any profits of any company or class of companies from any source, on any ground which appears to him sufficient."

See, e.g., Legal Notice No. 13 of 1962 (under Companies Income Tax Act, 1961), Income Tax (Exemption) (Interconsulting Limited) Order, 1962. The Federal Minister of Finance, effective April 1, 1962, exempted Interconsulting Limited of Zurich from the Companies Income Tax Act "in respect of all income earned by the company under an Agreement dated 4th January, 1962, appointing it as consulting engineer to the Government of the Federation of Nigeria for the designing and planning of an integrated iron and steel mill in Nigeria." This order is to continue in force as long as the company does not become a "Nigerian company" within §2 of the Companies Income Tax Act.

23. Official Gazette, Supplement (1958), p. A42.

24. The declining balance method of determining depreciation is used.

25. Companies Income Tax Act (above, n. 3), §27(g)(ii).

26. *Ibid.*, §33.

27. Agreement Relating to the Extension to Certain British Territories of the application of the Convention of April 16, 1945; Dec. 3, 1958 (1958) U.S.T. & O.I.A. 1459, T.I.A.S. No. 4141. Other nations with which Nigeria has similar agreements are: United Kingdom, Ghana, Canada, New Zealand, Sweden, Denmark, and Norway. See Companies Income Tax Act (above, n. 3), Fourth Schedule (Double Taxation Arrangements), A213.

A U.S. resident subject to U.S. tax, and not engaged in trade or business through a permanent establishment in Nigeria, is exempted from Nigerian taxes on dividends, interest, and royalties received from Nigerian sources, as a result of the treaty.

28. *Ibid.*, §37(1).

29. Under the U.S. Revenue Act of 1962, Nigeria has less-developed country (LDC) status. A U.S.-"controlled" foreign corporation, 80 per cent of whose assets and 80 per cent of whose profits are located in and derived from

an LDC, is not required to "gross-up" its earnings when they are remitted to the U.S. parent directly or through another LDC. It is entitled both to a deduction and to a credit for the income taxes paid to the LDC, and the result may be a combined LDC and U.S. tax considerably lower than the U.S. corporate-tax rate which is applicable when "grossing-up" is required. Dividends and interest from LDC subsidiaries and net gains, during the taxable year, on the sale of qualified investments in LDC's are excluded from Subpart F income, §954(b)(1)(A). Taxes on earnings of an LDC corporation that are remitted to a foreign holding company controlled by a U.S. firm may be deferred if they are reinvested in an LDC corporation within one year following the close of the taxable year, §954(b)(1).

30. Companies Income Tax Act, §28(c).
31. *Laws of the Federation of Nigeria and Lagos* A105 (1961).
32. Current regional tax rates on personal income may be obtained from the respective regional Ministries of Finance. See Diamond (above, n. 4), pp. 18F-18G for the rates in the Eastern and Northern Regions. A Joint Tax Board, representing all the governments, was constituted by the 1961 act to co-ordinate tax rates and collections. In 1963, the Minister of Finance reported that "it is the differences in the burden of income taxation in various parts of the Federation which causes us all the most concern. My colleagues in the Regions and I are determined to do something about this." Ministry of Information, *Modernisation Budget* (1963), p. 33.
33. See *Modernisation Budget* (above, n. 32), p. 32. A one-week tax-registration drive in Aba Division, in the Eastern Region, revealed 4,000 taxable adults who were not on the tax rolls. The drive, conducted by the Internal Revenue Office at Aba, covered Aba Township, and the urban areas of Ndiekoro, Eziukwn, Ogbor, and Ogbigbo. In Ogbigbo, where only 140 taxpayers were registered, 400 taxable adults were found never to have paid taxes. See *Nigerian Outlook* (Enugu), Aug. 1, 1962. The same issue of *Outlook* states, "Sixty prominent landlords including chiefs, professionals and legislators in Port Harcourt, who failed to pay their rate arrears [taxes] from March 1956 to 1962 are to be prosecuted."
34. The system is described in Federal Inland Department of Revenue, *Income Tax: The Employers Guide to "Pay As You Earn"* (Lagos, 1961).
35. E.g., General Agreement on Tariffs and Trade, Art. XVIII, 61 *Stat.* (5), (6); T.I.A.S. No. 1700; Treaty of Rome (EEC), Art. 133 (March 25, 1957).
36. Customs Tariff Ordinance, No. 60, Schedule II (1958).
37. 3 *Laws of the Federation of Nigeria and Lagos* c. 86 (1958).
38. Between 1960 and 1963, twenty-seven companies were granted import-duties relief, costing the government an estimated £502,000 in revenue. For a list of the companies, see *West Africa*, May 11, 1963.
39. Customs Duties (Dumped and Subsidized Goods) Ordinance, 1958, 2 *Laws of the Federation of Nigeria and Lagos* c. 47 (1958), gives the president in council power "to impose and vary duties of customs in such manner as he thinks necessary to meet the dumping or giving of the subsidy." Where there is no finding of harm to Nigerian industry, present or potential, the power may not be exercised if it appears that to do so would conflict with Nigeria's obligations under G.A.T.T., §3(1)(b). This statute is based on the English Act, Customs Duties (Dumping and Subsidies) Act, 1957, 5 & 6 Eliz. 2, c. 18 (1957).
40. In 1963, for example, import duties on tinned meats and poultry were increased from 25 per cent to 50 per cent *ad valorem*, on biscuits from 33⅓ per cent to 50 per cent, on shoes from 2/6 to 4 shillings per pair, and on suitcases a new duty of 4 shillings each, "all... intended solely to provide

increased needed protection to Nigerian industry." *Modernisation Budget* (above, n. 32), p. 29.

41. *Mobilisation Budget* (above, n. 1), p. 20.

42. Import duty drawback is authorized under the Customs Drawback Regulation, 1958.

43. Import procedures are set forth in detail in the various editions of the *Handbook of Commerce and Industry* published by the Ministry of Commerce and Industry.

44. The Western Nigeria Finance Corporation and the Mid-Western Nigeria Development Corporation grant loans when they are not available from private sources. The Eastern Nigeria Development Corporation has broadened its loan activities, from a major emphasis on agriculture, to include industrial ventures. The Industrial and Agricultural Co., Ltd., formed by the Eastern Nigerian government, in conjunction with the Commonwealth Development Corporation, makes both loans and direct investments; the Fund for Agricultural and Industrial Development is a source of small loans in the east. In the north, the lending and investing agency is Northern Nigeria Investments, Ltd., formed by the Northern Nigeria Development Corporation and the Commonwealth Development Corporation. The Northern Nigeria Development Corporation also makes loans directly.

At the federal level, the Nigerian Industrial Development Bank is the chief source of loans (see p. 22). The Revolving Loans Fund for Industry and the Federal Loan Board loan money at commercial rates, but their resources are limited.

In Western Nigeria, where the co-operative movement is strong, loans may be available from co-operative organizations.

45. *Business International*, April 3, 1964, agrees with this analysis. The situation, apparently, has not changed since 1961, when a delegation from the Federation of British Industries visited Nigeria and reported that the pioneer certificate "was not proving easy to administer, largely because the grant of the certificate involved the exercise of choices between rival projects sometimes located in different Regions. We came upon cases when these political difficulties had led to delays of many months in reaching decisions." Federation of British Industries, *Nigeria: An Industrial Reconnaissance* (London, 1961), p. 36.

46. *Laws of Nigeria*, A51 (1962).

47. All currencies, except the Nigerian pound, are now regarded as foreign currencies.

48. The earlier law was the Exchange Control Ordinance, 3 *Laws of the Federation of Nigeria and Lagos* c. 63 (1958).

49. *Mobilisation Budget* (above, n. 1), p. 23.

50. *Ibid.*, p. 24.

51. *Modernisation Budget* (above, n. 32), p. 24.

52. *Ibid.*

53. This has its counterpart in Nigeria's efforts to secure external financing. See the remarks of the Nigerian Minister of Finance at the 1962 Annual Meeting of the Board of Governors of the International Bank for Reconstruction and Development, complaining that negotiations for loans "tend to be slow, tardy, and time consuming." The minister was convinced that "without necessarily lowering the basic requirements of some lenders much could be done to reduce the frustrations...." 5 *Federal Nigeria* 15 (Nov., 1962).

54. It is too late to argue with the goals adopted, see Robert Theobald, *The Rich and the Poor* (New York, 1961), p. 18, but once adopted, it is appropriate to question the means to achieve them.

55. There are large numbers of Ibos in the Cameroun Republic, where it is said they are very much resented, and in Fernando Po, the Spanish islands in the Gulf of Guinea.

CHAPTER VII

1. In some cases, families might hold absolute title; in others, there may be involved an allegiance to an overlord requiring traditional payments. See the description of customary land tenure, made in 1898, by Rayner in his "Report on Land Tenure in West Africa," cited with approval, in 1921, by the Privy Council in *Amody Tijani v. Secretary, Southern Nigeria*, A.C. 399, 404-5 (1921).
2. See T. O. Elias, *Nigerian Land Law and Custom* (3rd. ed.; London, 1962), p. 155.
3. *Ibid.*, p. 163.
4. See p. 139.
5. See *Akpan Awo v. Cookey Gam*, 2 N.L.R. 97 (1913), where the defendant entered land contrary to native law and was in possession for over twenty-one years but with knowledge and consent of the plaintiffs. The fact that a third party, a European firm, had been permitted by the defendant to build a factory on the land may have been determinative. Within the family, *Sunmony v. Disy Raphael*, A.C. 881 (1927), would probably obtain; in this case, the Privy Council held that exclusive possession of Crown Lands by an individual must be presumed to have been taken on behalf of the family and gave no title to the individual vis-à-vis other members of the family.
6. Until 1900, the areas of Nigeria outside Lagos, except for the coastal areas to the east of Lagos (*i.e.*, the Oil Rivers and Niger Coast protectorates) were under the control of the Royal Niger Company.
7. Family claims, dating from allegedly faulty alienations made as long ago as the 1890's or based on residual rights recognized by certain statutes, nevertheless cloud what appear to have been perfect fee simple titles and are a source of frequent litigation in Lagos.
8. Ordinance No. 3 of 1863; Ordinance No. 4 of 1876.
9. Ordinance No. 17 of 1906.
10. Supreme Court Ordinance, 1914. Previously, English law was extended to the north by proclamations.
11. 29 Chas. 1, c. 3 (1677).
12. 8 & 9 Vict., c. 106 (1845).
13. 37 & 38 Vict., c. 78 (1874).
14. 43-45 Vict., c. 41 (1881).
15. 45-47 Vict., c. 39 (1882).
16. 54-56 Vict., c. 13 (1892).
17. 58-61 Vict., c. 65 (1897). Of these, only the acts of 1881 and 1897 have expressly been held "generally applicable," but the others have been accepted as such.
18. *Laws of Western Nigeria* c. 100 (1959).
19. 15 & 16 Geo. 5, c. 20 (1925).
20. Agreement may arise by implication if forms and documents based on the 1959 law are used by the parties. Property and Conveyancing Law (above, n. 18), §1(3).
21. The Land Tenure Law (1962). The predecessor statute, to much the same effect, was the Land and Native Rights Ordinance, 1916.
22. *Ibid.*, §10.
23. *Ibid.*, §19.
24. *Ibid.*, §5.

25. *Ibid.*, §34(3). In both cases where the revocation is to secure the land for public purposes, payment of compensation is provided for by §35.

26. *Ibid.*, §34(2).

27. *Ibid.*, §34(3).

28. This generally means the heads of immediate families within the extended family, including unmarried adult males, spinsters, illegitimate, or "natural," children, and *arotas* (strangers to, or descendants of slaves of, the family adopted into the family).

For an example of a sale set aside for want of consent "of a not unimportant minority of the family," see *Yesufu Esan and Others v. Bakare Faro and Others*, 12 W.A.C.A. 135 (1947). Such sales are not void but voidable.

29. E.g., *Agavan v. Mushi*, 1 N.L.R. 66 (1907); *Ajose v. Harworth*, 6 N.L.R. 98 (1925).

30. E.g., *Kugbiyi v. Odynjo*, 7 N.L.R. 57 (1926), right to harvest palm trees; *Lawani v. Tadeyo*, 10 W.A.C.A. 37 (1944), son's non-possessory right to live on the premises during good behavior.

31. James S. Coleman, *Nigeria: Background to Nationalism* (Berkeley, 1960), pp. 58-60.

32. Regarding the "white settler" problem in East Africa, see M. F. Hill, "The White Settler's Role in Kenya," 38 *Foreign Affairs* 638 (1960); *The Economic Development of Kenya* [IBRD Mission Report] (Nairobi, 1962), pp. 47-61.

33. Western Region: Native Lands Acquisition Law, 1952, and Regulations of 1958. Eastern Region: Acquisition of Land by Aliens Law, 1957. The Land Law of Western Nigeria is, for the time being, still applicable in the newly created Mid-Western Region, which came into being on October 1, 1963.

34. *Eyamba and Others v. Kouri*, 3 W.A.C.A. 186 (1937), decided under the Native Lands Acquisition Ordinance, 1917.

35. See p. 143. In the Western and Mid-Western regions, the applicable law is the Native Lands Acquisition Law, No. 4, 1952, and in the Eastern, the Acquisition of Lands by Aliens Law, No. 11, 1958.

36. Nigerian nationality is defined in the Republican Constitution, c. II.

37. Land Tenure Law (above, n. 21), §2.

38. The northern attitude toward southerners stems in part from the attitudes of colonial administrators. Marjorie Perham says, "...I fear that some of our officials became at least as northern as the northerners, fostering the local sense of difference, even of superiority, towards the south." M. F. Perham, *The Colonial Reckoning* (London, 1962), p. 116.

39. Land Tenure Law (above, n. 21), §6(2).

40. *Martins v. Molade and Two Others*, 9 N.L.R. 52 (1930).

41. Under the Registration of Titles Act, 1964.

42. Lagos Town Planning Ordinance, 1962, 4 *Laws of the Federation of Nigeria and Lagos* c. 95 (1958).

43. Obviously, this has even wider ramifications for the Nigerian economy as a whole, since the communal system of land tenure inhibits the use of land as security for credit. "[T]he value of land as a security increases in proportion to the absence of restraints upon its disposal." *East Africa Royal Commission* (1953-55). See the chapter on "Credit Transactions," p. 145, of this volume.

44. Leases on public lands may not be assigned or sublet without the consent of the responsible minister, nor may they be sold on attachment; a mortgagee may foreclose and take possession but may sell only to a buyer

approved by the minister. The lease usually includes conditions as to use and improvements, and variation requires the minister's prior consent.

45. Public Lands Acquisition Act, 5 *Laws of the Federation of Nigeria and Lagos* c. 167 (1958).

46. *Ibid.*, §2.

47. *Ibid.*, §3(1).

48. E.g., Land Tenure Law (above, n. 21), §§34-35, regarding acquisition of native lands for public purposes; for acquisition of other than native lands, the Public Lands Acquisition Act (above, n. 45) applies. See also note 33.

49. Republican Constitution, §31. See also Public Lands Acquisition Act (above, n. 45), §30.

50. See the discussion of fundamental rights, pp. 61-65.

51. *Chief Commissioner, Eastern Region v. S. N. Ononye and Others,* 17 N.L.R. 142 (1944).

52. Public Lands Acquisition Act (above, n. 45), §2(i). The amendment was supplied by Nigerian Law, No. 57, 1958, whereby public purpose was made to include "obtaining control over land required for or in connection with housing estate [sic], economic, industrial or agricultural development."

53. Transfer of a customary right of occupancy to an alien is not prohibited (see Land Tenure Law, above, n. 21, §27) but is simply not consented to.

54. The provincial secretary can approve a sublease of not over one year without reference to the minister. In the past, consent was rarely given to a sublease of more than five years, and sub-subleases were never approved. Today, practice is to approve leases for longer periods, and sub-subleases are authorized under §29, Land Tenure Law. These also require ministerial consent, as well as that of the holder of the right of occupancy.

55. It should be noted that certain lands in the Western Region have been transferred from the public domain (formerly known as Crown Lands) to commercial trustees and are covered by particular statutes. These are subject to the Native Lands Acquisition Law, 1952, but are administered by the Western Region Ministry of Lands.

56. State (formerly Crown) Lands Act, 1 *Laws of the Federation of Nigeria and Lagos* c. 45 (1958), §4.

CHAPTER VIII

1. *Halliday v. Alapatira,* 1 N.L.R. 1 (1881).

2. 32 & 33 Vict., c. 71 (1869).

3. A. E. W. Park, *The Sources of Nigerian Law* (Lagos, 1963), p. 32.

4. 1 *Laws of the Federation of Nigeria and Lagos* c. 37, §§129-230 (1958); unregistered companies are covered in §§233-38.

5. *Report of the Commissioners Appointed to Inquire into the Insolvency Law in Ghana* (1961), p. 23, as quoted by Anthony Allott, "Legal Development and Economic Growth in Africa," in *Changing Law in Developing Countries,* ed., J. N. D. Anderson (New York, 1963), pp. 204-5.

6. *Laws of Western Nigeria* c. 100 (1959).

7. T. O. Elias, *Nigerian Land Law and Custom* (3rd ed.; London, 1962), p. 187: "... The owner-occupier of land, in order to secure an advance of money or money's worth, gives possession and use of the land to the pledge creditor until the debt is fully discharged." See *Adjei v. Dabanka and Another,* I W.A.C.A. 63 (1930). A pledge may be with respect to specific usufruct of the land, such as palm trees, and, in such cases, the pledgor may remain in possession. A pledge is "perpetually redeemable," since no prescriptive right ever arises under native law and between natives. Elias notes

that "... cases have been known where the grandchildren of the pledgor family finally pay their ancestor's debt on the family land and so redeem it from the pledgee's living descendants" (p. 189).

8. The mortgagor also has the power to appoint a receiver. Both this and the power of sale derive from the English Conveyancing Act of 1881. These powers are, nevertheless, customarily expressed in the mortgage document.

9. Technically, under the pre-1925 English law, the mortgagee may take possession. 12 & 13 Geo. 5, c. 16, 2nd Schedule (1922). This was altered by the 1925 act, §§98, 99, 101(7) (iii), 109. It is common, in Nigeria, to insert in the memorandum of deposit of deeds a clause excluding the power of the mortgagor in possession, given by §18 of the Conveyancing and Law of Property Act of 1881, to lease the premises.

10. Native Lands Acquisition Law, 1962 (Western Nigeria); Acquisition of Lands by Aliens Law, 1957 (Eastern Nigeria); Land Tenure Act, 1962 (Northern Nigeria).

11. In Northern Nigeria and in Lagos, on land situated outside title registration districts, there is an additional ad valorem registration fee of 5 shillings per £100.

12. Cf. *Onashile v. Idown and Others*, [1963] All N.L.R. 313, interpreting §5 of the old Registration of Titles Ordinance. The Supreme Court there held that a legal mortgage of unregistered land, being an absolute conveyance of the fee simple, was subject to compulsory first-registration requirements pertaining to land within a registration district. The mortgagee having failed to register, the mortgage was void insofar as it purported to convey the legal estate, and the attempted exercise by the mortgagee of his power of sale was void. The decision immediately put into doubt the validity of most, if not all, legal mortgages on all unregistered land within registration districts, since it had been commonly thought that legal mortgages were not such transactions as compelled first registration. In fact, the registrar of titles was so far in agreement that he refused to accept proffered registrations. The decision, which reversed the high court, was technically correct but demonstrates the failure to adapt English law to local conditions, especially in view of the fact that the operative principle involved has long since ceased to apply in England. The old Ordinance was replaced by the Registration of Titles Act, 1964.

13. Cf., the situation in Northern Nigeria (above, p. 141).

14. Stamp duty on collateral or ancillary security raises a problem of other dimensions.

15. §101 of the Companies Act, 1 *Laws of the Federation of Nigeria and Lagos* c. 37 (1958). If not so registered, the mortgage shall "so far as any security in the Company's property or undertaking is thereby conferred, be void against the liquidator and any creditor of the company...." The registrar has no discretion to extend the filing period, but a high court may do so under §104 of the Companies Act.

16. T. O. Elias, *Groundwork of Nigerian Law* (London, 1954), pp. 240-42.

17. *Ibid.*

18. 17 & 18 Vict., c. 36 (1854), 41 & 42 Vict., c. 31 (1878), 45 & 46 Vict., c. 43 (1882), 53 & 54 Vict., c. 53 (1890), 54 & 55 Vict., c. 35 (1891).

19. 1 *Laws of the Federation of Nigeria and Lagos* c. 22 (1958).

20. Preamble, Bills of Sale Act, 17 & 18 Vict., c. 36 253-54 (1854).

21. The registrar was provided for by Notice 9 of 1937 under §2 of the Bills of Sale Ordinance (above, n. 19), and regional registrars by Law No. 131 of 1954, which amended the ordinance.

22. See *Joe Allen & Co., Ltd., v. Adewale and Lateju,* 9 N.L.R. 111, 116 (1929).
23. *Ollivant v. Akinsanya and Famu,* 10 N.L.R. 73, 74-75 (1930).
24. *Goodeve on Personal Property* (9th ed. by R. H. Kersley, London, 1949), p. 54.
25. A bill of sale may result by judicial construction where a hire-purchase agreement was intended or specified, when the transaction in reality was to secure a loan between the parties rather than to facilitate the sale of goods.
26. The Hire-Purchase Bill 1965, Explanatory Memorandum [signed by K. O. Mbadiwe, Minister of Trade], Supplement to Official Gazette No. 38, Vol. 52, April 29, 1965 (Part C). The full text was not yet available at the time of writing.
27. 56 & 57 Vict., c. 71 (1893).
28. 2 *Laws of the Federation of Nigeria and Lagos* c. 46, Part II (1958). The case so holding, binding in Nigeria, is *Helby v. Matthews,* A.C. 471 (1895).
29. 56 & 57 Vict., c. 71 (1893). The leading case binding in Nigeria is *Lee v. Butler,* 2 Q.B. 318 (1893), which so held under §9 of the Factors Act, 1889, an act identical with §25(2) of the Sale of Goods Act.
30. 8 Edw. 7, c. 53 (1908).
31. 1 & 2 Geo. 6, c. 53 (1938).
32. In England, the seller may insert a clause into the agreement giving him the right to terminate by notice after breach. If such notice has been served, the goods are no longer comprised in a hire-purchase agreement and are not subject to distress.
33. 37 Ch. 260 (1887).
34. *Ibid.,* p. 264.
35. *Edmons v. Balina Co.,* 36 Ch.D. 215 (1887).
36. *Ibid.,* p. 219.
37. Goodeve (above, n. 24), p. 443.
38. John E. Burke, Barrister-at-law, Lagos.
39. Goodeve (above, n. 24), p. 444.
40. *Government Stock Co. v. Manila Ry. Co.,* A.C. 81 (1897).
41. Often, the company is given up to three months after defaulting on payment of interest; the principal sum then becomes due, and the holder is able to pursue his remedies.
42. Companies Act (above, n. 15), §101(1)(f).

CHAPTER IX

1. *U.N.G.A.* Res. No. 1803 (XVII) (1962).
2. *Ibid.,* Art. I(4).
3. See Stephen M. Schwebel, "The Story of the U.N.'s Declaration on Permanent Sovereignty over Natural Resources," 49 *American Bar Association Journal* 463 (1963). It is Mr. Schwebel's view that "the force of the United States view that appropriate compensation in accordance with international law means prompt, adequate and effective compensation was enhanced by the General Assembly's treatment of the resolution." *Ibid.,* p. 466.
4. See Oscar Schachter, "The Quasi-Judicial Role of the Security Council and the General Assembly," 58 *American Journal of International Law* 960 (1964). France and South Africa voted against Res. No. 1803. The twelve abstainers were the Soviet Bloc (including Cuba) and, of the less-developed countries, only Ghana and Burma.
5. Res. No. 1803 (above, n. 1), Preamble.
6. *Ibid.,* Art. I (8).

7. *Ibid.*, Art. I (4).
8. *Ibid.*
9. §30 of the Independence Constitution (1960); §31 of the Republican Constitution (1963).
10. In the case of Cable and Wireless, Ltd., only a majority interest was nationalized, and the government and the nationalized owner joined to form Nigerian External Communications.
11. Investment Guarantees Agreement between the United States of America and Nigeria, Dec. 24, 1962, *T.I.A.S.* 5237. Expropriation is the only risk covered. The Nigerians were reluctant to sign such an agreement since it was viewed as "an infringement of sovereignty." Nigeria agreed to sign (the U.S. note was forwarded Aug. 28, 1962) after the U.S. committed itself to supplying £80 million for the 1962-68 Development Plan.
12. Financial pressures may then require a dilution of the criteria of compensation. In India, "the right to compensation for expropriations—which, as originally constituted and interpreted, gave the expropriated owner the market value, irrespective of the mode of deprivation—was amended so that he only gets what the Legislature says he may have...." Alan Gledhill, "Fundamental Rights," in *Changing Law in Developing Countries*, ed. J. N. D. Anderson (New York, 1963), p. 88. The right is contained in Article 31 of the Indian Constitution, and the change was effected by the Constitution (Fourth Amendment) Act of 1955.
13. "It is too easy to believe that a good civil servant, probably with a degree, will be able to make good business decisions or control the business decisions of others. But experience in other countries, and indeed under the colonial regime, does not confirm this." Guy Hunter, *The New Societies of Tropical Africa: A Selective Study* (London, 1962), p. 184. See also *ibid.*, p. 157.
14. E.g., Abukakar Tafawa Balewa, "Nigeria Looks Ahead," 41 *Foreign Affairs* 131 (1962); "Opportunities for Overseas Investment," a joint statement first issued by the federal and regional governments in 1956, reissued in 1959, and republished in Federal Ministry of Commerce and Industry, *Handbook of Commerce and Industry in Nigeria* (4th ed., 1960), p. 230, and (5th ed., 1962), p. 316: "Our Governments have no plans for nationalising industry beyond the extent to which public utilities are already nationalised, nor do they foresee any such proposals arising."
15. This was a complete contradiction of Chief Awolowo's earlier stand, as Chief Okotie-Eboh subsequently noted. Awolowo's change of view was, probably, attributable to his personal frustration, after independence, as leader of the opposition and the increased influence of radicals in the Action Group, owing to that party's failure to participate in the government.
16. Federal Ministry of Information, *No Nationalisation in Nigeria* (1961) (statement of policy made in Parliament by the federal Minister of Finance).
17. *Ibid.*
18. Parliamentary Debates, House of Representatives, March 21, 1964, p. 535.
19. Marketing boards were established by the colonial administration to stabilize supply and prices of agricultural products, to facilitate quality control and economical and orderly marketing, and to eliminate middlemen. The profits (or surpluses) of marketing boards have contributed substantial funds for economic development of the regions. A succinct description of a marketing board, its origins, and its operations is to be found in the Coker Commission of Inquiry, *Report into the Affairs of Certain Statutory Corporations in Western Nigeria*, Vol. I (1962), pp. 9-11. Marketing boards are described

more fully in A. H. Hanson, "Public Enterprise in Nigeria: II, Development Corporations," 37 *Public Administration* 21 (1959).

20. Ezekiel Mphahlele, *The African Image* (London, 1962), p. 25.

21. See Willie E. Abraham, *The Mind of Africa* (London, 1962), pp. 38-39.

22. *West Africa,* Nov. 3, 1962. "History... is the memory of nations, and one cannot live with another's memory or another's history. Consequently, we must rehabilitate our own history." Joseph Ki Zerbo, "African Personality and the New African Society" in *Pan-Africanism Reconsidered,* ed., American Society of African Culture (Berkeley, 1962), p. 281.

23. Thus, Marxism, too, requires "Africanization." Ki Zerbo (above, n. 21), pp. 277-78: "It is obvious that the choice of socialism is almost naturally and inevitably the end of African evolution, but, in my opinion, it is not the socialism elaborated by Marx on the basis of an analysis of a society fundamentally different from traditional African society.... I think it would be a basic methodological error to transpose Marxism to Africa as the general philosophy of society... and also an error of principle."

See also Emile Zinsou, "Comments," in *Pan-Africanism Reconsidered,* ed. American Society of African Culture (Berkeley, 1962), p. 194. "If we have felt the need to call it African socialism, it is because in our eyes it represents not an import thrust onto our situation from stem to stern, but an original search, fertilized by the facts of our lands. Our socialism... is not Marxism."

24. Abraham (above, n. 20), p. 182. Perhaps the most extreme definition of pragmatic socialism was that provided by members of an NCNC convention held in the Eastern Region in 1962: "Socialism is the right of everyone to start his own business."

25. See Rupert Emerson, *Political Modernization: The Single Party System* (Denver, 1962), p. 9.

26. See also Robert Theobald, *The Rich and the Poor* (New York, 1961), p. 19.

27. Hunter (above, n. 13), pp. 288-89.

28. Reported in *West Africa,* Dec. 29, 1962, p. 1449, in an article entitled "Who Is a Socialist?"

29. *Ibid.* Of course, what Dr. Biobaku forgets is that he is describing a preindustrial society, whose "humane" characteristics are not unique to Nigeria or Africa.

30. Hunter (above, n. 13), p. 289. See also *ibid.*, p. 182. The Mercedes has since replaced the Chevrolet as prime status symbol. See David Apter, "The New Nations and the Scientific Revolution," 17 *Bulletin of the Atomic Scientists* 60-64 (1961), where the high correlation, in the minds of African leaders, between socialism and technology and the resulting "anti-intellectualism" are discussed. See "What Kind of Dignity?" (Lagos) *Sunday Mirror,* July 29, 1962, p. 3: "For twenty-five years, you must look up only to the doctors, biologists, engineers as the only wise men of society...."

31. John Hennings, "The Attitudes of African Nationalism towards Communism," *Duquesne Review* (Spring, 1962), p. 69. Mr. Hennings, at the time of writing, was colonial attaché of the British Embassy in Washington. With respect to the capitalist/colonialist equation, Mr. Hennings, in the same article, p. 61, quotes President Nkrumah as having said to the Ghana National Assembly in April, 1961, "It would be the greatest mistake to imagine that all foreign powers are colonialists or that the interests of overseas investments are necessarily best served by a continuation of imperialism in an open or concealed form. On the contrary the existence of colonialism... is in direct contradiction to the essential elements of private capitalism."

32. Nigeria is one of the few African states that retains the parliamentary system with an opposition party. See Kalu Ezera, *Constitutional Developments in Nigeria* (Cambridge, Eng., 1960), p. 259.

33. Frank Moraes, "The Importance of Being Black," 43 *Foreign Affairs* 99-111, 106 (1964). Emerson points out that "in presenting the case for a one-party state in Ghana in 1962 the Minister of Defense, Kofi Baako, told the National Assembly that the multi-party system was unfitting to Ghana where tradition called for a council of elders, approved by the people and with a chief to lead them." Emerson (above, n. 25), p. 21.

34. "Among all the African states Nigeria has the best claim to have preserved a measure of multi-party constitutional democracy but the disturbances in the Western Region and the treason trials involving major opposition leaders have somewhat tarnished the Nigerian record." Emerson (above, n. 25), p. 15. See the chapter on "The Western Region Crisis of 1962-63," p. 175.

35. See Paul O. Proehl, "Private Investment Abroad," 9 *Journal of Public Law* 362 (1960).

36. "The situation grows, if anything, worse when a small minority of Africans are included in the European managerial levels and therefore in the circle of housing, club and social expenditure typical of the foreign group.... Neither the appointment of an African director nor the existence of African shareholders will disguise the social and environmental exclusiveness which has been the pattern in the past and remains all too evidently the pattern today." Hunter (above, n. 13), pp. 189-90.

37. *West Africa*, April 11, 1964. It was also the Minister of Economic Development, Mr. Waziri Ibrahim, whose comments in November, 1962, on the "discrepancies" in the 1962 census initiated a controversy that put the census under such a cloud that it was eventually nullified by a decision of the federal and regional premiers "in view of the loss of confidence in the figures for various regions." A new census, costing £2 million, was undertaken with U.N. assistance, in 1963, precipitating even sharper controversy. See p. 00.

38. *Ibid.*

39. *Ibid.*

40. Hunter (above, n. 13), p. 326. Peter Kilby, *Development of Small Industry in Eastern Nigeria* (U.S. AID, Lagos, 1962), p. 12: "The Nigerian entrepreneur insists that lack of capital is the only obstacle retarding his progress. Similarly the Government and many development planners emphasize the capital scarcity problem... [T]o ascribe to it the leading role in the small industry drama would be to err grievously. The provision of finance results in growth only when combined with the crucial ingredients of technical knowledge, marketing capabilities and management control."

41. Interestingly, a process of "Northernization" is being pursued in the Northern Region, to oust Southern Nigerians from important positions. In 1962, Northern Nigerians suggested that federal civil service requirements be lowered to accommodate less-well-educated applicants from the north. See *West Africa*, July 5, 1962, p. 6.

42. With respect to the "felt need" to own and its negative implications for development, there is a striking and useful parallel to be observed in the habits or attitudes of businessmen: "... [R]enting of the factory site, as opposed to land acquisition and construction, should be encouraged. The cost, the delay (seldom less than 18 months) and the administrative entanglements of procuring an industrial site, are serious handicaps to a fledgling entrepreneur.... Initially, ownership undertaking merely increases the risk without any corresponding benefit from the development viewpoint. Also

there is the risk that part or all of an industrial loan-financed structure may be directed to the real estate market." Kilby (above, n. 40), p. 14.

43. Foreign ownership can cause difficulties, even in highly advanced countries, because of its susceptibility to partisan purposes. Cf. the experience of General Motors in Australia in the late 1950's and present attitudes in France.

44. The remarks of the Minister for Economic Development were the occasion for the most recent pronouncement of the prime minister on this subject in the House of Representatives in April, 1964: "Believing, as we do, in an economy in which free enterprise and private capital can play their full part, we welcome the investment of private foreign capital in productive areas of the economy, and we recognise that the investor is entitled to look for a reasonable return from his investment.... We have never concealed our belief that Nigerian enterprise and Nigerian capital must play an ever-increasing part in the economic life of the nation. It must be obvious that no Nigerian can be content so long as any major sector of the economy is controlled by foreigners. But we are realists and we say that so long as there is a dearth of Nigerian capital, so long must there be an opportunity for foreign capital in Nigeria. We do not seek the withdrawal of foreign capital from any area of the economy before Nigerian enterprise is able to replace it. When the time for withdrawal has come, due notice will be given." *West Africa*, April 18, 1964, p. 441.

45. Apropos of the act requiring insurance companies that were doing business in Nigeria to invest a prescribed minimum of premiums paid in Nigeria, a reader's letter in *West Africa*, July 27, 1963, expressed a popular attitude: "While one thinks of the huge profits made by private firms in Nigeria, the fabulous salaries these firms pay to their own people ... in contrast to the very low and discriminatory wages paid to Nigerians working for them irrespective of their qualifications and status, one might urge that another bill be introduced compelling all private firms operating in Nigeria to invest substantially in our country's economy."

46. See President Azikiwe's 1964 Message to Parliament, in which he complains that "the economic factors which have kept our trade at a low ebb are due to the manipulation at the international level of the world commodity market...." 7 *Federal Nigeria* 6 (March-April, 1964). See also *Towards a New Trade Policy for Development* (Report by the Secretary-General of the United Nations Conference on Trade and Development), U.N. Doc. E/CONF. 46/3 (February 12, 1964), especially pp. 51-71; also the *Final Act of the United Nations Conference on Trade and Development*, U.N. Doc. E/CONF. 46/L.28 (June 16, 1964).

47. Global commodity agreements for the stabilization of supply and price tend, also, to perpetuate reliance on the commodity agreed upon. Of course, to the extent that commodity stabilization contributes to the stability of the country's economy, it may permit economic development and diversification that utilize other available resources.

CHAPTER X

1. An account of the Western Region Crisis is to be found in O. I. Odumoso, *The Nigerian Constitution: History and Development* (London, 1963), pp. 276-305, and in J. T. MacIntosh, "Politics in Nigeria: The Action Group Crisis of 1963," 17 *Political Studies* 126 (1963). A brief account of the 1965 election crisis is given in the Preface.

2. §31 of the Constitution of Western Nigeria provides that "the Governor may at any time prorogue or dissolve the Legislative Houses of the Region,

but only if the Premier recommends dissolution, if the House of Assembly passes a resolution of no confidence and the Premier does not within three days either resign or advise dissolution; and if the office of Premier is vacant and the Governor does not believe he can appoint a person capable of commanding majority support."

3. Whether the Awolowo forces could have commanded the necessary number of votes on a division of the House has been questioned. At any rate, it has been suggested that some of the signers would have shown more fortitude in standing with Akintola on the floor of the House than they did when solicited privately for their signatures. It was alleged by the counsel for Chief Akintola at the Privy Council hearing that, of the sixty-six signers, a substantial portion subsequently voted for Akintola. *West Africa*, May 4, 1963, p. 506. But there was no opportunity to "vote" for Akintola until after the crisis was over. However, in the debates in the Federal Parliament on May 29, Chief A. Akerele said, in discussing the list of signatures, "[M]ore than half of the list here had already given their names, affirming their support for Chief Samuel Akintola." Parliamentary Debates, House of Representatives, May 29, 1962, p. 17.

4. The exchange of letters and requests mentioned in this paragraph was read into the record by Chief A. Akerele during the debates on May 29 and is to be found at pp. 15-19 of the Parliamentary Debates, House of Representatives, May 29, 1962.

5. Under §108(1)(a) of the Independence Constitution, when a question concerning the interpretation of the constitution involves a substantial question of law, the high court shall refer it to the federal Supreme Court.

6. Odumosu (above, n. 1), p. 279.

7. Independence Constitution, §65(3)(a).

8. *Ibid.*, §65(3)(b).

9. *Ibid.*, §65(3)(c). Why should the third mode require a two-thirds vote? Would not Parliament always choose to act under subsection (b), which requires only a simple majority? Does this imply (b) must, therefore, necessarily be subject to *some* limitation?

10. *Laws of the Federation of Nigeria and Lagos*, No. 1, A1 (1961). This was a substantial re-enactment of the Emergency Powers Orders in Council, which were retained by virtue of §6 of the Independence Constitution until March 30, 1961, when the present act became effective. The first such Order in Council was promulgated in 1939. It is, therefore, essentially a colonial measure.

11. *Laws of Nigeria*, L.N. 54, B101 (1962).

12. *Ibid.*, L.N. 55-66, B104-B105; L.N. 69, B155; L.N. 71, B159; L.N. 103, B189 (1962). The Emergency Powers (Requisition) Regulation specifically provided for compensation for property requisitioned, §19(1), and provision was made for reference to the high court in case of a dispute on the amount of the claim, with interest thereon at 5 per cent (§20). Amendments of regulations are found in L.N. 107, B194, and in L.N. 134, B217.

13. *Ibid.*, A47 (1962).

14. The federal Supreme Court otherwise has original jurisdiction only in disputes between the federation and a region, or between regions. See §107(1), Independence Constitution. Parliament may confer original jurisdiction on the Supreme Court, except in criminal matters. See §107(2).

15. The federal government contended that the lawyers and journalists were not restricted as such, but as "politicians."

16. Emergency Powers (General) Regulations, §4.

17. *Ibid.*, §4(2).

18. *Ibid.*
19. *Ibid.*
20. *Akintola v. Governor of Western Nigeria* [*Aderemi*] *and Adegbenro*, F.S.C. 187/1962, subsequently reversed by the Privy Council, where the case was styled *Adegbenro v. Akintola*, A.C. (P.C.) 614 (1963). See the comments by Anthony N. Allott and C. Ogwurike in 7 *Journal of African Law* 95-99 (1963). Dr. Allott notes the parallel in the Congo, when President Kasavuba purported to dismiss Premier Lumumba: "[T]he Congolese *Loi Fundamentale* had borrowed the Belgian rule that the Sovereign could dismiss the Premier, but had not expressly taken over the well-accepted convention, established in Belgium just as in Britain, that the Sovereign could only exercise this power when Parliament had signified that it had lost confidence in the Premier." The contrast in the modes of settling the issue in Nigeria and the Congo is well known.
21. *Adegbenro v. Attorney General of the Federation of Nigeria*, F.S.C. 170/1962 reported in 4 *Nigerian Bar Journal* 58 (1963).
22. *Williams v. Majekodunmi*, F.S.C. 166/1962 reported in 4 *Nigerian Bar Journal* 74 (1963).
23. The cases are fully discussed by S. G. Davies, "Nigeria—Some Recent Decisions on the Constitution," 11 *International and Comparative Law Quarterly* 919-36 (1962).
24. High Court of Lagos 595/1962, 598/1962, and 599/1962, reported in 4 *Nigerian Bar Journal* 63 (1963).
25. Earlier, the defendants in the case of *Akintola v. Adegbenro* had sought to bring Chief Williams out of restriction as counsel. After this was denied them, they retained a British barrister, Mr. Dingle Foot, who shortly arrived in Nigeria. Upon arrival, Foot was ordered to leave the country within twenty-four hours. This time was extended, but he was expelled after making submissions to the federal Supreme Court.
26. Western Region Official Gazette, April 7, 1961, p. 410.
27. In 1954, Bauer warned, "It is not unlikely that African political parties gaining power will use the machinery and funds of the [Marketing] Boards to further the general political aims of the parties." P. T. Bauer, *West African Trade* (Cambridge, Eng., 1955).
28. 44 & 45 Vict., c. 69 (1881). The act survives independence, and the substitution of an extradition treaty, under which Britain could properly have refused to return Enaharo (because of the political nature of the crime), had apparently not occurred to anyone. Under the Fugitive Offenders Act, Britain was clearly obliged to comply with Nigeria's request.
29. Until October 1, 1963, the decision of the Privy Council was binding in Nigeria, *Thomas v. Ademola*, 18 N.L.R. 12, 23 (1945).
30. See above, n. 20.
31. James S. Coleman, *Nigeria: Background to Nationalism* (Berkeley, 1960), pp. 170 ff.
32. In the debate on May 29, 1962, on the resolution to declare an emergency in the Western Region, Chief Awolowo cited both the Tiv riots and riots reported to have taken place in Okrika, in Eastern Nigeria, as not having occasioned the declaration of an emergency. See Aliyi Ekineh, *Democratic Rights during a "Period of Emergency"* (Lagos, 1963), p. 13.
33. See above, note 26.
34. *West African Pilot*, June 4, 1962, p. 5, quoted in Odumoso (above, n. 1), p. 300. The answer to the premier's question is that the Nigerian barrister would be let in and could, if any British lawyer could, appear in an English court. However, Parliament is supreme in England; in Nigeria the constitution is.

35. *West African Pilot*, June 5, 1962, *ibid.*, p. 300.
36. *West African Pilot*, June 8, 1962, *ibid.*
37. *Daily Express*, May 4, 1962, *ibid.*, p. 301.
38. *Ibid.*
39. Parliamentary Debates, House of Representatives, May 29, 1962, p. 23.
40. *Akintola v. Aderemi and Adegbenro*, F.S.C. 187/1962.
41. Davies (above, n. 23), p. 935.
42. A.C. (P.C.) 614 (1963).
43. See p. 180.
44. Davies (above, n. 23), p. 935; Anthony Allott, "Comment," 7 *Journal of African Law* 95 (1963).
45. Allott (above, n. 44). Allott suggests, "The constitution did not in terms say what the people of Western Nigeria apparently wanted...the terms must therefore be changed." *Quaere*: Could one not as easily say that the legislature, by amending, was bringing the constitution into conformance with the judgment of the federal Supreme Court, which had correctly interpreted the intended meaning of §33(10)? See also A.E.W. Park's letter in 1 *The Lawyer* 84 (1963) (Bulletin of the Law Students of the University of Lagos).
46. Odumosu (above, n. 1), p. 296.
47. C. Ogwurike, "The Governor's Power to Remove a Premier from Office in Western Nigeria," 7 *Journal of African Law* 95 (1963).
48. *Ibid.*, p. 99.
49. "The end to be attained in the development of the law of contract is the supremacy, not of some hypothetical, imaginary will, apart from external manifestations, but of will outwardly revealed in the spoken or the written word." Benjamin N. Cardozo, *The Growth of the Law* (New Haven, Conn., 1924), p. iii. Cardozo was speaking only of commercial transactions. His more general views of the law are well known: "The final cause of law is the welfare of society...I do not mean...that judges are commissioned to set aside existing rules at pleasure in favor of any other set of rules which they may hold to be expedient or wise. I mean that when they are called upon to say how far existing rules are to be extended or restricted, they must let the welfare of society fix the path, its direction and its distance." Benjamin N. Cardozo, *The Nature of the Judicial Process* (New Haven, Conn., 1921), pp. 66-67.
50. The view of British drafters of constitutions for former colonial territories that constitutions should be precise instruments and are to be regarded by courts as such is believed to be at the root of much of the difficulty. The view accounts for the length of these documents but has not insured clearness.
Compare §38(1) of the Constitution of Western Nigeria with §33(1). §38(1) says that in the exercise of his functions under this constitution, the governor shall act on the advice of the executive, except (1) where the constitution requires that he act on the advice of "any person or authority other than the Executive Council," and (2) where he shall act "in accordance with his own deliberate judgment" in performing four specific functions, which are listed and which include the appointment of a premier under §33(2) but *do not include* the removal of a premier under §33(10). *Quaere*: Since the governor obviously cannot act on the premier's advice on the premier's own dismissal, and since he is not authorized under §38(1) to use his own judgment, must he not act under §33(10) on the advice of "authority other than the Executive Council," viz., Parliament? See also the comment in note 9.
51. See pp. 61-65.
52. [1961] All N.L.R. 604. Substantial parts of the Commissions and Tribunals of Inquiry Act, 1961, were held unconstitutional. The Privy

Council affirmed on July 3, 1963, shortly after reversing the decision in the *Akintola* case.

53. Alternative pleadings, directed toward particular regulations and parts thereof were also made. See the report in 4 *Nigerian Bar Journal* 58-62 (1963).

54. *Ibid.*, p. 59.

55. *Ibid.*

56. Davies (above, n. 23), p. 932.

57. §4 provides that, "(1) Parliament may alter any of the provisions of this Constitution or (insofar as it forms part of the law of Nigeria) any of the provisions of the Nigeria Independence Act, 1960:

"Provided that, insofar as it alters any of the provisions of this section ... [the applicable provisions are here listed]... or any of the provisions of the Nigeria Independence Act, 1960, an Act of Parliament shall not come into operation unless each legislative house of at least two Regions has passed a resolution signifying consent to its having effect.

"(2) A bill for an Act of Parliament under this section, not being an Act to which subsection (3) of this section applies, shall not be passed in either House of Parliament unless it has been supported on second and third readings by the votes of not less than two-thirds of all members of that House."

58. Independence Constitution, Chap. III, §§22-26.

59. *Nigerian Bar Journal* (above, n. 22).

60. See the discussion following, p. 00.

61. Ekineh (above, n. 32), p. 20.

62. See p. 63.

63. Emergency Powers Act, §5, *Laws of the Federation of Nigeria and Lagos*, No. 1, A-1 (1961). The case relied upon was *Shannon and Others v. Loner Mainland Dairy Products Board* (Attorney-General for British Columbia intervening), A.C. 708, 722 (1938).

64. See p. 178, n. 17.

65. *Nigerian Bar Journal* (above, n. 22), p. 79.

66. Quoted in Davies (above, n. 23), p. 930.

67. A. E. W. Park finds no fault: "My general view of Section 65(3)(b) is not altered by the suggestion that Parliament may abuse the procedure contained therein in order to establish and maintain dictatorial powers of government. It is to me an unacceptable constitutional doctrine that violence may be done to the clear wording of the Constitution in order to permit a non-elected and largely irremovable group of five judges to enquire into allegations of bad faith on the part of a majority of the elected representatives of the Nigerian people." 1 *The Lawyer* 89 (1963). The formula would appear to be: A written constitution which contains a "clearly worded" §65(b)(3) equals an English unwritten constitutional system.

68. *Awolowo v. Sarki and the Attorney-General*, L.D. 595 (1962). Reported in 4 *Nigerian B. J.* 63-73 (1963).

69. *Ibid.*, pp. 71-72. Obviously, Justice Udo-Udoma's characterization of the constitution as one meant "for Nigerians" is much too restrictive. Of the chapter on fundamental rights, only §§37 (freedom of movement and residence) and 28 (freedom from discrimination, based on membership in a particular community, tribe, place of origin, religion or political opinion) are limited to citizens of Nigeria. All others, including §21, specify only "person" or "any person" (§§22 and 32); begin with the words "No person shall be..." or "every person shall be..." (§§23-26); or specify property (§§18-21) without respect to the citizenship of the owner (§31, on the compulsory acquisition of property).

70. See note 25.
71. Ekineh (above, n. 32), p. 32.
72. *Laws of Nigeria* A393 (1962). See "The Legal Practitioner's Act, 1962" in 4 *Nigerian Bar Journal* 9-18 (1963).
73. Under authority of yet another regulation, Emergency Powers (Statutory Corporation Inquiries) Regulations, 1962, promulgated as Legal Notice No. 71 of 1962 in Official Gazette, No. 47 (June 16, 1962).
74. Coker Commission of Inquiry, *Report into the Affairs of Certain Statutory Corporations in Western Nigeria*, Vol. I, p. 3 (1962).
75. *Ibid.*, Vol. IV, p. 67.
76. *West Africa*, Jan. 12, 1963, p. 29.
77. Coker Report (above, n. 74), Vols. I-VI.
78. *West Africa*, Jan. 12, 1963, p. 29.
79. Coker Report (above, n. 74), Vol. I, p. 4.
80. The election crisis is briefly discussed in the Preface.

Index

NOTE: Items preceded by an asterisk (*) are foreign statutes, in most cases of England or the United Kingdom.

A

Aba Riots, 181
Abraham, Willie E., 167
Absenteeism, 90
Accounts, 73
Acquisition of Land by Aliens Law (Eastern Nigeria), 143
Action Group, 7, 71, 176-81
Advisory Committee on Aids to African Businessmen, 100
Adebo, Chief S. O., 11
Adegbenro, Chief A. O., 179
Adegbenro v. Akintola, 56
Adegbenro v. Attorney General of the Federation of Nigeria, 187-88
Ademola, Sir Adetokunbo, 6, 11, 184
African Civil Servants' Technical Workers' Union, 111
Africanness (*négritude*), 108, 166
Agreement to purchase, 151
Agricultural Development Corporation (Northern Nigeria), 31
Agriculture, 91
Akintola, Chief, 56, 176 ff.
Akintola v. Adegbenro, 181, 183 ff.
Albania, import license required, 127
Alcan Aluminium of Nigeria, Ltd., trust deed, 155-56
Alkali courts, 48, 204 (n. 55)
All-Nigeria People's Conference, 112
All Nigeria Trade Union Federation (ANTUF), 111-13
Allott, A. N., 39, 40, 45, 185
Aluminum, 29
Amachree, Godfrey K., 11
Appeal commissioners (tax), 119
Appeals, 52-53, 57
Apprenticeship, 90, 95-96, 216 (n. 21)
Approved status
  For branch, 81
  In general, for exchange control purposes, 130
Arbitration, 55
Arbitration Act, 55
Ashby Report, 217 (n. 22)
Attitudes
  American, 9
  Nigerian, 9, 44
    Social security, 108
    Private enterprise, 127
    In government, 132-33
    Foreign business, 172
    Courts, 182-83
    Investment in stock, 199 (n. 31)
Automobile assembly plant, proposed, 8
Automation, 217 (n. 26)
Awolowo, Chief O., 176 ff.
Awolowo v. Minister of Internal Affairs, 179, 190
Azikiwe, Nnamdi, 4, 34, 111

B

Bairamian, Justice, 63
Balewa, Sir Abubakar T.
  And Sardauna of Sokoto, 50

Statement on foreign capital, 159
Statement on Western Region Crisis, 177
Statements on courts, 182-83
Statement on foreign private capital, 233 (n. 44)
Balewa v. Doherty, 57
Bankruptcy
  Absence of statute, 146
  Ghana's statute, 147
  Commercial liquidation, 147
*Bankruptcy Act, 146
Banks
  Commercial savings accounts, 24
  Deposits, 24
  Credit controls, 24-25
  Reserve ratio, Central Bank, 198 (n. 21)
  Treasury bill ratio to revenue, Central Bank, 200 (n. 39)
Bar Association, 190
Bello, Alhaji Ahmadu (Sardauna of Sokoto), 3, 50, 182
Best man principle, 50
Bill of sale, 150 ff.
Bill of Sales Act, 150-51
*Bill of Sales Act of 1854, 150
Biobaku, Dr., 168
Board of Inland Revenue
  Administers company tax, 118
  Appeal from, 119
  Investigative Branch, 123
Borha, L. L., 112
Boulding, K. E., 13
Branches, doing business through, 81
Brett, Justice Lionel, 62, 184 ff.
Bretton, Henry L., 75
Budget, 21, 22, 34
Bureaucracy, 132
Business associations
  Aversion to, among Nigerians, 72 ff.
  Forms of, 82 ff.
Buying in Nigeria, 82

C

Capital
  Private, 7, 19
  Amortization, 8, 121
  Repatriation, 28
  Indigenous, 134
Central Bank, 23, 25, 34, 130-31
Census
  1952-53, 91
  Work force, 92
  1963 census and election crisis, 194
  Statistics, 215-16 (n. 6)
  Discrepancies, 232 (n. 37)
Certificate of Occupancy, 139, 143
Chitty, Justice, 153
Chiefs and elders
  Role in customary law, 49 ff.
  Selection of, 50, 205 (n. 68)
Children and Young Persons' Law (Northern Nigeria), 63
China, Red, import license required, 127
Citizens Insurance Co. of Canada v. Parsons, 64
Civil rights. *See* Fundamental rights
Civil service, 5
Civil Service Union, 109
Co-determination, German, 77
Coker, Justice G. B. A., 191
Coker Commission, 7, 9, 179-80, 191-94
Collado, Emilio G., 37
Collective bargaining, 102
Calloway, 96-97
*Colonial Development and Welfare Act of 1940, 110; of 1945, 14, 94
Colonialism, 4, 11, 170
Colony Province
  Acquisition of land by aliens in, 81
  Land tenure, 139-42
  Mortgages, 149
Commissioner of Labour, 105
Commission on Company Law Revision, 77
Commission on the Working and Administration of Company Law in Ghana, 75
Commissions and Tribunals Inquiry Act, 62
Commissions of inquiry, to investigate wages, 102
Committee of Trade Unionists, 111
Commodity markets, world, 173, 233 (nn. 46 and 47)
Common law
  English, 38 ff.
  Nigerian, 46
Common market, African, 9
Communism, 168
Companies Act
  Securities regulation, 26
  Adoption of English act, 39

Index

In general, 74-78
Need for revision, 76-77
Commission on Company Law Revision, 77
Survey by English experts, 77-78
Draft legislation, 78
Bankruptcy, 146
Mortgages, 149
Debentures, 154
*Companies Act of 1862, 76
*Companies Act of 1908, 39, 76
*Companies Act of 1948, 78
*Company Code Bill, 76
Compensation, for nationalization
  Under U.N.G.A. Res. No. 1803, 160
  Nigeria, 161
Congo, compared to Western Region Crisis, 235 (n. 20)
Constitutional Conference of 1963, 60, 180-81
Constitutional law
  Amendment, 50 ff.
  Appeals, 52
  Jurisdiction, 52
  Fundamental rights, 61-65
  Western Region Crisis, 183 ff.
  Interpretation, 185-87
Constitution of 1960 (Independence Constitution)
  Effect on existing law, 39
  Amendment process, 51
  Judicial Service Commission, 58
  Fundamental rights, 61-65, 70
  Labor, 104
  Western Region Crisis, 177 ff.
Constitution of 1963 (Republican Constitution)
  Effect on existing law, 40
  Interpretation Act, 41
  Compensation for land taken, 142
  Omission of appeal to Privy Council, 185
Constitution of Western Nigeria
  §33(10)(a), 176-77
  Retroactive amendment, 180, 185
Consumer goods, 20
Consumption, 15, 25
Continuing Education of the Bar, 69
Control, government, over business, 81-82, 200 (n. 49)
*Conveyancing Acts of 1881, 1882, and 1892, 139
Coroners, 55

Corruption and bribery
  In general, 133-34
  Western Region, 173, 191-92
Cost of living, 103-4
Council of Legal Education (Nigeria), 69
Council of Legal Education (U.K.), 65-66
Court of Resolution, 48, 53
Courts
  Customary, 45-49
  Superior courts, 52-55
  Privy Council and, 55-61
  Nigerian attitudes towards, 60
  Attitudes toward expatriate creditors, 152
Credit
  Bank policy, 24
  Controls, 24-25
Creditors, 146 ff.
Criminal Codes, 48, 49, 55, 64
Crisis, election, 1964-65, xi
Crisis of 1962-63, Western Region. See Western Nigeria
Crown lands. See State lands
Customary law
  In general, 39, 42, 45-52
  Customs Tariff Ordinance, 125
  Land tenure, 138 ff.
  Eminent domain, 142
  Pledges or pawns of land, 147
  Pledges or pawns of chattels, 150
  Description of court activities, 203 (n. 38)
  Under regional control, 204 (n. 43)
  Courts in Northern Nigeria, 204 (n. 55)
  Abuses in courts, 205 (n. 75)

D

Daily Express (Lagos), 61
Daily Times (Lagos), 26
"Dash." See Corruption and bribery
Davies, S. G., 184, 187
Debentures
  In general, 153-58
  Description, 154
  Formal, 155-57
Debt service, statistics, 20, 198 (n. 22)
Deeds, registration of, 141
Defense, 22, 33
Demogue, René, 145
Descent and distribution

Intestacy, 73
Marriage, 73
Wills, 73
Design protection, 84
Detribalization, 108
Development corporations listed, 224 (n. 44)
Development Plan of Technical Education, 94
Diop, Alioune, 166
Director of Public Prosecutions v. Obi, 62, 64
Disincentives, 132-36
  Delay, 132
  Bureaucracy, 132-33
  Corruption and bribery, 133-34
  Personnel shortages, 134-35
  Capital shortage, 134
  Quotas, expatriate personnel, 134
  Undeveloped markets, 134
  Racism, 135
  Xenophobia, 135
Distributive trades
  Reserved to Nigerians, 80
  Expatriate retrenchment, 218 (n. 33)
Doctors, 6
Doherty v. Balewa, 62, 187
Double-taxation agreements, 122
Dunlop Nigerian Industries, 26, 33
Duties, rates, 223 (n. 40)

E

East Africa, 44
Eastern bloc nations, import licenses required, 127
Eastern Nigeria
  Economic Plan, 31
  Best man principle, 50
  Survey of small industry, 79 ff.
  Attitudes toward private enterprise, 127, 134
  Land tenure, 139-43
  Mortgages, 147
Eclecticism, legal, 42 ff.
Economic development
  In general, 6-7, 13-35
  Postwar planning, 14-15
  Growth, 1950-60, 15
  Foreign exchange position, 15-16, 19-20
  Objectives, 16-17
  Public sector, 17-18
  Private sector, 18-19
  Foreign public capital, 19-20

Financing internal costs, 21-29
Savings institutions, 22-28
Review of 1962-68 Plan, 32-35
Education
  In general, 5-6
  Development Plan, 18, 30, 31
  Of lawyers, 65-68
  Federal responsibilities, 200 (n. 45)
  National Universities Commission Report, 200 (n. 46)
Egba Uprising, 181
Ekineh, Aliyi, 68, 188
Elias, Dr. T. O., 11, 40, 41, 48, 86, 175
Elizabeth II, 4, 181
Emergency Powers Act, 177-78, 187
Emergency Powers (Jurisdiction) Act, 178
Emergency Powers Regulations, 178, 187
Eminent domain, 142-43
Emirs and emirates, 50
Election Crisis, 1964-65, xi, 8, 194
Electricity, 10, 29
Electricity Corporation of Nigeria, 95
Employment, 91-94
Enahoro, Chief Anthony, 180
Ente Nazionale di Idrocarburi, 101
Entrepreneurship, 71-82
  Indigenous, 72-80
  Alien, 80-82
Equitable mortgage, 148
Equity, 38 ff.
Equity of redemption, 147
Exchange Control Act, 81, 129
Exchange license, 81
Expatriate employees
  Quotas, 98
  Statistics, 99-100
  Nigerianization, 100
Export crops, 20, 196 (n. 19)
External financing
  Economic Plan, 18-20
  Delay, 224 (n. 53)

F

Factories Ordinance, 105
Family life
  Ties, 73
  Enterprises, 80
  As social security, 108
Fatal Accidents Acts, 105

Federated Trades Union Congress (TUC), 111
Federation of Unions of Government and Municipal Nonclerical Workers of Nigeria, 111
Five-year economic plans (1955), 14
Fixed charges. *See* Debentures
Fliedner, H., 137
Floating charges, 154-55, 157
Foot, Dingle, 182, 190, 235 (n. 25)
Forced labor, 90
Ford Foundation, 16
Foreclosure, mortgage, 147
Foreigners, treatment of, 135-36, 141
Foreign exchange controls, 128-32
Foreign investment, by countries, 197 (n. 3)
*Foreign Jurisdiction Act, 38
France, diplomatic break with, 11
Free enterprise, 233 (n. 44)
*Fugitive Offenders Act, 180
Fundamental rights, 61-65

G

Gas, natural, 200 (n. 42)
General Council of the bar, 69
Germany, East, import license required, 127
Germany, Federal Republic of, 19, 77
Ghana
  Attitudes toward, 44, 45
  Preventive detention, 60, 70
  Company Code Bill, 76
  Central planning, 167
Government securities traded, 27
Gower, L. C. B., 75 ff., 147
Gratiaen, E. F. N., 190
Gross domestic product (GDP), 15, 19
Gross national product (GNP), 6
Grove, David, 61 ff.
Guinea, 44, 167

H

Harbison, Frederick, 89, 96
High Court of Lagos, 151
High courts, 39, 53
Hire-purchase, 151-53
Hire-Purchase Act, 151-53
*Hire Purchase Acts of 1938 and 1954, 152
Holland, Denys C., 62

Hong Kong, as origin of Japanese-made goods, 127
Hours, working, 104
Housing Corporation (Northern Nigeria), 31-32
Hunter, Guy, 73, 168

I

Immigration Act
  In general, 98, 190
  Statement by Minister of Internal Affairs, 217 (n. 28)
Imodu, M. A. O., 111-12
Imperial statutes, 38 ff.
Imports
  Levels, 20
  Controls, 123-26
  Procedures, 126-27
  Re-export, 126
  Prohibited articles, 126-27
  Discrimination, 127
Incentives
  Taxation, 8, 119-22
  Tariff protection, 124-26
  Regional, 127-28
  Fiscal measures, 129-32
  See also Disincentives
Income Tax (Amendment) Act, 121
Income Tax Management Act, 122
Income Tax Ordinance, 122
Incorporated private partnership, 75-77
Independent United Labour Congress (IULC), 113
India
  Identity of interests, 43-44
  Preventive detention, 60
  Civil rights enforcement in courts, 210 (n. 159)
Individualism, 72
Industrial Development Corporation (Northern Nigeria), 31
Industrial Development (Import Duties Relief) Act, 124
Industrial Development (Income Tax Relief) Act, 119
Industrial estates, 142
Industry
  Infant industry, 8, 124
  Small, 78 ff.
  Labor-intensive, 98
In re Southern Rhodesia, 45
Insurance
  Tax incentives, 25
  Under trust receipt, 158

Statement on nationalization of, 165
General risk, 199 (n. 30)
Insurance (Miscellaneous Provisions) Act, 165
Interest rates, 134, 150
International Commission of Jurists, 6
International Convention for the Protection of Industrial Property, 83
International Development Association, 19
International Finance Corporation, 19, 23
International Labour Organisation, 11
International Sugar Agreement, 127
International Wheat Agreement, 127
*Interpretation Act, 41
Investment
 Inducements, 8, 119-22
 By individuals, 26
 By areas, 128
Investment Unit, 34
Islam
 Influence on customary law, 46 ff.
 North African ties, 203 (n. 33)
 Schools of Jurisprudence, 205 (n. 57)
Israel
 Contribution to Economic Plan, 19
 Legal system compared, 203 (n. 30)
Italy, 19, 29

J

Japan
 Membership in IBRD Consulatative Group, 20
 Discrimination against, 127
Jebba Dam. *See* Niger Dam
Jenkins Commission, 78
Johnson, Chief Joseph M., 11
Joint Action Committee (JAC), 114
Joint (Economic) Planning Committee, 14
Journalists, 69
Journal of Africa Law, 61
Judges
 Estimate of, 6
 Colonial, 39
 Appointment of, 58-59
 Superior courts, 61
 Customary courts, 205 (n. 63)
Judgments, enforcing
 Enforcement of, 53
 Levy of execution, 153
Judicial Committee of the Privy Council. *See* Privy Council
Judicial Service Commissions, 58 ff., 69
Jurisdiction of courts, 52 ff.
Justices of the peace, 55
Juvenile courts, 55

K

Kainji Dam. *See* Niger Dam
Kaldor, Nicholas, 117
Kassim, J. O., 191
Kilby, Peter, 79
Korea, North, import license required, 127

L

Labor and social legislation, 93, 104-8
Labor health areas, 103
Labor
 In general, 89-116
 Work force, 90-94
 Labor and social legislation, 93, 104-8
 Strikes, 1963-64, 93, 114
 Training, 94-96
 Under Economic Development Plan, 96, 116
 Manpower needs, 96-101
 Industrialization, 97
 Management personnel shortage, 98, 134-35
 Expatriates, 99-100
 Women, 101
 Wages and hours, 101-4
 Minimum-wage legislation, 101, 115
 Wage inquiries, 102
 Collective bargaining, 102
 Wage costs, 102-3
 Cost of living, 103-4
 Maximum hours, 104
 Overtime, 104
 Holidays, 104
 Trade unions, 109-14
 Morgan Commission (1964), 115
 Leadership, 220 (n. 96)
Labour Code (Amendment) Act, 109
Labour Code Ordinance, 104 ff.
Lagos Executive Development Board, 141

Lagos Stock Exchange, 22, 25-27, 77
Lagos Stores, Ltd. v. Elackstock & Co., 85
Land, for foreign business, 81, 140-41
Land officers, federal, 143-44
Land tenure
  In general, 138-44
  Native law, 138
  English law, 138
  Fee simple, 138, 142
  Regional law, 139
  Right of occupancy, 139
  White settlers, 140
  Rights of aliens, 140-41
  Leases, 140, 143-44
  Economic development, effect on, 141-44
  Registration of title, 141
  Eminent domain, 142
  Certificate of Occupancy, 143
Land Tenure Law (Northern Nigeria), 141
*Land Transfer Act of 1897, 139
*Law of Distress Amendment Act of 1908, 153
*Law of Property Act of 1925, 139, 147
Law schools and training, 48, 65-68
Lawyers
  Attitude toward customary law, 48
  Numbers of, 65, 67
  Qualification and status, 65
  Training of, 48, 65-68
  Fees required, 68
  Non-Nigerian, barring entry of, 190
Law of Lagos, 6
LDCs (Less Developed Countries, under U.S. law), 222 (n. 29)
Leases
  General use, 140
  Public lands, 143
  Assignment of, 148
  Governmental consent to sublease, 226 (nn. 44 and 54)
Legal Practitioners Act, 68, 190
Legal profession. *See* Lawyers
Levantines, attitudes toward, 100, 135
Levy v. Abercorris, 153
Licensing, 83
Little, A. D., Co., 10, 35
Loans, development, 23, 28, 199 (n. 38)

Losses, carried forward, 121
Lugard, Lord, 140

M

Magistrates
  Courts, 54-55
  Appointment of, 59
Majekodunmi, Dr. Moses, 11, 178 ff.
Maliki School of Islamic law, 48, 205 (n. 57)
Management
  Trainees, 97
  Personnel shortage, 98, 134-35
  Contract, 212 (n. 31)
  Consultation, 213 (n. 40)
Manpower
  High-level, 97
  Skill-levels, 97
Marketing boards, 32, 230 (n. 19)
Markets, Nigerian, 135
Marriage, under English law, 73
Marxism, 44, 231 (n. 23)
Mbanefo, Sir Louis, 6, 11
  Commission, 218 (n. 46)
Michelin Tyre Co., 33
Mid-West State, 182
Minister (Ministry) of Commerce and Industry
  Application for pioneer status, 119
  Tariff protection, 124-25
  Import licenses, 126-27
Minister (Ministry) of Economic Development
  Economic Plan, 1962-68, 16
  Statement reserving certain businesses to Nigerians, 80
  Statement on foreign enterprise, 172
  Statement on 1962 census, 232 (n. 37)
Minister (Ministry) of Finance
  Foreign aid gap, 19
  Annual budgets, 21
  Nigerian Industrial Development Bank, 22
  Credit controls, 24
  National Savings Campaign, 24
  Investment of National Provident Fund moneys, 27, 107
  Treasury bills, 28
  Exchange control, 81, 128-32
  Statement on taxation, 118
  Power to exempt from tax, 121
  Statement on tariff protection, 125-26

Statement on nationalization, 163-65
Socialism, 166
Minister of Labour
  Power to establish wage boards, 101
  Responsibility, 105
Minister of Trade, power to regulate hire-purchase, 152
Ministry of Lands and Housing (Western Nigeria), 143
Ministry of Lands and Survey (Northern Nigeria), 143
Ministry of Posts and Telegraphs, 95
Ministry of Town Planning (Eastern Nigeria), 143
Ministry of Works and Surveys, 95
Mobil Oil Nigeria Limited, 67
Morgan, Justice, 114
Morgan Commission, 114-15
Mortgages, chattel
  In general, 150-53
  Pledge, indigenous, 150
Mortgages, on land
  In general, 147-49
  Customary law, 147
  Pre-1925 English mortgage, 147
  Fees, 148-49
  Second mortgage, 148
  Corporate-owned land, 149
  Registration, 149
Mphahlele, Ezekiel, 166

N

National Council of Nigeria and the Cameroons, 111
National Council of Nigerian Citizens (NCNC), 111
National Council of Trade Unions, Nigeria (NCTUN), 112
National Development Plan, 1962-68
  In general, 16-35
  Objectives, 17
  Financing, 17-21, 33
  Quantified economic targets, 17
  Relation to company law, 76
  Vocational training under, 96
  Effect of 1964 wage increases, 116
  Exchange controls, 132
National Economic Council, 14
National Investment and Properties Co. (NIPC), 192
Nationalization
  Nigerian Airways, 30, 162, 164
  In general, 160-66
  U.N.G.A. Res. No. 1803, 160-61
  Compensation, 161, 230 (n. 12)
  Investment guarantee agreement with U.S., 161
  Nigerian National Lines, 162, 164
  Cable and Wireless (Nigerian External Communications), 162, 164
  Government policy, 163
  "Public utility" defined, 164
National Manpower Board, 93, 96
National Provident Fund (NPF)
  As savings institution, 27-28
  Act, 106-7
  Rate of contributions, 106
  Coverage, 106-7
  Advisory Council, 107
  Investment Committee, 107
  Voluntary participation, 107
Native Lands Acquisition Law (Western Nigeria), 143, 149
Native Lands Acquisition Ordinance, 141
Native law. See Customary Law
Négritude. See Africanness
Netherlands, 19, 29
Niger Coast Protectorate, 38
Niger Dam, 10, 18, 29, 200 (n. 40)
Nigerian Airways, nationalization of, 30, 162, 164
Nigerian Bar Association, 68-70
Nigerian Bar Journal, 68
Nigerian Chamber of Mines, 95
Nigerian External Communications (Cable and Wireless), nationalization of, 162, 164
Nigerian Federation of Women's Clubs, 70
Nigerian Fermentation Co., 33
Nigerian Indutrial Development Bank (NIDB), 8, 22-23
Nigerianization
  Credit base, 19
  Law, 42, 203 (n. 29)
  Corporations, 82
  Employment, 98-99, 100
  Recognition of by foreigners, 134
  Distinguished from socialism, 170
Nigerian Labour Congress (NLC), 111
Nigerian Federation of Labour, 111
Nigerian National Lines, nationalization of, 30, 162, 164
Nigerian Railway Corporation, 95

Nigerian Sugar Co., 26, 33
Nigerian Trades Union Congress (NTUC), 112
Nigerian Union of Teachers, 109, 111
Nkrumah, 167, 209 (n. 131), 231 (n. 31)
North Africa
  Influence of, on law, 44
  Islamic ties of Northern Nigeria, 203 (n. 33)
Northern Cameroons, 38
Northern Nigeria
  Economic Programme, 31
  Emirs, 50, 52
  Attitude toward foreign enterprise, 127
  Land tenure, 139-43
  Mortgages on land, 148-49
  Islamic ties, 203 (n. 33)
  "Northernization," 232 (n. 41)
Northern Nigeria Development Bank, 32
Nuclear tests, French, 11
Nwabueze, B. O., 53, 54
Nyhart, J. D., 72

O

Oba of Lagos, 50
Odumoso, O. I., 182, 185
Ogwurike, Dr. C., 185
Oil, 5, 10, 20, 31, 165
Oil Rivers Protectorate, 38
Okpara, Dr. M. I., 182
Okuboyejo, N. A. A., 71
Olawoyin v. Attorney General of the Northern Region, 63, 64
Orders in Council, 38
Overtime, 104

P

Palming off, 86
Pan-Africanism, 11
Park, A. E. W., 40, 41
Parliament, Federal
  New legislation, 6
  Position of chiefs in, 50-51
  Power to confer jurisdiction, 52
  Supremacy of, 60
  Power to declare emergency, 177, 187-89
Partnership, 74, 75, 79
Patents, 84
*Patents and Designs Acts, 1907 to 1932, 84

Penal Code of Northern Nigeria, 42, 48, 62, 204 (n. 45)
Permanent Sovereignty Over Natural Resources (U.N.G.A. Res. No. 1803, 1962), 160-61
Pioneer industry,
  As control factor, 81
  In general, 119-20
  Delay in securing, 128, 224 (n. 45)
Police
  Detention by, 60
  Powers, 81
Population. *See* Census
Ports Authority Technical and Craft Training Centre, 95
Precedent
  English, 40 ff.
  American, 42
Preventive Detention Act, proposed, 60-61
Private capital, 7, 18-19, 23-27, 233 (n. 44)
Privy Council, Judicial Committee of
  Appeals to, from Commonwealth courts, 4, 208 (n. 115)
  Judgment in *In re Southern Rhodesia*, 45
  As Nigeria's highest court of appeal until 1963, 52, 57
  Role in Western Region Crisis, 55 ff., 180 ff.
  Role in removal of Nigerian judges, 58 ff.
  Judgment in *Akintola* case, 180, 184
  Appointment of first African to, 207 (n. 107)
Process, service and execution, 53
Production
  Industrial, 9-10
  Feasibility list, 10
Productivity, compared with European workers, 215 (n. 1)
Profits, 73
Project Evaluation Unit, 34
Property and Conveyancing Law (Western Nigeria), 139
Protectorate of Nigeria, 38, 85
Protectorate of Northern Nigeria, 38
Protectorate of Southern Nigeria, 38, 85
Public Lands Acquisition Act, 142
*Public Law 480, 19
"Public purpose," 143

248   Index

Public utility, for nationalization purposes, 164

Q

The Queen v. Amalgamated Press, Ltd., 65
Quotas, expatriate, 100, 134

R

Racism, 11, 108, 135, 166
Railway Workers' Union, 107
*Real Property Act of 1845, 139
Regionalism
    Law schools and, 66
    Affecting foreign enterprise, 127-28
Regional ministries of economic planning, 14
Registration of Business Names Act, 72
Registration of title, 141
Republic, changeover to, 57, 181
Reserves, foreign exchange, 15-16, 20, 34
Restrictive-business practices act, 82
Revenue, sources, 199 (n. 26)
Rockefeller Brothers Fund, 80
Royal Niger Co., 38, 139
Rule of law, 56, 185
Rumania, import license required, 127

S

*Sale of Goods Act of 1893, 153
Sardauna of Sokoto. *See* Bello, Alhaji Ahmadu
Sardauna Province, 139
Savings
    By public, 6, 23, 199 (n. 28)
    Government spending, 21
    Deposits, 24
    National Campaign, 24
    Insurance, 25
    Stock purchases, 25
Savings certificates, 23
Securities regulation, 26
Sedition
    Cases, 64-65, 210 (n. 169)
    Definition of, 210 (n. 169)
Selling in Nigeria, 82
Senghor, L., 167
Sharia Court of Appeals, 48, 52, 53
Shell-B.P. Petroleum Development Co. vocational training program, 95

Shiroro Gorge Dam. *See* Niger Dam
Sick leave, workers, 104
Single-party systems, and socialism, 168-69
Skill levels, worker, 97
Slave trade, 90
Social development, 90
Socialism
    Influence on law, 44
    In general, 166-70
    Content, 166-67
    Single-party systems, 168-69
    Distinguished from economic nationalism, 170
Social legislation, 93, 104-8
Sole proprietorship, 72, 79
South Africa (and South West Africa), import license required, 127
Stamp duties, on mortgages, 149
State lands, 141, 143-44, 149
*Statute of Frauds, 139
Statutory corporations, 34, 95
Steel mill, 29, 165
Strikes, labor
    Man-days lost, 1963-64, 93
    1964 wage increase, 114
    Factors preventing, 200 (n. 97)
Subsidiaries, 81
Supreme Court, Federal
    Jurisdiction, 52
    Appeals to, 52-53
    Privy Council and, 55-61
    Fundamental rights cases, 61-65
    Williams case, 70, 189
    Western Region Crisis cases, 181-91

T

Tariff protection, 8, 124-26
Taxation
    Licensing fees and royalties, 83
    Licensing without equity participation, 83
    In general, 118-23
    Policy, 118
    Corporate rate, 118, 220 (n. 2)
    Exempted income, 118
    Appeal Commission, 119
    Appeal to high court, 119
    Appeal to Supreme Court, 119
    Source of income, 119
    Penalties, 119
    Incentives, 119-22
    Private companies, 121-22

Index

International agreements, 122
Individuals, 122-23
Deductions, 122
Evasion, 122-23
Withholding, 123
Oil companies, 221 (n. 3)
Ghanaian, compared, 221 (n. 4)
Allocation of income, 221 (n. 14)
Exemption from, 222 (nn. 21 and 22)
Applicability of U.S. law to LDCs, 222 (n. 29)
Regional, 223 (nn. 32 and 33)
Taylor, Justice, 187
Technical assistance, 198 (n. 18)
Technical institutes, 95
Tiv Riots, 235 (n. 32)
Touré, Sékou, 167
Trade dispute, defined, 219 (n. 67)
Trademarks
  In general 83, 85-87
  Revision of law, 213 (n. 53)
  Federal control, 214 (n. 75)
*Trademarks Act of 1905, 86
Trade Marks Proclamation, 85
Trades Disputes (Arbitration and Inquiry) Ordinance, 105
Trades Union Congress (of Nigeria) (TUC[N]), 112
Trade unions
  In general, 109-14
  ICFTU, 109, 111-12
  WFTU, 109, 111-12
  Membership, 112
  Political role, 113
Trade Unions Ordinance, 105
Trading of workers, 93-96
Transportation and communications,
  Nationalization, 30, 162, 164
  Economic Plan projects, 31-33
Treason, felonious, 180-81
Treasury bills, 28
Treaties and agreements
  International Convention for the Protection of Industrial Property, 83
  Universal Copyright Convention, 83
  Double-taxation agreements, 122
  International Wheat Agreement, 127
  International Sugar Agreement, 127
  Investment guarantee agreement with U.S., 161

Trust receipts, 157-58
Turnover, 90

U

Udo-Udoma, Justice, 190
Ugochukwu, Chief, 23
Unemployment, effect of industrialization, 97
United Africa Co.
  Vocational training program, 95
  Investment in industry, 101
United Kingdom, Economic Plan contributions, 19, 29
United Kingdom Designs (Protection) Ordinance, 84
United Labour Congress (ULC), 113
United People's Party (UPP), 180
United States
  Agency for International Development (U.S. AID), 6, 10, 35
  Contributions to Economic Plan, 19, 29
  Decisions of courts as precedent, 42
  Double taxation agreement, 122
  Position on U.N.G.A. Res. No. 1803, 160
  Investment guarantee agreement, 161
Universal Copyright Convention, 83
Universities, 5-6, 66, 200 (n. 46)
Urbanization, 90
U.S. AID, 6, 10, 35

V

Vacations, of workers, 104
*Vendor and Purchaser Act of 1874, 139
Vietnam, North, import license required, 127
Visas, 8, 80
Vocational schools, 94-96

W

Wages
  Levels, 101 ff.
  Authority to review, 101-2
  Costs, 102-3
  Levels, minimum, 1964, 115
  Minimum, legislation proposed, 115
  Increases, 1964, 115-16
  Unskilled labor, 218 (n. 37)
Wages Board Ordinance, 101-2, 104
War Chiefs of Lagos, 50

Warehousing, bonded, 158
West Africa, 60
West African Court of Appeals, 57, 84
West African Pilot
  Editorial on courts, 182
Western House of Assembly, 177, 181, 183
Western Nigeria
  Crisis of 1962-63, 7, 22, 56, 63, 69-70, 176-94
  Economic plan, 15, 30-31
  Constitution, amendment of, 56
  Business aids, 79
  Wage survey, 1959, 114
  Land tenure, 139-43
  Mortgages, 147-49
  Coker Commission of Inquiry, 191-94
Western Nigeria Development Corporation, 192
Western Region Finance Corporation, 192
Western Region Marketing Board, 179, 191-92
White Cap Chiefs of Lagos, 50
Williams, Akintola, 191
Williams, Chief F. R. A. (Rotimi), 63, 69, 70, 178 ff.
Williams v. Majekodunmi, 63, 70, 188-89
Witnesses, compulsory attendance of, 53
Work force
  School-leavers, 90
  Statistics, 91 ff.
  Training, 93
  Characteristics, 93-94, 215 (n. 1)
  Educational background, 97
  Skill-levels, 97
  Women, 101
Workmen's Compensation Ordinance, 105
World Bank (IBRD), 16, 19, 29
  Consultative Group (Nigeria), 20
World Health Organization, 11
Writs and processes, service of, 53

X

Xenophobia, 135, 172

Y

Yugoslavia, import license required, 127